A Director's Voyage Through Risk Management

Dean A. Yoost

RMA is a member-driven professional association whose sole purpose is to advance sound risk management principles in the financial services industry.

RMA helps our members use sound risk management principles to improve institutional performance and financial stability, and enhance the risk management competency of individuals through information, peer sharing, and networking.

Edited by Frank Devlin

Cover design by Arielle Morris

Text design and composition by Stephen Druding

Front cover photo by Shutterstock, Inc.

RMA Product Number: 641140

ISBN: 978-1-57070-345-4

Library of Congress Control Number: 2016 954 039

Printed in the United States of America.

A Director's Voyage Through Risk Management

Ralph Waldo Emerson wrote,
"Men are what their mothers made them."
This book is dedicated to our mother, Delores Lillian Yoost,
whom we lost on February 9, 2016.

Contents

Why I Wrote This Book

"The real voyage of discovery consists not in seeking new lands but seeing with new eyes."

—Marcel Proust

I experienced a diverse and extraordinarily satisfying 33-year career with one professional services firm as an advisor, a builder and leader of businesses, and a mentor—one-half of the time resident in Tokyo and Beijing.

After retiring from the firm, I embarked on the next leg of my voyage by joining the board of directors of four international companies, three publicly traded and one privately owned, in four different industries: banking, insurance, technology, and manufacturing. At the time, I believed that my value to these boards was to showcase my skills and experience in corporate finance, accounting, and taxation and to demonstrate global savvy and business acumen.

To an extent, this was true. However, I learned that much more value is created by a director's ability to understand the business and the environment; to deal with unstructured, complex problems; and to offer insight and unique perspectives. I observed that a director's worth is in the capacity to think carefully about the big opportunities and risks; to raise questions that represent new approaches, new thinking, and subtle differences; and to make informed decisions.

Given the intensity of the expectations of shareholders, regulators, and other stakeholders—and the dynamism of business and the risks—fulfilling board responsibilities is no placid stroll down the 18th fairway. The somewhat whimsical approach of some past practices to board governance and risk oversight are in the rear-view mirror. Today, as a board member of both a large global bank and a large global insurance company, and as an advisory committee member of a captive finance company, I spend considerable time and energy, both inside and outside the boardroom, attempting to understand the trends, developments, and particularly the risks—both global and local—that impact these industries and businesses, now and in the future.

An ever-increasing proportion of the risks relate to the challenges of operating in complex and highly regulated industries. The banking and insurance regulators are knowledgeable, persistent, and laser-focused on current and emerging risks and the risk management framework. Although some of the risks impact strategy, many of the threats are operational and financial in nature.

Another broad spectrum of risks is dynamic and more global. These threats are associated with disruptive megatrends such as the propulsion of the emerging-country markets, shifts in demographics including the aging population, and advances in technologies and the proliferation of data. Directors are spending much more time on these forces because of their potential impact on business models.

ix

My intent in writing this book is to share my voyage as a director and impart whatever wisdom I may have gleaned so far in dealing with the rather daunting challenges in overseeing risk management. Like all directors, I take very seriously my duties and responsibilities in the boardroom and want to contribute to the further development of best practices.

Each chapter in this book is written from my perspective as a director who has the curiosity, the thirst, and the need to identify important risks and emerging threats and to obtain sufficient insight to be able to effectively challenge management. Included in each chapter are questions directors should ask. I am hopeful that these suggested inquiries will facilitate even more thoughtful and provocative discussions in the boardroom.

Dean A. Yoost
November 2016

Acknowledgments

My sincerest thanks to Ed DeMarco and Frank Devlin of The Risk Management Association, who provided their support, wisdom, and counsel in conceptualizing and editing this book. I am both humbled and honored to be associated with RMA, which has served the financial services industry since 1914.

I am also grateful to the board members and executives who provided the many insightful comments quoted herein. Their collective views greatly expanded the breadth, depth, and quality of the content.

Special and heartfelt thanks to Bernard F. (Bud) Mathaisel, Eric V. Zwisler, and D. J. Peterson, who were my co-authors on earlier published articles that formed the foundation of some chapters, and Mary Benbrook. Mary's administrative contributions and diligence kept *A Director's Voyage Through Risk Management* on track.

Director's Duties and Responsibilities

Introduction to Part I: Director's Duties and Responsibilities

"Voyage upon life's sea,
To yourself be true,
And, whatever your lot may be,
Paddle your own canoe."
— SARAH T. BOLTON

The business affairs of a corporation are, as a matter of law, managed under the direction of a board of directors. The board delegates to a full-time executive team the management of the institution's operations. This positions the directors to provide oversight of, and serve as an independent check on, management. The board is responsible for making statutorily identified decisions, for selecting the chief executive officer, and for providing oversight of the business and affairs of the institution and its management. Management is responsible for the day-to-day operations.[1]

The board's authority comes from both law and custom. Directors have a great number of duties and responsibilities under federal and state law, stock market listing requirements, and the institution's governing documents, which include the corporate charter, articles of incorporation, and by-laws. In addition to its legal responsibilities, the board is expected to fulfill expectations placed upon it by tradition and current practice.

Under general and longstanding principles of corporate law, the fundamental obligations of the board are its fiduciary duties of loyalty and care owed to the institution and its shareholders. The "duty of loyalty" requires directors to avoid conflicts of interest with respect to the matters they decide for the institution. The "duty of care" means that directors exercise the same level of care that any ordinary person would in overseeing his or her own investments.

The articles of incorporation will rarely place limits on the board's authority, so it is assumed that board approval is required for any material commitment of corporate resources, adoption of or change in corporate policy, or transactions out of the ordinary course of doing business. Thus, proposals to issue debt securities; to acquire or dispose of significant assets; or to initiate, terminate, or compromise major litigation are situations that are typically reserved for action by the board.[2]

The role of directors at banking institutions, in particular, is established by a matrix of federal banking statutes and the regulations and pronouncements made by the regulators. The Board of Governors of the Federal Reserve System also recognizes that, in the exercise of their duties, directors of banking institutions are governed by federal and state banking, securities, and antitrust statutes, as well as by common law.

The specific obligations imposed on bank directors are largely intended to protect the safety and soundness of the institutions. These requirements are not intended to be viewed as altering the board's traditional duties or creating new fiduciary duties, but

---

[1]"Guiding Principles for Enhancing US Banking Organization Corporate Governance," The Clearing House, 2015.

[2]"A Practical Guide: Fundamentals for Corporate Directors," National Association of Corporate Directors, 2012.

rather as providing specific directives that inform the manner in which the directors undertake their responsibilities.

The Basel Committee on Banking Supervision issued guidelines in July 2015 describing the duties and responsibilities of directors. These guidelines are illustrative and not intended to be all-encompassing.[3]

The Basel guidelines indicate that the board has overall responsibility for the institution, including approving and overseeing management's implementations of the strategic objectives, governance framework, and corporate culture. Directors have the ultimate responsibility for business strategy and financial soundness, key personnel decisions, internal organization and governance structure and practices, and risk management and compliance obligations. The guidelines indicate that the board may delegate some of its functions, though not its responsibilities, to board committees. The guidelines also note that directors should establish and be satisfied with the institution's organizational structure. This enables the board and management to carry out their responsibilities and facilitate effective decision making and good governance, including the establishment of key responsibilities and authorities of the board itself and management, and those responsible for the risk management and control functions.

The guidelines further indicate that the board should do the following:

- Actively engage in the affairs of the institution and keep up with material changes in the institution's business and the external environment, as well as act in a timely manner to protect the long-term interests of the institution.
- Play a lead role in establishing the institution's culture and values.
- Oversee the development of and approve the business objectives and strategy, as well as monitor their implementation.
- Oversee implementation of the governance framework and periodically review it to ensure it remains appropriate in the light of material changes to the institution's size, complexity, geographical footprint, business strategy, markets, and regulatory requirements.
- Establish, along with management, the institution's risk appetite, taking into account the competitive and regulatory landscape and the firm's long-term interests, risk exposures, and ability to manage risk effectively.
- Oversee the institution's adherence to the risk appetite statement, risk policies, and risk limits.
- Approve the approach and oversee the implementation of key policies pertaining to the capital adequacy assessment process, capital and liquidity plans, compliance policies and obligations, and the internal control systems.
- Require that the institution maintain a robust finance function responsible for accounting and financial data.
- Approve the annual financial statements and require a periodic independent review of critical areas.
- Approve the selection and oversee the performance of the CEO, key members of management, and heads of the control functions.
- Oversee the institution's approach to compensation, including monitoring and

---

[3]"Guidelines: Corporate Governance Principles for Banks," Bank for International Settlements, 2015.

reviewing executive compensation and assessing whether it is aligned with the risk culture and risk appetite.

■ Oversee the integrity, independence, and effectiveness of the institution's policies and procedures for whistleblowing.

The Basel guidelines also indicate that directors should ensure that transactions with related parties are reviewed to assess risk and are subject to appropriate restrictions, by requiring that such transactions be conducted on arm's-length terms and that corporate or business resources are not misappropriated or misapplied.

Finally, in discharging these responsibilities, directors should take into account the legitimate interests of depositors, shareholders, and other relevant stakeholders. Directors should also ensure that the institution maintains an effective relationship with the regulators.

The aforementioned roles and responsibilities of directors are pervasive and carry a heavy burden, requiring that they have suitable experience and knowledge, the available time and energy, and the passion and commitment. Directors need to possess a strong moral compass and mature leadership abilities.

Part I of this book expands on these descriptions and presents the expectations and challenges confronting directors. Chapter 1 outlines how directors can best fulfill their duties and responsibilities. The current environment demands that directors have an informed perspective and wide lens. Chapter 2 focuses on the regulators' minimum standards for the board and describes how directors can meet the new expectations and provide a credible challenge to management.

Parts I and II are written from the perspective of a director for a large bank, given that the practices and prescriptions in banking are more established, and the regulatory guidance more defined, than in insurance or most other industries.

Directors Need an Informed Perspective and Wide Lens

"Rank does not confer privilege or give power. It imposes responsibility."
— PETER F. DRUCKER

As directors confront growing scrutiny from stakeholders and the regulators, board practices are evolving by necessity. Directors want to spend more time on areas impacting shareholder value creation, like strategy, but they continue to be consumed by regulatory pronouncements, actions, and heightened standards. The regulators have become increasingly uncompromising and want more from both the board and management.

Directors recognize the criticality of establishing the right "tone at the top" and culture, as well as the importance of balancing short-term results with a focus on the longer-term horizon. They are heavily vested in assisting management in identifying, monitoring, and mitigating risks, while recognizing the demarcation between oversight and management. Directors are challenged by the rapid pace of change and the inherent risks in a global, digitalized world. They are committed to staying abreast of the latest business, governance, and regulatory developments to remain informed, notwithstanding the increasing volume of materials and diversity of issues. They want management to help them fulfill their duties and responsibilities by enhancing the content and format of board materials and targeting the dialogue in the boardroom. In fulfilling their duties and responsibilities, board members know this requires wisdom and a strong commitment.[4]

The growing complexities of business and the enhanced oversight role mandate that directors have an informed perspective and use a wide lens to meet the challenges in the boardroom. It is a new world in corporate governance. "The rapid pace of change is due to transformative advances in technology, heightened expectations of investors, regulators, and other stakeholders, and shifting markets and political environments around the world. This makes it sometimes difficult for directors to rely on historical precedents and past experiences, and their impact on strategy and business models," noted Robert H. Herz, a board member of Morgan Stanley, Workiva, and Fannie Mae.

---

[4]"Governing for the Long-term: Looking Down the Road with an Eye on the Rear-view Mirror," Annual Corporate Directors Survey, PricewaterhouseCoopers, 2015.

Regulators' Expectations

The regulators have increased their emphasis on corporate governance as a critical element in their goal of promoting safety and soundness. Their governance principles not only outline key legal and regulatory requirements, but also incorporate enhancements to governance that not infrequently extend beyond what is required by law. The Office of the Comptroller of the Currency's issuance of its heightened or minimum standards, "Guidelines Establishing Heightened Standards for Certain Large Insured National Banks, Insured Federal Savings Associations, and Insured Federal Branches," issued on September 11, 2014, significantly raises the bar on directors.

While protecting shareholder interests and maximizing shareholder value are fundamental in the board's decision making, the regulators have become an important stakeholder for boards and management to manage in order to ensure that the institution's strategy delivers the highest shareholder returns.

The Risk Management Association observes that the American Association of Board Directors has identified 800 legislative and regulatory provisions that have accumulated over many decades and impacted the responsibilities of directors. Some believe that this ever-increasing regulatory burden has created a diversion from the board time needed for effective risk oversight of the business and other essential board responsibilities. RMA notes that the increasing threats of regulatory actions and personal liability are forcing boards of financial institutions to become almost "compliance boards," where attention is focused on satisfying laws, regulations, and regulatory guidance that pertain to duties that may properly be the function of management.[5]

The regulators also have established expectations that institutions should focus on conduct and consumer outcomes at every level of decision making. Richard Cordray, director of the Consumer Financial Production Bureau, has suggested that a stated objective of the CFPB is to bring clarity to the financial markets by instituting disclosures that allow consumers to compare the terms, conditions, and pricing of similar financial products and services. The goal is to make sure the costs and risks of financial products and services are clear, and to act as necessary to ensure access to credit and fair treatment.[6]

As a result, directors are broadening their perspectives in boardroom discussions, going beyond growth and profitability to more narrowly consider customer outcomes. In addition, directors need to insist, now more than ever, that the firm's strategy and execution consider the wider public interest and, in the case of large institutions, the financial risks to taxpayers.

"Directors need to understand the expectations of the regulators. While the board's primary responsibilities are to its shareholders and other stakeholders, failing to meet regulatory standards brings with it serious risks in terms of reputation, fines, and penalties, and perhaps even personal accountability," commented David L. Rosenblum, a board member of Hamni Financial Corporation.

---

[5] Letter from The Risk Management Association to the Office of the Comptroller of the Currency, March 23, 2014.
[6] Remarks by Richard Cordray at the American Bar Association, April 3, 2014.

'Tone at the Top'

Setting the proper "tone at the top" is fundamental to establishing a sound corporate culture, a core responsibility of directors. The tone sets the moral compass of the institution. The culture reinforces appropriate norms for responsible and ethical behavior, especially critical to the institution's risk awareness, risk-taking behavior, and risk management.

"Tone at the top" describes the institution's atmosphere in the workplace as established and led by the board and management. Having the right tone reinforces the culture and prevents inappropriate behavior and unethical practices. Whatever tone is established will have a trickle-down effect on employees. If the tone upholds strong ethics and high integrity, and allows for zero tolerance for bad behavior, employees will be motivated to uphold these values.

The regulators are keenly focused on the board's oversight of the institution's tone and culture, and they expect directors to be actively engaged in aligning the institution's values with its strategic objectives. The culture permeates the entire institution and all significant decisions and ensures that an appropriate balance is struck between risk and reward, consistent with the risk appetite.[7]

The establishment of a culture of risk and compliance that respects the spirit of the law, as well as the technical rules, is an essential element of successful risk management. Accordingly, directors and management need to work to create the right "tone at the top" emphasizing the importance of risk and compliance at every level.

Longer-Term Perspective

All management teams strive to make their institutions better and stronger over the longer term. Yet, when it comes to priorities and plans of action, few have visions beyond the next quarter or, at most, a year or two. The reality is that immediate concerns and the uncertainty of the future lead management to focus on the short term. This tension between long-term intention and short-term action is perhaps the biggest failure today of corporate governance.

The dichotomy between long-term and short-term thinking has had a polarizing effect in the boardroom. Directors tend to look down the road with a focus on enhancing long-term shareholder value. Yet, they are simultaneously preoccupied with a need to look in the rear-view mirror and meet short-term expectations in the form of quarterly earnings. This pressure often results in decisions that may satisfy the expectations of stakeholders for the next quarter, but not necessarily the next decade.[8]

The power of a board is derived from one of its key remits, which is to consider the longer-term strategy and the future shape and direction of the institution. Stable, sustainable growth often requires putting long-term goals ahead of short-term gains. Especially in uncertain times, having a board that can stand for a longer-term strategy instills

---

[7]"Aggregate Impact of Regulation and the Work of Boards: Rising Above the Detail," Deloitte, 2015.
[8]"Governing for the Long-term: Looking Down the Road with an Eye on the Rear-view Mirror," 2015.

in management the strength to weather the challenges and make the right decisions on big-ticket items like acquisitions, investments, divestitures, and right-sizing.[9]

Overseeing Risk Management

The higher speed and broader impact of change increases risk and reduces viable reaction time. The speed at which change can occur, and the impact it can have, increases the need for appropriate risk management and the board's oversight. This makes preparing for change and crisis more critical than ever, especially since institutions are often judged more harshly for their responses to a crisis than the fact they had the crisis in the first place.[10]

The OCC's minimum standards require directors to actively oversee the institution's risk-taking activities and to challenge management decisions that could cause the risk profile to exceed the institution's risk appetite or jeopardize safety and soundness.

"Risk management is not a function, in my opinion, but a capability for improving decision making and avoiding catastrophic risks. It is about empowering people throughout the institution to make smart, risk-adjusted decisions," commented Anand K. Nallathambi, president and CEO, CoreLogic Inc.

The National Association of Corporate Directors (NACD) outlines three principles for directors in overseeing risk management:

1. Directors must understand the specific risks facing the institution they serve and ensure there is a process in place to alert them to the occurrence of those risks.
2. Directors need to ensure that management has identified all the specific material risks the institution faces.
3. Directors and management should agree on plans not only for addressing risks but also for mitigating their impact.[11]

An informed and well-functioning board can help management curb the impact of risks at each step along the way. Directors exercise risk oversight by providing counsel and input into significant policies and frameworks, offering guidance and challenge of strategic decisions and the calibration of the risks, overseeing the outcomes of management's execution of the strategy, and determining the accountability for risk outcomes.

Even the most sophisticated institutions are finding it difficult to achieve profitable growth with the requirement to meet greater regulatory expectations and manage increasingly complex risks. Directors can help management by bringing new perspectives and ideas to the boardroom about which risks the institution faces and what should be done about them.

Directors are in a position to prevent management from taking the risks that could lead to the crisis in the first place. Of course, some risks are beyond the control of management. But even in those cases, timely and comprehensive information provided to

---

[9] "New Challenges for Boards," by Michael Wagner, Oliver Wyman, 2013.
[10] "Risk Oversight: Board Lessons for Turbulent Times," Report of the NACD Blue Ribbon Commission, National Association for Corporate Directors, 2006.
[11] Ibid.

the board potentially can lessen damages.[12] Moreover, a forward-looking view of strategy and risks is critical. Directors can easily get sidelined dealing with historical requirements and past issues. Although these are important, retaining a forward-looking perspective and assessing not only current risks but also emerging risks is a board imperative.

Understandably, neither boards nor management should be expected to identify and prepare for every possible risk an institution could face. Risk management and oversight should focus on the material risks—that is, risks of a magnitude that a reasonably prudent person would consider important in the context of the institution's business because they would have significant adverse impacts.

Directors also need to move beyond merely understanding risks to focusing on resiliency plans and the processes to deal with the impact of unexpected events. The board must ensure that response and recovery plans are in place when an incident occurs. Many institutions have preparedness plans, but wider resilience planning in the face of cybersecurity breaches, reputational damage, operational failures, and strategic risks is sometimes lacking. Importantly, directors need to be comfortable with their role when an incident occurs, both in the near term (for example, potentially moving from oversight to hands-on management) and the longer term (for example, focusing on recovery and managing outcomes).[13]

Oversight vs. Management

Directors ensure good management; they are not meant to provide it.

A central tenet of good corporate governance is the distinction between the board's responsibility for oversight of the business and the affairs of the institution and management's responsibility for the day-to-day operations.

Directors are responsible for providing leadership through decision making and oversight. Absent extraordinary circumstances, the board should not involve itself in the day-to-day operations as this will likely reduce efficiency, impair the board's ability to perform its oversight role objectively, and create uncertainty as to roles and responsibilities. In addition, directors attempting to exercise active day-to-day management or control could create a myriad of operating issues because directors normally lack the experience, expertise, time, and knowledge to perform such a role and they could compromise the board's independence.

The delineation between the oversight responsibilities of directors and the day-to-day operations of management has been recognized by the regulators. The Federal Reserve states that the board should delegate the conducting of the business to management and employees. The OCC notes that the role of directors is to oversee the institution, and one of their fundamental responsibilities is to select and retain competent management with the ability to manage day-to-day operations. Similarly, the Federal Deposit Insurance Corporation, in its "Pocket Guide for Directors," states that the role of the board is to oversee the conduct of the institution's business.[14]

---

[12] Ibid.

[13] "Aggregate Impact of Regulation and the Work of Boards: Rising Above the Detail," 2015.

[14] "Guiding Principles for Enhancing U.S. Banking Organization Corporate Governance," The Clearing House, 2015.

Questions Directors Should Ask About Their Roles and Responsibilities

- Which indicators suggest to directors that the board and management are meeting the minimum standards of the regulators?
- How can the board become comfortable that the proper "tone at the top" and culture have been established?
- How does the board ensure that it takes the long-term view, yet satisfies the short-term requirements? How can the board better support management's long-term strategies?
- What are the specific risks facing the institution? What processes are in place to alert directors to these risks? What are the risk mitigation plans?
- What areas, if any, cause concern about the board's over-reaching into management?
- What are the gaps in the qualifications and the experiences of directors? What are the specific board's capabilities in the areas of global markets and technology?
- How can board and committee time be used more effectively? What improvements can be made to board and committee agendas? Are more (or fewer) meetings required?
- What is the content and quality of the director education programs? Which topics should be covered?
- How can directors gain more interaction with the broader management team, employees, and the regulators?
- What is the design of the board's self-assessment process? Who will lead the evaluation? What are the results and action plans for areas of improvement?
- How can board materials be improved? Are the materials properly contextualized and annotated? How can the volume of materials be reduced?
- How can directors best determine that the minutes to board and committee meetings meet the expectations of the regulators, yet avoid overly detailed transcripts?

From time to time, enforcement actions by the regulators have imposed expanded responsibilities on the boards of the penalized institutions. The Clearing House[15] describes consent orders entered into by the regulators and certain banking institutions in regard to their mortgage servicing operations. These consent orders require the board to ensure that the institution achieves and maintains effective mortgage servicing, foreclosure, and loss mitigation activities, as well as associated risk management, compliance, quality control, audit, training, staffing, and related functions.[16]

In addition, the board may, as a practical matter, become more active when an institution experiences financial difficulty. Directors of an insolvent institution, for example, may decide to more actively participate in key decisions to the extent necessary to protect the interests of stakeholders. Furthermore, the actions of directors reacting to a threatened change in control may be subject to enhanced judicial scrutiny, such that the directors' level of involvement in decision making can intensify. Also, when directors are

---

[15]The Clearing House is a banking association that advocates on regulatory, legislative, and legal public policy issues on behalf of the largest U.S. commercial banks before policy makers, courts of law, and standards setters in the U.S. and abroad.

[16] "Guiding Principles for Enhancing U.S. Banking Organization Corporate Governance," 2015.

deciding to sell the institution or large portions of the business, they are charged with the duty to seek the best price for the shareholders. In these circumstances, the board will often need to be much more closely involved in making decisions and, in certain circumstances, may rely on its own legal and financial advisors in addition to management.[17]

Although the foregoing situations can lead to greater involvement by the board on a temporary basis, directors are nevertheless still acting in an oversight role. There also may be exceptional circumstances when the board's role may go beyond oversight, such as in the event of a sudden departure or incapacitation of one or more senior executives. In these circumstances, it may be necessary and appropriate for a director selected by the board to assume a management role on a temporary basis pending successor appointments. This level of involvement, however, is not a normal function of the board.[18]

"It is the board's responsibility to form policy, approve strategy, and provide the proper oversight. Management is tasked with execution and the day-to-day operations of the business, which is an important and critical distinction," said William S. Thompson Jr., a board member of Citigroup Inc.

Qualifications of Directors

In order to have an informed perspective and provide effective oversight, boards need to possess individuals with a mix of up-to-date skills and experience that encompass the major areas of the business. Collectively, the directors should bring to the boardroom experience, expertise, diversity of views, and wisdom. However, this does not mean expertise is required in every aspect of a large, complex financial institution.

In some cases, boards may lack directors who have the requisite backgrounds and in-depth experience in critical areas, such as international business or technology.

How can boards address these gaps? There are at least three possible approaches:

1. Recruit and appoint a new director or directors with global or technology expertise.
2. Form a separate committee of the board to focus on global or technology opportunities and risks.
3. Appoint one or two designated directors to serve as the board's facilitator on global or technology matters.

Depending on the complexity and importance of issues facing the institution, the board may decide to consider whether it needs at least one director with a sophisticated understanding of key global issues and geographies or technology specifications. The recruitment and appointment of a new director or directors who are experienced in these areas can be very helpful in paving the way and enhancing the board's knowledge. Moreover, these directors may add something to the board that is harder to quantify than specific market know-how or technology expertise, but potentially of even greater value: that is, creating a more open and diverse mind-set and thereby enhancing the board's deliberation and problem-solving skills.

---

[17]Ibid.
[18]Ibid.

How would you describe the importance of having the following attributes on your board?

	(% described as "very important")
Financial expertise	91%
Industry expertise	70%
Operational expertise	66%
Risk management expertise	62%
International expertise	41%
Gender diversity	39%
IT strategy expertise	37%

Source: "Governing for the Long-term: Looking Down the Road with an Eye on the Rear-View Mirror," Annual Corporate Directors Survey, PricewaterhouseCoopers, 2015.

Some boards believe, however, that the appointment of a new "global director" or "technology director" may be limiting, given that no candidate would have all of the required knowledge in these areas. In fact, this may result in an extraordinary burden on these directors regardless of their experience or expertise. The board may also have a false sense of security if it relies on one director for all things global or technology specific.

The complexity and importance of international or technology issues also should be considered in relation to the organization of the board's work through its committee structure.

More specifically, the board needs to determine whether global or technology issues are sufficiently significant to warrant the dedicated attention from a specialized committee or subcommittees. The board should decide where the responsibility for the oversight of global or technology risks is covered, either with the full board or one of its committees.

Some boards form a separate committee, such as a "global markets committee" or a "technology committee," or a subset of an existing committee, focusing on the opportunities and risks in these areas. However, the formation of a separate committee inherently would be populated by the same pool of existing directors, which could result in the over-crowding of committee and board calendars.

In order to facilitate the board's oversight of international or technology matters, the board could also designate a director or two to serve as primary liaison or facilitator for the board or one of its committees. The designation would relate solely to global or technology issues, as defined. The designated director would keep apprised of significant international or technology developments and institutional initiatives, participate in periodic reporting and key meetings, join in site visits, and regularly counsel management. The designated director would be responsible, with management, for keeping the board and its committees informed and facilitating the board's agenda on global or technology matters. The designated director would not have authority to make decisions or otherwise act on behalf of the board or its committees.

As an additional note, directors are striving to become better educated, particularly on global matters. Robert E. Denham, a partner with Munger, Tolles & Olson and a board member of Chevron Corporation, said that "many boards are developing a global mind-set by holding meetings outside the U.S., adding directors with international experience, and working closely with consultants, attorneys, accountants, and other external advisors to leverage their expertise."

Commitment and Allocation of Time

The National Association of Corporate Directors advises that directors need to thoroughly understand the institution's business and its strategy and the underlying assumptions. Such an understanding includes fluency regarding the industry and the environment, in addition to the emerging forces that could shift or even overturn industry norms. Directors must become familiar with the institution's business model and market dynamics. As a result, the NACD concludes that the level of preparation required of individual directors is not only substantial, but increasing significantly.[19]

In addition, as mentioned, directors are increasingly challenged, particularly in regulated industries such as banking (and, to a lesser degree, insurance), to balance the time they spend dealing with regulation and compliance rather than discussing more strategic opportunities and issues.

Many boards struggle to get through long lists of priority items. For example, 10 years ago conduct-related reporting to the board was typically limited to a short summary and update. It now takes up a large portion of board and committee meetings with reports sometimes running into hundreds of pages.[20]

The time commitment of directors depends on the institution's facts and circumstances. Directors need to fully prepare for board and committee meetings, which involves study, reflection, and the formulation of relevant questions. They must also be prepared for unanticipated demands on their time. Although a significant portion of the post-crisis regulatory reform agenda has already been implemented, even more regulation can be expected. Complying with the breadth and volume of regulatory change can consume up to 80% of both board and committee time, according to Deloitte's estimate.[21]

Directors want to make more productive use of their time, according to PwC's Annual Corporate Directors Survey. The survey notes that many directors believe they allocate sufficient time to important topics during boardroom discussions, and nearly two-thirds "very much" believe this is the case. But 56% of directors "somewhat" wish management presentations were less formal and included more spontaneous discussion,

---

[19] "The Board and Long-Term Value Creation," Report of the NACD Blue Ribbon Commission, National Association of Corporate Directors, 2015.
[20] "New Challenges for Boards," 2013.
[21] "Aggregate Impact of Regulating and the Work of Boards: Rising Above the Detail," 2015.

and nearly half of directors want the dialogue with management to be more open and less controlled or scripted.[22]

Board members are generally reluctant to take on additional duties unless the board is convinced that directors have the necessary expertise and time to appropriately perform those duties and, in doing so, will not create confusion as to decision-making authority. Of course, unusual circumstances may require an enhanced level of oversight by the board. When an institution is subject to an enforcement action by the regulators, for example, directors may be obligated to oversee in a more active manner the timely implementation of corrective actions and assess the compliance. It is critical that the specific requirements with respect to corrective actions should not be permitted to distract the board from its broader oversight functions.[23]

"While some directors may be closer to the specifics of regulation or the details of the business, boards collectively need to maintain the 'big picture' perspective and not drown in the details. In today's boardroom, committing and allocating the time of directors is a big challenge," said David E. I. Pyott, a board member of Avery Dennison Corporation, BioMarin Pharmaceuticals Inc., Alnylam Pharmaceutical Inc., and Royal Phillips.

Board 'Best Practices'

Directors need to consider board "best practices" and other measures of excellence in this era of increased scrutiny from stakeholders and heightened regulatory expectations.

Directors' Continuing Education

The OCC's minimum standards provide that, in order to ensure each director has the knowledge, skills, and abilities needed to meet the regulators' expectations, the board should establish and adhere to a formal, ongoing education program for directors. The program should consider the directors' knowledge and experience and the institution's risk profile. The OCC notes that the frequency, scope, and selection of the program's presenters are left to the discretion of the board and management.

Director education and its importance cannot be overemphasized, as the complexity and breadth of issues confronting directors today can be overwhelming. The sessions, presented by either or both internal and external specialists, often cover topics such as industry trends, new products and services, technical reporting pronouncements, peer company profiles, and the larger and more global developments. Committing to an annual board education calendar is a good discipline. In addition to the practical effect of educational sessions on enhanced decision making, the regulators likely will take into account the nature and scope of director education in determining whether the directors sought in good faith to discharge their fiduciary responsibilities.[24]

---

[22] "Governing for the Long-term: Looking Down the Road with an Eye on the Rear-view Mirror," 2015.

[23] "Guiding Principles for Enhancing U.S. Banking Organization Corporate Governance," 2015.

[24] "Fiduciary Duties of Financial Institution Directors and Officers in the Post-Dodd-Frank Era," by Rodney R. Peck and Michael J. Halloran, *International Journal of Disclosure and Governance,* 2015.

Meeting with Key Constituents

The interactions of directors with management and other employees are, in many cases, confined to the boardroom as directors have limited time and few opportunities to meet and discuss issues with broader groups. Such interaction needs to happen more often. "Attendance at management's leadership conferences, which many institutions hold regularly, and access to the buildings to walk the halls, can be helpful for directors to informally talk with management and employees to discern what is actually happening and whether the corporate values are being lived every day," commented M. Christian Mitchell, a board member of Grandpoint Capital, Parsons Corporation, Reis Inc., Stearns Holdings, and Western Asset Mortgage Capital Corp.

In addition, directors should seek to meet and establish a personal rapport with the regulators, including the on-site examiners. The regulators can provide independent, objective advice and information to directors on compliance matters, management's performance, and weaknesses and potential areas for improvement, which can be very informative and particularly insightful.

It is important to recognize, however, that examinations by the regulators do not diminish the board's responsibilities to oversee the business. Directors are responsible for obtaining information from management and other sources as to the condition of the institution and should not rely on the regulators as their principal source of information to identify or surface problems. Instead, directors should also look to management, internal auditors, and outside experts to provide information and perspectives and to identify the important issues.[25]

Board's Annual Self-Assessment

The OCC's minimum standards require that the board conduct a self-assessment, including an evaluation of the board's effectiveness in meeting the heightened standards. The self-assessment is intended to result in a productive dialogue among directors that identifies opportunities for improvement and leads to specific changes that are capable of being tracked, measured, and evaluated. Both the OCC's minimum standards and the listing requirements of public companies require board self-assessments annually.

Board and committee self-assessments can be very productive exercises and useful in uncovering concerns of directors and motivating recommendations for improvement.

An assessment of the board's effectiveness aims to determine the extent to which the board demonstrates effective behaviors that contribute to good governance. The assessment typically includes 1) consideration of how successfully the board communicates and demonstrates the "tone at the top" and the ethical and cultural values of the institution; 2) the opportunity for candid and informed communication among directors; 3) the calibration of how effectively the board interacts with management; 4) the extent to which the board understands and takes into consideration strategic goals and business objectives; and 5) the extent to which directors have access to information that allows them to exercise board responsibilities.

---

[25] "Guiding Principles for Enhancing U.S. Banking Organization Corporate Governance," 2015.

Recommendations to Directors for Long-Term Value Creation

- In order to build and maintain a sufficiently thorough understanding of the institution's business model and industry context, directors need to factor substantial preparation time into their board duties.
- Institutions need to maintain a direct connection between short-term viability and long-term value creation.
- The board's CEO selection and evaluation processes should include an assessment of the extent to which he or she is an effective advocate for the long-term strategy.
- To enhance discussions of short- and long-term strategy, directors should seek information from a range of internal and external sources.
- Boards should ensure that major capital allocation and annual budget decisions reflect long-term strategic objectives as well as short-term priorities.
- A component related to progress against long-term goals and objectives should be included in the annual incentive plans for the CEO and management.
- Directors should approach board composition and succession planning with long-term needs in mind, based on the director skills that will be most relevant in three, five, or more years.
- Make clarifying the connection between the institution's short- and medium-term actions and its longer-term strategic objectives a primary objective of investor communications.
- Boards should consider recommending a move away from quarterly earnings guidance in favor of broader guidance parameters tied to long-term performance and strategic objectives.
- The shareholder communications plan should include preparing selected members of the board to engage directly with investors on selected governance matters, including the oversight of long-term strategy.

Source: "The Board and Long-Term Value Creation," Report of the NACD Blue Ribbon Commission, National Association of Corporate Directors, 2015.

Many assessments are conducted by the board's chairman or lead director, or led by the nominating and governance committee. Although the evaluations are well intentioned, directors nevertheless are sometimes unwilling to disclose perceived weaknesses to those most responsible for the effective functioning of the board. As a result, best practices suggest engaging an independent third party to design the assessment process and conduct the interviews. This may not be necessary every year, but can be used on a rotating basis. In fact, counsel is often engaged to help protect the results of the exercise under attorney-client privilege.

The board evaluation process needs to be appropriately organized, conducted, and documented to avoid creating a misleading, and potentially harmful, record. The use of written questionnaires, if not properly managed, can create a record that does not accurately reflect the overall views of the directors and could be taken out of context. As an alternative, the board may want to structure the evaluation as an open discussion with individual directors that is ultimately condensed into a written report or PowerPoint presentation to the board.[26]

Board Materials

The board's ability to effectively deliberate and provide proper oversight is only as good as the information it receives. Effective board governance requires that directors receive the right information, in the right format, and in a timely fashion. There is much room for improvement in this area. PwC's Annual Corporate Directors Survey notes that two-thirds of directors "somewhat" or "very much" wish their materials would better highlight the risks associated with the topics presented. A similar percentage would like more management summaries and insights.[27]

In carrying out its monitoring function, the board may rely on reports prepared by management if the directors are confident that they are reliable. Directors must believe in good faith that the reports are accurate and contain sufficient details to allow for effective monitoring. To that end, the board should satisfy itself that the information and reporting systems are designed to provide timely and accurate information sufficient for the directors to reach informed judgments.

Board materials should reflect the scale, scope, and complexity of the institution. Too many boards drown in a mass of information that does not permit appropriate preparation given the time available. Therefore, all board reports, to be meaningful, need to be contextualized and annotated, and include an executive summary that allows directors to focus on the important items. Directors should be consulted about which materials they will require to make informed decisions, to avoid overloading the reports with irrelevant or repetitive information.

In addition, management presentations to the board need to be succinct, yet still provide an appropriate level of detail. Presenters should assume that directors have read the board materials in advance so that the discussion gets right to the main points and stays within the allotted time.

Directors need to be aware that the regulators regularly review materials distributed to the board, especially those involving risk management issues and major deliberations and decisions. Deficient board materials can be a source of criticism.[28]

Many high-performing boards employ electronic board books, which eliminate the need for voluminous and unmanageable hard-copy board materials. However, the use of iPads and similar devices to store board books often results in an even greater volume of board and committee materials. Directors need to counsel management that the intended use of electronic board books is to make board packages more efficient and they should not be viewed as an opportunity to substitute quantity for quality.

Finally, it needs to be a priority that, prior to the meeting, all board materials are provided to the directors in sufficient time for them to study the content, seek addi-

---

[26] Ibid.
[27] "Governing for the Long-term: Looking Down the Road with an Eye on the Rear-view Mirror," 2015.
[28] "Fiduciary Duties of Financial Institution Directors and Officers in the Post-Dodd-Frank Era," 2015.

tional information, and consult with management. Being well prepared not only means attempting to be informed on matters before the board, but also being equipped with important questions and observations. For directors to attend a meeting without adequate preparation is a missed opportunity.

Board Minutes

Boards and their committees are required by state corporate law to keep minutes of their proceedings, which constitute an important part of the books and records.

In order to demonstrate the degree of care taken by the board on important issues, the minutes of board meetings need to be comprehensive. In other contexts, however, corporate lawyers often advise that minutes should be primarily a record of actions taken, rather than a burdensome detailing of the deliberations. Today, in response to the regulators' expectations, it is advisable for the minutes to include appropriate narratives to demonstrate the board's credible challenge to management.[29]

There is wide variation with respect to the level of detail presented in minutes. There is no single correct approach to recording minutes, and the board should agree on one based on its circumstances and specific needs. The Clearing House believes the minutes should not be a verbatim transcript of the meeting and, in particular, should not attribute specific views to particular directors in a way that could chill discussion. But the minutes should cover, at a minimum, a description of significant subjects discussed, the nature of the debates, the decisions reached, and any dissenting votes or abstentions.[30]

"We generally prefer limited minute-taking in board and committee meetings to avoid inappropriate use in the event of possible litigation. However, the regulators expect, and we need to be responsive to, the need for sufficiently detailed minutes and robust documentation in board and committee books," commented Michael F. Coyne, general counsel, MUFG Union Bank.

Final Comments

Directors must never forget that they have been chosen for a position of special trust and confidence. Serving on a board is a cooperative, collegial endeavor in which the ultimate goal is to advance collective interests. Individual ego and personal interests must therefore be subordinated to the interests of the board and the interests of all stakeholders. Accordingly, while directors should approach all matters with an open mind and be receptive to the ideas of others, in the end they must rely on their own sense of what is fair, equitable, and in the best interests of the institution.[31]

---

[29] Ibid.

[30] "Guiding Principles for Enhancing U.S. Banking Organization Corporate Governance," 2015.

[31] "A Practical Guide: Fundamentals for Corporate Directors," National Association of Corporate Directors, 2012.

'Credible Challenge' and the Search for Excellence

"Judge a man by his questions rather than by his answers."

— VOLTAIRE

Following the 2008 financial crisis, the regulators and elected government officials responsible for ensuring the safety and stability of the capital markets launched a plethora of commissions and special inquiries aimed at determining why risk management processes were ineffective.

The prevailing view is that the financial crisis could be traced, in large part, to the failure of corporate governance and risk management systems. At some institutions, this view suggests that boards and management did not sufficiently comprehend aggregate risk and that the institutions lacked sufficiently robust risk frameworks. In other words, the people, systems, and processes for monitoring the complex galaxy of risks failed.

In some cases, compensation programs were structured to share upside benefits but not the downside risks. Inadequate and fragmented technology infrastructures hindered efforts to identify, measure, monitor, and control risk. Some of these institutions had risk cultures lacking effective challenge from independent risk managers, audit, and control personnel. While these problems existed to some extent at institutions of all sizes, the regulators embrace the view that the problems were most pronounced in the largest, most complex institutions and that they posed the greatest threat to the stability of the financial system.

In response to the crisis, the Office of the Comptroller of the Currency resolved to raise the standards for corporate governance and risk management systems. The OCC developed an informal set of heightened expectations, also referred to as the "getting to strong" program, to enhance its supervision and strengthen the governance and risk management practices of large institutions. The heightened expectations were meant to reflect the OCC's experience during the financial crisis and address certain weaknesses observed in the governance and risk management practices of large institutions. Although most of the regulatory attention since the financial crisis has been focused on mandating higher levels of capital at institutions of all sizes, the OCC's heightened expectations program was primarily directed at risk management processes.

Remarks by Comptroller Curry

The OCC's intent with its heightened expectations program was to clarify and raise the bar for corporate governance at the largest and most complex institutions. In doing so, it significantly ratcheted up the expectations for independent directors. Thomas J. Curry, the Comptroller of the Currency, suggested that the regulators expect directors to present a "credible challenge" to management and to have a thorough knowledge of not only the risks their institution is taking on, but also how management is addressing these risks. It means that the OCC is no longer willing to accept risk management systems that are simply satisfactory. Comptroller Curry and the OCC seek excellence. The expectation is that large institutions will meet high standards and that risk management functions and independent directors will take a strong hand in ensuring compliance.[32]

Comptroller Curry also said that, in the wake of the financial crisis, more is expected of financial institutions of all sizes in terms of their operations and financial profitability. He noted that there are heightened expectations for the regulators as well—in particular, for them to do their job in a way that keeps the banking system safe and sound and avoids anything like what was endured during the crisis.[33]

The OCC's Guidelines

As mentioned, in September 2014, the OCC issued "Guidelines Establishing Heightened Standards for Certain Large Insured Banks, Insured Savings Associations, and Insured Federal Branches." The guidelines, which are frequently referred to as heightened or minimum standards, apply to national banks, federal savings associations, and insured federal branches of foreign banks with average total consolidated assets of $50 billion or more measured on the basis of average total consolidated assets for the previous four calendar years. Once the threshold is crossed, there is no turning back, even if the institution has four quarters with less than $50 billion in total consolidated assets.

The guidelines also apply to institutions with less than $50 billion in assets if they are determined by the OCC to be highly complex or likely to present heightened risk.

The OCC recognizes that insured federal branches are not required to have a statutory board of directors and that their risk governance frameworks will vary owing to the variety of activities performed in the branch. As a result, the OCC intends to apply the guidelines to insured federal branches in a flexible manner.

While the guidelines apply specifically to large institutions, directors need to be cognizant that the regulators are expecting a strong industry commitment toward the proper oversight of risks. It is likely, and even probable, that the regulators will impose on virtually all banks various elements of the OCC's guidelines. "All institutions irrespective of size need to take notice of these guidelines and calibrate and adjust board and management practices accordingly," noted Philip B. Flynn, president and CEO, Associated Bank.

The guidelines are intended to advance the heightened expectations program, as memorialized by the OCC's informal set of heightened expectations. Using these guidelines,

---

[32] Remarks by Thomas J. Curry at the 49th Annual Conference on Bank Structure and Competition, Chicago, Illinois, May 9, 2013.

[33] Remarks by Thomas J. Curry at the ABA Risk Management Forum, Orlando, Florida, April 10, 2014.

examiners now assess risk management practices and the effectiveness of the board's oversight to identify weaknesses and to communicate to the board and management those areas requiring improvement.

The guidelines establish six minimum standards for the board in providing oversight to the risk governance framework's design and implementation:

1. Require an effective framework. Directors should oversee compliance with safe and sound practices and require management to establish and implement an effective risk governance framework that meets the guidelines' standards.
2. Provide active oversight of management. The board should actively oversee risk-taking activities and hold management accountable for adhering to the framework.
3. Exercise independent judgment. Directors are expected to exercise sound, independent judgment when providing oversight.
4. Include independent directors. Board membership should include at least two independent directors.
5. Provide ongoing training to all directors. The board should establish and adhere to a formal, ongoing education program for directors that considers the directors' knowledge and experience as well as the institution's risk profile.
6. Conduct self-assessments. The board should conduct an annual self-assessment that includes an evaluation of its effectiveness in meeting the standards established for the board in the guidelines.

The guidelines indicate that directors should be financially knowledgeable and committed to conducting diligent reviews of management, the financials, and business plans. The OCC will evaluate each director's knowledge and experience, as demonstrated in his or her written biography and in discussions with examiners.

The guidelines reemphasize the OCC's expectations that the board provide a "credible challenge" to management. The OCC believes that directors will be able to exert this challenge if they have a comprehensive understanding of the risk-taking activities and actively engage in providing oversight to those activities. As noted, the OCC seems to believe that some directors, almost solipsistically, had an incomplete understanding of their institutions' risk exposures during the financial crisis. To the OCC, this suggests a failure to exercise adequate oversight of management and to critically evaluate management's recommendations and decisions during the years preceding the financial crisis.

In issuing the guidelines, the OCC did not intend to impose managerial responsibilities on the board or to suggest that the board must guarantee results under the risk framework. The guidelines do indicate, however, that the directors should require management to establish and implement an effective framework with the board's oversight.

The guidelines also provide that the board or its risk committee should approve significant, but not all, changes to the risk framework and monitor compliance. Directors are required to monitor compliance by overseeing management's implementation of the framework and holding management accountable.

As part of its program of minimum standards, the OCC expects management to provide the board with enough information on the institution's risk profile and management practices to ensure operation within the board-approved risk appetite. (Risk appe-

The Board's Credible Challenge: Areas of Regulatory Focus

	Areas of Focus
Corporate Strategy	Evaluation of capital, liquidity, funding, and risk management in the creation of the annual strategy and the funding plan.
Budgeting and Planning	Review and consideration of key financial and nonfinancial metrics informing the budget.
Institutional Performance	Maintenance of a thorough understanding of the institution, the industry, emerging trends and risks, and management's assumptions in order to ensure performance objectives are met.
Significant Transactions	Evaluation of proposed transactions to ensure they align with strategic and risk objectives, are sufficiently planned and financed, and have the appropriate infrastructure in place.
Risk Management	Enforcement of a risk management framework that contemplates trends, is clearly communicated and consistently applied, and is incorporated into all aspects of business planning.
Compensation	Development of compensation practices that retain top talent and do not encourage irresponsible risk management behaviors.
Succession Planning	Formulation of a succession plan in the event of a planned or unplanned change in leadership.
Culture and Ethics	Creation of an environment requiring adherence to a code of ethics that cascades through the enterprise, including management and all employees.
Capital Stress Testing (CCAR)	Evaluation of the institution's capital stress-testing program.
Resolution Planning	Development of resolution planning by requiring business management involvement and creating initiatives to enhance resolvability.

Source: "Board of Directors: Effective Challenge," PricewaterhouseCoopers, 2015.

tite defines the aggregate level and types of risk the board and management are willing to accept to achieve strategic objectives and business plans.) If variances arise, the OCC expects directors to offer a challenge to management.

In providing oversight, directors may rely on independent risk management and internal audit. In addition, some boards periodically engage third-party experts to assist them in understanding the risks and to make recommendations to strengthen board and institutional practices. While the guidelines are focused on independent risk management and internal audit, they do not prohibit boards from engaging third-party experts to also assist them in carrying out their responsibilities.

The OCC believes that the capacity to dedicate sufficient time and energy to reviewing information and developing an understanding of the key issues related to risk-taking activities is a critical prerequisite to being an effective director. Informed directors are well positioned to engage in substantive discussions with management in which the board provides approval to management, requests guidance to clarify areas of uncertainty, and questions the propriety of strategic initiatives. Therefore, the guidelines provide that directors, in reliance on information they receive from independent risk management, internal audit, and other sources, should question, challenge, and, when necessary, oppose recommendations and decisions made by management that could cause the institution's risk profile to exceed its risk appetite or jeopardize the safety and soundness of the institution. In addition to resulting in a more informed board, the OCC expects that this provision will enable directors to make a determination as to whether management is adhering to, and understands, the risk framework.

As an illustration of this point, recurring breaches of risk limits or actions that cause the risk profile to materially exceed the risk appetite may demonstrate that management does not understand or is not adhering to the framework. In these situations, the guidelines recommend that the directors take action to hold the appropriate party, or parties, accountable.

The OCC does not intend the guidelines to become a compliance exercise or lead to scripted meetings between the board and management. Instead, the OCC will assess compliance primarily by engaging its examiners in frequent conversations with directors.

Likewise, the OCC does not expect directors to evidence opposition to management during every board meeting. Instead, the OCC expects directors to oppose management's recommendations and decisions only when necessary. The OCC believes that an environment in which examiners, directors, and management openly communicate will benefit the institution.

These guidelines effectively hardwire the informal expectations program into the OCC examination process.

The minimum standards are prescribed by the OCC in the form of guidelines rather than formal regulations. "Minimum standards give the OCC more flexibility in determining whether to require a noncompliant institution to submit a formal remediation plan or to tailor a different remedy, taking into account the institution's circumstances and its self-corrective or remedial efforts," said Rodney R. Peck, partner, Pillsbury Winthrop Shaw Pittman, and a board member of Bank of the West.

Other Regulatory Initiatives

The OCC's guidelines represent only one, albeit an important, part of the latest trends in rulemakings and pronouncements that focus on an institution's risk management framework and corporate governance structure in addition to the board's responsibilities.

When it comes to risk management, the regulators expect the whole to be greater than the sum of its parts. The Federal Reserve is focused on the enterprise-wide consolidated view of the institution, while the OCC expects the institution to evaluate and manage risk separate from its parent in order to protect the national bank charter. Both views are aligned and have the fundamental requirements of stronger risk management and governance.

Building upon lessons learned from the crisis, the Board of Governors of the Federal Reserve System also has taken a number of important steps to improve its supervisory program for large institutions. These initiatives have focused not just on the amount of capital an institution maintains, but also on the internal practices and policies an institution uses to determine the amount and composition of capital that would be adequate, given the institution's risk exposures and strategies as well as regulatory expectations and standards. Corporate governance, risk appetite, and risk management are viewed as important aspects of these initiatives.

In December 2012, the Federal Reserve issued SR 12-17, "Consolidated Supervision Framework for Large Financial Institutions." The framework has two primary objectives. First, each institution is expected to ensure that the consolidated institution and its core business lines can survive under a range of internal or external stresses. This requires financial resilience, achieved by maintaining sufficient capital and liquidity, and operational resilience, achieved by maintaining effective corporate governance, risk management, and recovery planning. Second, each institution is expected to ensure the sustainability of its critical operations under a range of internal and external stresses. This requires, among other things, effective resolution planning that addresses the complexity and the interconnectivity of the institution's operations.

In August 2013, the Federal Reserve issued "Capital Planning at Large Bank Holding Companies: Supervisory Expectations and Range of Current Practice" (the ROPE guidance). These guidelines describe the Fed's expectations for internal capital planning at the large, complex institutions subject to its capital plan rules, referred to as the Comprehensive Capital Analysis and Review (CCAR).

The ROPE guidance indicates that the board has ultimate oversight responsibility and accountability for capital planning and should be in a position to make informed decisions.

Directors should receive information sufficient to understand the material risks and exposures in order to inform and support decisions on capital planning and adequacy. The information needs to include a discussion of key limitations, assumptions, and uncertainties within the capital planning process so that directors are fully informed of any weaknesses in the process and can effectively challenge reported results before making capital decisions. The ROPE guidance suggests that boards with stronger practices have sufficient expertise and a level of engagement to understand and critically evaluate the information provided by management.

Federal Reserve Chair Janet Yellen notes that, while there is some evidence of improved risk management, internal controls, and governance at the biggest institutions, compliance breakdowns in recent years continue to undermine confidence in risk management and controls. Given the size, complexity, and interconnectedness of the institutions, she said that this could have implications for financial stability.[34]

The trend toward greater regulatory expectations for directors will continue in the foreseeable future as the following events unfold:

- The Federal Reserve implements the Dodd-Frank Act's enhanced risk management standards for large U.S. bank holding companies, large foreign banking organizations, and systemically important nonbank financial companies.

---

[34] Remarks by Janet L. Yellen at the Committee on Financial Services, U.S. House of Representatives, Washington, D.C., November 4, 2015.

Effective Oversight of Risks

Regulatory Expectations

- The board should receive information from management sufficient to understand the material risks and exposures. The information should be received at least quarterly or when there are significant developments.
- Reports to the board should include a discussion of key limitations, assumptions, and uncertainties within the risk framework, to fully inform directors of any weaknesses in the process so they can effectively challenge reported results.
- Reports to the board should include management's strategies to address key limitations identified in the risk management framework so that directors can assess reported strategies and take appropriate action to address weaknesses.

Industry Best Practices

- Reports to the board should provide timely, concise, and accurate information, with key takeaways concerning
  - Current and expected market conditions.
  - Enterprise-wide risk issues and mitigating measures.
  - Risk and performance profiles of each line of business.
- Reports to the board should include management's assessment of end-to-end risk management and reporting. This assessment outlines the strengths and limitations of the information provided to the board, including those related to data, models, and report production.
- Reports to the board need to include high-level summaries of efforts to improve risk-data quality and accuracy, as well as assessments of the controls used in producing and aggregating risk information.

Source: "Board Governance: Higher Expectations, But Better Practice?" PricewaterhouseCoopers, January 2016.

- Banking institutions design and implement comprehensive compliance and risk governance programs for the Volcker Rule, the Dodd-Frank liquidity risk management standards, capital planning and stress testing, the changing derivative regulatory landscape, and other important legal and regulatory developments.
- The Federal Reserve and Federal Deposit Insurance Corporation apply similar risk governance principles to large state banks, and all U.S. banking agencies apply over time some or all of these principles to mid-size banks.[35]

Given these pronouncements, it is apparent that minimum standards for risk governance are here to stay, and their criticality for the regulators will continue to increase. "The focus of regulators on such issues as capital adequacy, liquidity, operational risk, governance, and culture is driving change throughout the financial services industry. The minimum standards of the regulators place serious new responsibilities on both directors and management," noted Eugene A. Ludwig, founder and CEO, Promontory Financial Group.

---

[35] "Introduction to Risk Governance and the OCC's Guidelines," Davis Polk, 2014.

Siren Call to Directors

The financial services industry has faced significant challenges since the financial crisis. The pace of change is unprecedented and, at times, bewildering. Many boards and management must contend with multiple jurisdictions and timetables for new regulations and expectations, while facing higher penalties for noncompliance. The regulators seem determined to avoid putting taxpayers on the hook for another round of bailouts.

The primary driver of the OCC's guidelines is that there needs to be an entity or body—ultimately, the board—that serves to establish the acceptable level of risk. The expectation is that directors will establish and monitor the level of risk and that they will need to push back on management and the business lines, which naturally want to increase risk as a trade-off for greater profitability.

The Risk Management Association supports the notion of credible challenge and believes that the appropriate role of the board is to provide oversight by critically evaluating management's recommendations and decisions. In this regard, directors need to understand the content of these recommendations and decisions, the desired outcomes, and the material risks. They must determine whether management has properly assessed the risks and has either developed appropriate mitigation strategies or willingly accepted the risks known at the time.[36]

Risk Management in the Banking Sector
Survey Results

Key Challenges

Difficult economic climate   Demanding regulations   Competition from digital innovators

Signs of Growth

41% of respondents have raised risk appetites for new products.

79% think risk functions play an important role in enabling growth.

14% say they have achieved fully risk-based decision making.

Source: "Global Risk Management Study: Banking Report," Accenture, 2015.

The guidelines are intended to encourage and in fact compel the board's challenge to management, but they are not meant to promote confrontation between directors and management at board and committee meetings or even outside forums. However, directors are expected to expand their oversight of risk in meaningful ways, a notion that is becoming widely emphasized by the regulators. It is not simply that directors question each and every decision of management. These guidelines require a board that is active and informed when it comes to risk matters. At the same time, the board does not operate at the front lines of the business. Directors rely on management and a network of reporting processes to remain informed about the risks.

---

[36] Letter from The Risk Management Association to the Office of the Comptroller of the Currency, March 25, 2014.

The Clearing House believes that the board's challenge should consist of informed and probing questions to management, inside or outside of the boardroom, rather than a formal record of disagreements with management or rejections of management recommendations. In particular, The Clearing House does not believe that the effectiveness of challenge can be evaluated based on the number of challenges recorded in the minutes or elsewhere.[37]

Some believe that the biggest handicap directors face today in overseeing risk is self-inflicted. Many directors, for a variety of reasons, including the rationales "This is how we have always done it" or "It would be impolite to ask," have simply not asked management for the type, quality, and quantity of information necessary to meet increased risk oversight and risk governance expectations.[38]

Directors are compelled to pursue new approaches in effectively challenging management decisions. Directors need to help management establish a "tone at the top" that fosters transparency in decision making and communication, as well as vigorous adherence to a code of ethics. Additionally, directors should create independence in board decision making by incorporating objective advice from both internal and external sources. Pointed questions that allow directors to consider broader institutional objectives, culture, and the risk appetite when approving budgets, financial plans, and executive compensation are essential and very effective.[39]

Directors must undertake a process that allows them to receive sufficient information about the business, risks, and performance in real time, including formal written opinions on the effectiveness of the risk management process from assurance providers. The board must then take this information and use it to challenge assumptions, projections, and strategic initiatives of management. Directors must be comfortable that management has thought through the plans and is responding appropriately to questions and comments.

A dilemma for boards in obtaining more and better information is the risk of asymmetric data, or simply the gap between the information known by management and the information presented to the board. The role of a director, by nature, is less than a full-time position. As such, directors rely heavily on management to provide the information needed to evaluate risks and performance. Management cannot, and should not, provide every piece of data to the board. As a result, gaps can arise in what management knows versus what it presents to the board. Directors need to have confidence that the information reflects the facts and the realities of the business. The regulators are often helpful in identifying and helping to remedy information gaps when they occur.

Creating and fostering a culture that actively supports a credible challenge is extraordinarily difficult. Conflict, which generally is avoided at all cost, can be a key ingredient in searching for the facts, reaching the right conclusions, and making the best decisions. In all businesses and in many boardrooms, there is a fine line between being a "challenger" and

---

[37] "Guiding Principles for Enhancing U.S. Banking Organization Corporate Governance," The Clearing House, 2015.
[38] "Risk Oversight: Evolving Expectations for Boards," by Parveen P. Gupta and Tim J. Leech, The Conference Board Governance Center, January 2014.
[39] "Board of Directors: Effective Challenge," PricewaterhouseCoopers, December 2015.

Questions Directors Should Ask As a Credible Challenge

- What information is being shared with the board? Is the information sufficiently detailed, yet not overwhelming, for directors to understand and evaluate the critical risks?
- Are the proper resources in place to manage risks? Are the risk management capabilities improving regularly enough to ensure that risks are being managed properly in a dynamic environment?
- How are risk appetite and the risk management framework embedded into the business?
- Are the directors and management aligned with regard to the appetite for risk? How do directors evaluate the impact of the compensation program on management's risk taking?
- As new initiatives, products, and services are introduced, which processes are in place to evaluate the risks in advance of decision making? What are the thresholds for when matters need to be brought to the board before a decision is finalized or risks escalated?
- How is risk management used to add competitive advantage and value by addressing the gaps in the operations?
- What is the quality of the internal controls supporting the risk management framework?
- Which mechanisms are in place for the board to assess management's data against industry trends and other objective sources to ensure performance is measured accurately?
- In dealing with the regulators, are the institution's risk management initiatives and activities properly and comprehensively described? What is the level of the documentation demonstrating directors' credible challenge?
- Which gaps in directors' experience and expertise need to be addressed in order for the board to provide credible challenge to management?

---

being an "obstructionist." Success in this space is predicated on a culture that truly values challenge and debate.[40]

According to the guidelines, active oversight does not mean that directors should be assuming management functions. Although Comptroller Curry's commentaries and the OCC's guidelines are helpful in determining the director's role and responsibilities regarding the oversight of risk, it is likely that some directors will occasionally be drawn precariously close to management functions as they perform their own investigations and engage in overseeing management.

Considerable management support is required as it relates to overseeing risk and exercising a credible challenge. Directors will need more documentation to support management's assertions about risks and how they are being managed. Directors should be receiving high-level information and key current and emerging risk data and actionable reports. Management's reports will need to be able to highlight the current state of risk and emerging themes in ways that are understandable so that directors can assess the information in greater depth. Best practices are focused on quality data that is supported by sufficient analysis and synthesis to make it relevant and transparent. As a result, enhanced oversight likely requires more board and committee meetings, better analytics

---

[40] "Barriers to Achieving Credible Challenge," by Robert A. Prentice and Yousef A. Valine, *The RMA Journal,* July-August 2015.

of the information, a commitment to board education, and a much greater command of each specific risk's details.[41]

As the guidelines bring a new level of detail to board-level issues, it may be necessary, in some cases, to perform a gap analysis of the institution and the board to ensure compliance and meet the expectations of regulators. Both the board and management need to be committed to addressing the gaps or deficiencies appropriately.

The levels of litigation and regulatory risks have become more than likely elevated as boards and management implement more transparent and demonstrable risk management systems. Better and more formal risk management processes and improved information can, as a by-product, burden directors with detailed and documented knowledge of the risk acceptance and risk tolerance decisions that have the potential for controversy. These new risks of greater scrutiny and the possibility for more litigation must be fully understood by directors, and mitigation strategies need to be thoughtfully developed.[42]

Care must be exercised in what is documented and in the level of detail supporting the board's credible challenge. The regulators will focus on the number of risk committee meetings and their duration, the quality of information provided, and the active engagement of the directors. All of these factors serve to demonstrate the level of interaction, the presence of effective challenge, and the perceived importance of risk. It is also important to document in the minutes and in the board materials that management is working through the issues that have been raised by the directors' challenges. [43]

Final Comments

The standards for board oversight are evolving rapidly, and many directors are facing significant challenges in meeting the new expectations. The notion of the board's credible challenge presents a serious next step for directors in the search for excellence.

Directors need to digest the regulatory requirements and understand the expectations of the regulators. Each board member is expected to have knowledge and meaningful experience to add value to the discussion of risks and the risk framework. Directors also need to dedicate ample time and energy to understanding the business and the institution's inherent and emerging risks. This understanding is achieved not only by studying and absorbing board materials and presentations, but also, in many cases, by walking the halls of the institution to become acquainted with its people, programs, and processes.

Credible challenge is presented by those directors who apply their knowledge, invest the requisite time and effort, and have both the confidence to ask difficult questions and the tenacity to pursue acceptable responses.

---

[41] "Stronger: OCC's Heightened Expectations, Enhancing Risk Management and Driving Growth," Deloitte, 2014.

[42] "Risk Oversight: Evolving Expectations for Boards," January 2014.

[43] "OCC Final Guidelines Establishing Heightened Standards for Certain Large Insured Banking Institutions," KPMG, September 2014.

PART

Oversight of the Risk Framework

Introduction to Part II: Oversight of the Risk Framework

"It is not the ship so much as the skilled sailing that assures a prosperous voyage."
—GEORGE WILLIAM CURTIS

The National Association of Corporate Directors maintains that the greatest risk any institution faces is the potential failure of its board to provide effective oversight—particularly risk oversight through proper corporate governance.

The board's role in risk governance continues to attract the attention of the regulators, who expect the appropriate tone at the top to be established by the board and management. While the largest institutions have made significant progress toward meeting expectations, many still have work to do.

"Risk oversight" describes the board's role in the risk management process. Effective risk oversight determines that the institution has in place a robust process for identifying, prioritizing, sourcing, managing, and monitoring its critical risks. By contrast, "risk management" is what management does to execute the risk management process in accordance with established performance goals and risk tolerances. As a result, the role of risk oversight becomes the process by which directors and management develop a mutual understanding of the institution's risks.

The financial crisis exposed inherent weaknesses in risk management, evidenced by inconsistent governance, siloed infrastructures, disparate systems and processes, fragmented decision making, inadequate forecasting, and a dearth of cohesive reporting. The negative impacts on many institutions shocked the financial services industry, resulting in a very notable shift in the attitudes toward risk. Directors are at the forefront of this transformation.

The regulations that emerged from the financial crisis and the fines that were levied in its wake triggered a wave of change in the risk functions of financial institutions. These include more detailed and demanding capital leverage, liquidity, and funding requirements, as well as higher standards for risk reporting. The management of nonfinancial risks has become more important, and the standards for compliance and conduct have tightened. Stress testing has emerged as a major regulatory tool in tandem with the rise of expectations for risk appetite statements and frameworks. Financial institutions also have invested in strengthening their risk cultures and are involving their boards more closely in key risk decisions.

Risk is a much riskier proposition than it used to be. New risks are emerging as markets get disrupted, political instability interrupts initiatives and programs, and new technology pushes boundaries and limits across the risk spectrum. Yet, while some directors see risk as a negative, effective risk management can actually help businesses grow faster and pursue new opportunities.

In addition, public opinion and the perception of fairness are changing fundamentally. Consumers are less willing to accept the principle of "caveat emptor" when it comes to financial products and services. This provides institutions with a fundamental challenge given that what is acceptable today may be unacceptable tomorrow.

Boards and management are reconstituting strategies to reflect the enhanced focus on risk, both short term and longer term, and the risk culture. Changes required to institutionalize a strong risk culture are far-reaching, so that risk becomes the business of everyone, led by the directors and management but championed by all employees. Directors are challenging management to clearly define the risk appetite and drive its implementation throughout the institution and align risk-related responsibilities and accountabilities. As a result, institutions are investing heavily in time and technology to strengthen the processes and tools to manage risk more effectively.

Directors who understand the threats and vulnerabilities are much more able to effectively challenge management and provide guidance and leadership. The board's role of providing proper oversight is best accomplished when risk is woven into virtually every discussion in the boardroom and not set aside and addressed as a discrete activity. Board members need to recognize that establishing and overseeing a risk framework that attempts to adopt best practices is an interactive process. It requires the board and management to continuously monitor and reevaluate the responses to emerging risks, new technologies, and regulatory issues, as well as develop thoughtful mitigation plans.

In addition, directors face increasing challenges in balancing the time they spend on regulatory matters with business issues. Complying with the volume and breadth of regulatory change can be daunting. The regulators are themselves under pressure in today's changing and complex environment and are struggling to provide "bright line" rules and definitions for institutions to follow. Consequently, directors and management need to find their own definitions of what constitutes a sustainable business and profitable operating model with an acceptable risk profile.

A director's voyage through risk management begins with understanding the risk governance framework. The framework includes overseeing the methods and processes used to manage risks and seizing opportunities related to achieving objectives. It involves identifying events or circumstances relevant to the risks, assessing them in terms of likelihood and magnitude of impact, determining a response strategy, and monitoring progress.

Financial risks and controls are now well understood, and as a result established frameworks exist. Operational risks are supported by developing risk and control frameworks, while the more elusive strategic risk and reputation risk frameworks for many institutions remain works in progress.

The board has two primary areas of focus in overseeing the risk framework: 1) how to ensure the key risks are identified and prioritized; and 2) how to integrate risk management into the fabric of the institution so that it does not become a layer of bureaucracy or disconnected from those who really know and are accountable for the operations.

Directors should be regularly asking the following five questions as they oversee the risk framework:

1. Does the risk profile reflect the significant risks facing the institution? What are the gaps?
2. What is the extent of continuing improvements being made to risk management capabilities to ensure that risks are being effectively managed in a changing environment?

3. What is the alignment of the board and management with regard to the appetite for risk?

4. What is the risk culture and is it encouraging the right behaviors?

5. How is risk management integrated with other management processes?

Part II focuses on specific aspects of the board's oversight of the risk framework. Chapters 3 and 4 address the criticalness of the culture and the importance of establishing and monitoring the risk appetite framework. Chapters 5 to 12 discuss strategic risk, reputational risk, risks with information technology, cybersecurity threats, IT budgets, risk and capital, model risk, and third-party risks. For bank directors in particular, these are some of today's more challenging areas.

Part III expands on the coverage of risks by addressing global megatrends and the growing threats posed by these disruptive forces.

Risk Culture Is an Enigma

"Culture is what is left after everything we have learned has been forgotten."
—G. Bromley Oxnam

Risk culture is an enigma. It is critical, yet difficult to define, and a challenge to change once it becomes embedded in the fabric of an institution.

The Group of Thirty,[44] a consultative group that examines global economic and monetary affairs, suggests that banks and banking today stand in disrepute. The Group maintains that poor cultural foundations and significant cultural failures were major drivers of the financial crisis and that they continue to be factors in the scandals since then, exacerbated by employees with questionable conduct and values who move from bank to bank with impunity. The Group says that unhealthy cultural norms or subcultures within large institutions (including in some cases criminal behavior) have hurt the public, caused reputational damage and loss of public trust, and been financially costly in terms of fines, litigation, and regulatory actions. This has been economically costly to society at large and a major distraction for both boards and management. According to the G30, banking is at a low point in terms of customer trust, reputation, and economic returns, and steps must be taken to reverse this situation.[45]

Regulators across the world are focusing on culture and introducing changes that require boards to establish, shape, and monitor the risk culture. Repeated conduct failures in the financial services industry have caused directors, with the urging of the regulators, to demand significant, tangible enhancements to governance, structure, and controls in order to improve risk behaviors.

Culture is a major factor impacting the severity of risks. Weaknesses in risk culture are often viewed as a root cause of headline risk and compliance events. "In my experience, virtually all large, systematic risk incidents are linked to a cultural root cause," said Richard C. Hartnack, board member of Synchrony Financial.

---

[44] The Group of Thirty is an informal group composed of 30 of the world's central bankers, practitioners, academics, and others. Based in Washington, D.C., the G30 meets twice annually to discuss economics, foreign exchange, capital markets, and other matters.
[45] "Banking Conduct and Culture: A Call for Sustained and Comprehensive Reform," The Group of Thirty, July 2015.

It has been reported that, since the financial crisis, over $100 billion in fines have been imposed on the six largest U.S. banks for credit and mortgage-related activities, confirming that the solution to misbehavior is not achieved simply by developing new policies and prescribed procedures. Additionally, both the OCC and the Consumer Financial Protection Bureau are specifically investigating the sales cultures at major financial institutions. The regulators want to know whether the institutions are pushing employees too hard to meet sales quotas, yet failing to prevent questionable behaviors.

The board has a significant responsibility in fostering a culture of accountability, one that does not tolerate bad behavior. The regulators are holding directors and management directly responsible for establishing and maintaining the risk culture.

Directors need to establish expectations on how management will hold employees accountable for bad behavior and how the CEO and management will be held accountable. The regulators expect business strategies to be implemented that place the interests of customers and the integrity of the markets ahead of profit maximization, supported by tangible actions and the proper behaviors of both directors and management.

Risk culture does not operate in a vacuum. The institution's overall culture influences its risk culture in many ways, and they are virtually one and the same. A strong risk culture maintains a healthy tension between the institution's entrepreneurial activities for creating enterprise value and its risk activities for protecting value, ensuring that neither one is disproportionately strong relative to the other.

Getting the right culture is extremely challenging, particularly as an institution grows and becomes more complex, so evaluating and overseeing risk awareness and sensitivity throughout the institution is no easy task. "Culture can range from how a clerk interacts with customers to how highly paid managers and traders make impactful decisions. It entails a kaleidoscope of essential touchpoints," noted Julia S. Gouw, board member of Pacific Life Insurance Company.

Culture is reflected in the choices, behaviors, and conduct of directors, management, and all employees. William C. Dudley, president of the Federal Reserve Bank of New York, described culture as the implicit norms that guide behavior in the absence of regulations or compliance rules—and sometimes despite those explicit restraints. He says that it exists within every institution whether it is recognized or ignored, whether it is nurtured or neglected, and whether it is embraced or disavowed.[46]

Dudley also stated that the Dodd-Frank Act did little to curb misconduct. He commented that if those managing capital cushions and liquidity buffers view these tools as sufficient mitigants for the costs of misconduct, or if powerful incentives encourage workarounds of the new regulations, then the connection between post-crisis reforms and greater financial stability becomes threatened.[47]

---

[46] Remarks by William C. Dudley at the Federal Reserve Bank of New York Conference, New York City, October 20, 2014.

[47] Remarks by William C. Dudley at the Federal Reserve Bank of New York Conference, New York City, November 5, 2015.

The OCC's Guidelines

The OCC's guidelines on minimum standards provide that an institution should have a comprehensive written statement that articulates the risk appetite and includes a description of a safe and sound risk culture and how the institution assesses and accepts risks.

The guidelines do not specifically include a definition of culture. However, the OCC suggests that setting an appropriate "tone at the top" is critical to establishing a sound risk culture. The guidelines indicate that directors and management should describe the core values expected of employees carrying out their respective roles and responsibilities. These values should serve as the basis for risk-taking decisions and need to be reinforced by the actions of directors, management, and all employees.

The OCC's guidelines further suggest that evidence of a sound risk culture includes, but is not limited to, the following: 1) an open dialogue and transparent sharing of information between the lines of business, independent risk management, and internal audit; 2) consideration of all relevant risks and views of independent risk management and internal audit in risk-taking decisions; and 3) compensation and performance management programs and decisions that reward compliance with the core values and quantitative limits established in the risk appetite statement and that hold accountable those who do not conduct themselves in a proper manner.

FSB's Guidance

In April 2014, the Financial Stability Board,[48] which establishes international standards for the financial services industry and provides advice to regulators, released "Guidance on Supervisory Interaction with Financial Institutions on Risk Culture," which provides a framework for assessing risk culture.

The guidance puts forward the idea that culture is complicated because it involves behaviors and attitudes. Nevertheless, efforts should be made to understand the culture and how it affects safety and soundness.

The guidance expects employees in all parts of the institution to conduct business in a legal and ethical manner. An environment that promotes integrity should be created across the institution as a whole, including fair outcomes for customers. The guidance makes it clear that regulators will look to directors to confirm that risk-taking behavior is acceptable.

While various definitions exist, risk culture focuses on the institution's norms, attitudes, and behaviors related to risk awareness, risk taking, and risk management. The guidance notes that an institution's risk culture plays an important role in influencing

---

[48] The Financial Stability Board has been established to coordinate at the international level the work of national financial authorities and international standards-setting bodies and to develop and promote the implementation of effective regulatory, supervisory, and other financial-sector policies in the interest of financial stability. It brings together national authorities responsible for financial stability in 24 countries and jurisdictions, international financial institutions, sector-specific international groupings of regulators and supervisors, and committees of central bank experts. The FSB is hosted by the Bank for International Settlements, which is also the host for the Basel Committee. It is generally understood that the regulators in the U.S. will place at least "advisory reliance" on the views put forth by the FSB.

the actions and decisions of employees and in shaping the institution's attitude toward its stakeholders, including the regulators. The risk culture supports appropriate risk awareness, behaviors, and judgments about risk taking within the governance framework. The guidance emphasizes that a sound risk culture bolsters effective risk management, promotes sound risk taking, and ensures that emerging risks or risk-taking activities beyond the institution's risk appetite are recognized, assessed, escalated, and addressed in a timely manner.

The guidance suggests that regulators need to consider whether an institution's risk culture is appropriate for the scale, complexity, and nature of its business and is based on sound, articulated values that are led by the board and management. In this regard, the regulators expect directors to oversee management in fostering and maintaining a sound risk culture. This requires regulators to describe these expectations to directors and management and ensure ongoing follow-up on whether these expectations are being met.

The guidance points to four indicators of a sound risk culture: "tone at the top," accountability, effective challenge, and incentives.

1. *"Tone at the top"* – The board and management are responsible for articulating the values that underline the risk culture, demonstrating through action the desired behaviors, holding staff accountable for their behavior, and monitoring behavior. The guidance highlights the importance of leading by example, assessing espoused values, ensuring a common understanding and awareness of risk, and learning from risk culture failures.

2. *Accountability* – Employees need to understand the core values of the risk culture and know they will be rewarded or held to account for their behavior. The guidance outlines the criticalness of the ownership of risk, the escalation process, and enforcement.

3. *Effective challenge* – An effective risk culture will facilitate constructive challenges in the line of business and in control functions. The guidance refers to the importance of allowing open dissent and enhancing the stature of risk management.

4. *Incentives* – In an effective risk culture, compensation and career development will be geared toward the long-term interests of the institution and linked to risk management, business conduct, and compliance considerations. The guidance outlines the importance of remuneration and performance processes, talent development, and succession planning.

The guidance notes that by asking relevant questions, directors can confirm that their risk culture message is appropriately impacting behavior. Asking the right questions is crucial to ensure that all elements of the process are aligned and that actions taken to deliver the right outcomes are mutually reinforcing.[49]

---

[49] "Assessing Risk Culture: Questions Firms Should Be Asking," Ernst & Young, January 2014.

Recommendations by the G30 on Conduct and Culture in Banking

- Institutions should aim for a fundamental shift in the overall mind-set on culture, raising the bar to consistently take difficult sanctioning decisions in response to bad behaviors.
- Boards should ensure that oversight of embedding values, conduct, and behavior remains a sustained priority.
- Institutions should ensure that their performance management does not reward employees who do not meet a threshold of acceptable behavior in alignment with the institution's values and conduct expectations.
- Institutions should continue to establish robust processes to explain and regularly reinforce to employees what is expected of them.
- All employees and all levels of management should adhere to values, conduct, and behavioral expectations.
- Addressing cultural issues must, of necessity, be the responsibility of the directors and management.

Source: "Banking Conduct and Culture: A Call for Sustained and Comprehensive Performance," The Group of Thirty, July 2015.

Strong Risk Culture

The values, goals, and priorities chosen by an institution to define "business success" work together to create the culture. A strong risk culture is marked by integrity, trust, and respect for authority. Culture evolves over time in relation to the events that affect the institution, such as mergers and acquisitions, as well as changes in the internal and external environments.

Moreover, although subcultures within institutions almost always exist, these subcultures need to adhere to the values that support the institution's overall risk culture.

Strong risk cultures are led by the directors and management, who project the core values of the institution through their actions and deeds. The risk strategy, and the value contributed by the risk culture, needs to be clear, communicated regularly, and supported by transparent and coordinated decision making. A strong risk culture encourages debate and constructive challenges of assumptions, decision making, and actions based on analytical insight and information sharing at all levels. Threats and concerns are escalated rapidly and failures are used as learning opportunities rather than openings for criticism. And importantly, a strong risk culture encourages directors, management, and employees to "do the right thing" consistently.[50]

"While there is no doubt that the 'tone at the top' is shaped by the CEO's operating objectives, style, and personal conduct, directors exercise significant influence over an institution's attitude toward risk, the aggressiveness of its policy choices, and its commitment to responsible business behavior," commented Joseph B. Ucuzoglu, chairman and CEO, Deloitte & Touche.

---

[50] "Establishing and Nurturing an Effective Risk Culture," Protiviti, 2014.

Since culture is about behavior, the longer someone has been immersed in a culture and the stronger that culture is, the greater the likelihood that the values and behavior reflect the culture. "First we make the culture, then the culture makes us."[51]

McKinsey & Company summarizes four traits of a strong risk culture, as follows:

1. *Encouraging Transparency*
   A strong culture actively seeks information about and insight into risk through appropriate risk models, detailed risk reporting, and the establishment of a shared responsibility to communicate potential issues. A lack of transparency on current and future risk exposures not only hinders early risk mitigation, but can also prevent measured risk taking.

   At the same time, it is important to foster a common understanding of the boundaries of individual risk taking. A clear risk tolerance derived from an overall risk appetite statement, expressed in specific guidelines that limit which risks are allowed, is an important element of a strong risk culture.

2. *Acknowledging Risk*
   It takes a confident management to acknowledge risk. Doing so requires working through the issues that could lead to crisis, embarrassment, or loss. The cultural differences are stark between institutions that acknowledge risk and those that do not.

3. *Responding to Risks*
   The most effective institutions move risk issues up the chain of command as quickly as they emerge. This requires well-defined, yet nimble, risk escalation processes along with the willingness to break through rigid governance mechanisms to get the right experts involved, regardless of whether they sit on a formal management committee. Very often, responsiveness can be bogged down by the very processes intended to support a strong risk environment. Responsiveness also requires instilling at the employee level a cohesive sense of personal accountability for risk management.

4. *Ensuring Respect for Risk*
   In the best of cases, the respect for rules is a powerful source of competitive advantage. Managements most often understand the need for controls that alert them to trends and behaviors they should monitor in order to better mobilize resources in response to evolving risks. While too few controls can leave an institution in the dark as a situation develops, too many can be equally problematic.[52]

Risk awareness is important because even isolated pockets of poor culture can thwart efforts to improve the management and control of risks. Without a strong risk culture, risk management can become overly encumbered with processes and controls, often in conflict with the business strategy. An unsupportive risk culture can be distracting,

---

[51] "Merging Credit Cultures," by John E. McKinley, *The RMA Journal,* March 2015.
[52] "Managing the People Side of Risk: Risk Culture Transformation," by Cindy Levy, Alexis Krivkovich, Mehdi El Quali, and Julia Graf, McKinsey & Company, March 2015.

expensive, frustrating for directors, and exhausting and confusing for management and employees.[53]

Importantly, a strong risk culture is not a risk-adverse culture. "A threat in today's environment is standing still in a changing world. The board and management need to properly balance risks with the rewards and continue to sensibly pursue profitable opportunities based on sound judgment," commented David W. Paul, senior vice president, American Honda Finance Corporation.

A Strong Risk Culture:

- **Reduces** the risk of misconduct.
- **Diminishes** the risk of regulatory scrutiny, action, and monetary fines, as well as other potential costs, such as operating expenses and capital committed.
- **Strengthens** asset quality.
- **Enhances** an institution's reputation with customers and clients, employees and management, shareholders, and regulators.
- **Promotes** innovation and new product development designed to serve customers.
- **Attracts and retains** highly qualified talent that similarly values a strong, positive culture and behavior, and reduces counterproductive behavior and employee turnover.
- **Protects** the brand.

Source: "Approaching the Crossroads of Conduct and Culture: Improving Culture in the Financial Services Industry," KPMG, 2015.

Alignment with Talent and Compensation

Having the right culture takes people with the knowledge, skills, and abilities to understand the importance of risk and the know-how to execute in a risk-sensitive manner—all of which places the issues of hiring and retaining talent in the spotlight, with a special focus on learning, development, and succession planning. This focus extends to compensation. The benefits structure should account for risk sensitivity, foster and encourage desired behaviors, and balance risk and rewards. Why all the focus on culture? A strong risk culture promotes accountability, consistency, transparency, and strategic alignment, even as risk requirements and the overall risk environment evolve.

As they move their focus to the qualitative aspects of risk management, the regulators are increasingly looking beyond quantitative measures to assess whether institutions have created a culture that encourages employees to take appropriate risks and promotes ethical behavior more broadly. In this effort, it is essential that incentive compensation schemes are aligned with an institution's risk appetite and behaviors.[54]

---

[53] "Getting to the Heart of Culture within Financial Services," by Matt Gosden, Kevan Jones, Michelle Daisley, and John-Paul Pape, Oliver Wyman, 2014.
[54] "Operating in the New Normal: Increased Regulation and Heightened Expectations," Global Risk Management Survey, Ninth Edition, Deloitte University Press, 2015.

The regulators suggest that compensation structures, by tying employee compensation to performance, are essential in enhancing culture and discouraging unnecessary risk taking. According to Daniel K. Tarullo, a member of the Board of Governors of the Federal Reserve System, employees, assuming they discern the factors that explain patterns of hiring, raises, promotions, demotions, and dismissals, receive very strong signals as to what the institution's leaders actually value. He notes that this set of signals has considerably more influence on employee behavior than a corporate statement of values or purposes, particularly if the system of rewards and punishments appears at odds.[55]

"Employee programs communicating cultural expectations such as periodic policy messages, awareness campaigns, and training sessions are helpful but not impactful standing alone. The risk culture should be part of an integrated approach. When culture is included in a comprehensive program that aligns performance expectations and compensation structures to risk-taking behaviors, they reinforce the critical elements of a strong risk culture," noted Ann F. Jaedicke, a board member of MUFG Union Bank.

Based on Deloitte's analysis, however, only 43% of U.S. banks of all sizes have so far integrated risk management with compensation, a regulatory expectation and an essential ingredient to strengthening the risk culture.[56]

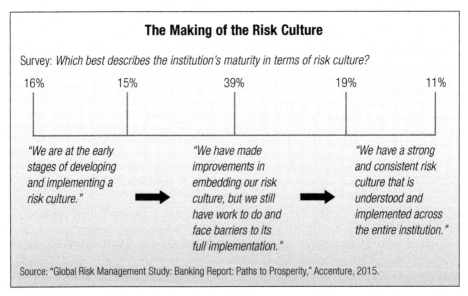

The Making of the Risk Culture

Survey: *Which best describes the institution's maturity in terms of risk culture?*

| 16% | 15% | 39% | 19% | 11% |

"We are at the early stages of developing and implementing a risk culture."

"We have made improvements in embedding our risk culture, but we still have work to do and face barriers to its full implementation."

"We have a strong and consistent risk culture that is understood and implemented across the entire institution."

Source: "Global Risk Management Study: Banking Report: Paths to Prosperity," Accenture, 2015.

A strong risk culture requires the support of compensation and incentives frameworks, including clawback and forfeiture provisions, designed to take into account conduct, credit, and market risks, as well as customer outcomes. This aligns the interests of management and employees with the values, goals, and expectations of the institu-

---

[55] Remarks by Daniel Tarullo at the Federal Reserve Bank of New York Conference, New York City, October 20, 2014.

[56] "Bank Board Risk Governance," Deloitte Center for Financial Services, Deloitte University Press, 2015.

tion. Regulators look to the relationships between incentive structures and individual accountability, and they are increasingly initiating actions against management and employees to account for their misconduct in addition to taking actions against the institution. Such actions can include monetary fines, sanctions, and industry bars.[57]

"The importance of the impact of compensation programs on culture and risk management cannot be underestimated. This requires a strong, identifiable linkage between behavioral expectations and performance achievements," said Carol Sudbeck, senior vice president, Human Resources and Public Affairs, Pacific Life Insurance Company.

Championing Culture

Building and maintaining a robust risk culture is critical to ensuring the success of the risk function. Although recognizing the importance of risk culture is gaining traction, many organizations are only beginning to institutionalize it. Many others are doubling down on culture because the regulators expect compliance with not only the letter of the laws but also the spirit. Surveys, videos, and direct discussions are being used to reinforce culture and behavioral messages. The following are some illustrations, as reported in *The Wall Street Journal.*

JPMorgan Chase & Co. held an exhibit and week-long speaker series, including presentations by a risk officer and the heads of diversity, administration, and corporate strategy. Employees were asked to sign a "How We Do Business" wall to show their commitment. This followed a message sent from chairman and CEO Jamie Dimon that focused on how the institution does business, including compensation practices, employee feedback, and the keeping of one set of books. The institution plans to add metrics to track performance that include client satisfaction and employee survey results, code of conduct issues, and regulatory actions.

Citigroup Inc.'s board created a committee on ethics and culture, telling its shareholders it is aware of the public's perception that many in the banking industry do not behave ethically. It released videos on its internal website of management personnel recounting ethical dilemmas they have faced. In a letter to employees, CEO Michael Corbat said he is confident that the overwhelming majority of employees "always do the right thing." But, he added, there are some people who still do not get it, and he told employees they would be held responsible not just for their own wrongdoing but for turning a blind eye to others.

And, Bank of America Corp. has been encouraging employees to identify and escalate as a reminder to report questionable behavior. Since 2011, it has sent more than 10,000 managers through a risk "boot camp" where they brush up on regulations and work through sample scenarios.[58]

---

[57] "Approaching the Crossroads of Conduct and Culture: Improving Culture in the Financial Services Industry," KPMG, 2015.
[58] "What Banks are Doing to Improve Their Culture," *The Wall Street Journal*, February 2, 2015.

The Weak End of Culture

Transparency

- Poor communication: A culture where warning signs of internal and external risks are not shared.
- Unclear tolerance: A culture where the leadership does not communicate the risk appetite or fails to present a coherent approach or strategy.
- Lack of insight: A culture where the institution fails to understand the risks it is running, or believes that such an understanding is the preserve of risk specialists.

Acknowledgment

- Overconfidence: A culture where employees believe that the institution is insulated or even immune from risk because of their superior position or people.
- No challenge: A culture where employees do not challenge each other's attitudes, ideas, or actions.
- Fear of bad news: A culture where management and employees feel inhibited about passing on bad news or learning from past mistakes.

Responsiveness

- Indifference: A culture that discourages responding to situations or fosters apathy about the outcome, owing either to bad faith or incompetence.
- Slow response: A culture where the institution perceives external changes, but acts too slowly or is in denial about innovation or the likely impact of change.

Respect

- Beat the system: A culture where the risk appetite is misaligned with the risk profile, leaving room for the conception and implementation of inappropriate activities.
- Gaming: A culture where business units take risks or embrace projects that could benefit the unit but are out of line with the risk appetite.

Source: "Taking Control of Organizational Risk Culture," McKinsey & Company, February 2010.

Measuring Effectiveness

The FSB's guidance sets aside the issue of how regulators and institutions should assess culture, recognizing that there are many varied approaches. Nevertheless, risk culture can and should be measured. Typically, a combination of different metrics is used to measure various aspects of risk culture.

McKinsey & Company suggests the following:

- Behavioral scores from annual surveys, sampling employees about their views on a set of prevailing outcomes and practices along all risk culture dimensions.
- Risk culture knowledge scores, such as the share of employees that attend risk culture training modules, the frequency of risk-focused communications sent out by management, etc.
- Outcome-based metrics, including total operational losses, the number of compli-

ance incidents, the amount of audit findings resolved in a timely manner, and the number of risk limit breaches.[59]

A "red flag system" sometimes is introduced in which management issues red flags to employees for nonadherence to policies and procedures (such as not fulfilling mandatory training requirements on time, breaching limits, and using unapproved models). The specific number of red flags issued depends on the frequency and severity of individual breaches. Red flags are then considered during performance reviews and constitute one criterion for decisions regarding individual promotions and compensation.[60]

In addition, Deloitte suggests 10 ways that directors and management can evaluate the "tone at the top," which is a critical element of the risk culture.

1. *Extent and nature of wrongdoing.* Benchmarking against other institutions the number and nature of known incidents of wrongdoing may highlight the extent to which "tone at the top" has led to compliance with policies. If management dismisses minor violations as unimportant, this may indicate a culture of noncompliance that could heighten the risk of more serious violations.

2. *Use of anonymity in incident reports.* If the institution has a significantly higher than average proportion of whistleblower reports made anonymously, this may suggest that employees are afraid to report wrongdoing or that employees believe that protection of previous whistleblowers has been inadequate.

3. *Social media reputation assessment.* Monitoring comments and criticism in social media and other online venues can help identify views of the culture that could suggest an inadequate "tone at the top."

4. *Employee surveys/questionnaires.* Many institutions use annual employee surveys to gather information on their employees' engagement and to monitor trends.

5. *Tone of management communications.* Reading communications from management to employees for tone, in addition to content, may provide insight. Notice boards, office walls, and intranets may communicate a "tone at the top" quite different from the one on display in the boardroom.

6. *Group discussion.* Having a normal meeting agenda item for board and management to share their observations regarding activities, communications, and style may provide an opportunity to develop a cohesive perspective on the "tone at the top."

7. *Facility visits.* Rotating the location of board and management meetings can allow directors to observe different parts of the business. Establishing contact with local management can facilitate future communication if issues arise.

8. *Exit interviews.* Some departing employees, concerned about burning bridges, may be unwilling to mention ethics and integrity issues that might have contributed to their departure. Others may welcome the opportunity to discuss their experiences, but may provide this information only if prompted.

9. *Interviews and focus group.* Interviews can be effective in assessing the "tone at the top" when they employ a structured approach and when people are comfortable stating their views openly.

---

[59] "Managing the People Side of Risk: Risk Culture Transformation," March 2015.
[60] Ibid

10. *Customer complaints.* Monitoring trends in customer feedback can provide insight into the culture. The swift and open handling of grievances may indicate a dedication to compliance and ethics.[61]

Implications for Directors

Fostering a strong risk culture is as much a board responsibility as a management responsibility. Directors need to oversee performance and compensation arrangements and their alignment with risks. Building incentive structures that place a premium on risk awareness is critical.

McKinsey & Company foreshadows that building and maintaining a robust risk culture will be critical to ensuring the success of the future risk function. A robust risk culture is also likely to be a prerequisite in future competitive advantage. McKinsey suggests that the risk function of the future is expected to have an explicit aspiration with values and norms that the institution can use to manage risk. These values will most likely promote informed risk-taking based on the risk appetite, coupled with the necessary checks and control systems to detect, assess, and mitigate risks, as well as transparent procedures to follow up on breaches and deviations.[62]

Institutionalizing a strong risk culture that creates a tangible sense of risk ownership requires a long-term commitment and significant investment. It entails constant, repetitive processes involving a variety of channels, tools, policies, and procedures. To be successful, directors and management need to be committed to devote a considerable amount of time and money to determining, communicating, and instilling the institution's values, culture, and code of conduct.

A well-defined risk appetite framework that is cascaded through the institution and reflected in strategy and business decisions is the core to building a strong risk culture. The board approves the risk appetite, but its development and execution must involve the broader management team. Directors need to monitor the definition of risk appetite and clarify the risk ownership roles and responsibilities in order to hold management and employees accountable, recognizing that accountability involves both communication and the enforcement of the rules.

To avoid becoming merely a theoretical concept, the risk culture needs to be reflected in the overall risk governance process. Accountabilities for risk management and the right behaviors should be reinforced through board and committee charters, policies, job descriptions, risk appetite statements, limit structures, procedures, and escalation protocols.

Directors need to encourage a culture of transparency in exposing and evaluating risks. Risk transparency plays a central role in developing mitigation strategies. If the board and management cannot properly recognize and assess risks, or are unable to identify when behavior is moving away from expected norms, then the risk culture will be in jeopardy.

---

[61] "The Tone at the Top: Ten Ways to Measure Effectiveness," Deloitte Forensic Center, 2011.
[62] "The Future of Bank Risk Management," by Philipp Härle, Andras Havas, Andreas Kremer, Daniel Rona, and Hamid Samandari, McKinsey & Company, December 2015.

Questions Directors Should Ask About Risk Culture

"Tone at the Top"

- Are the mission, vision, and values clearly aligned and communicated throughout the institution?
- Do the board and management lead by example? What is the "tone from the top"?
- Is management displaying the right behaviors? What processes ensure the message is consistent, understood, and accepted?
- Is the strategy appropriate given the risk appetite, and does the risk appetite framework ensure that decisions throughout the institution are consistent with the risk appetite?
- Is the risk appetite considered in corporate strategy and capital planning? Are risk outcomes articulated in strategy?
- Are returns commensurate with risks assumed in the various businesses?
- Are new businesses or products approved before controls are in place?
- Which products and businesses are growing most rapidly and have the highest returns? Do directors understand why? Is it because of excessive risk taking?
- Does the board track outstanding recommendations from internal audit and the regulators?
- How long do issues remain open?

Accountability

- Is it clear that the front office is responsible for all aspects of risk stemming from its activities, including reputation and operational risks?
- How is emerging risk information transmitted across the institution? Are businesses taking the lead in the self-identification of risks?
- Is the board aware of the escalation process for control breaches? Are there reports indicating how often controls are breached in the different business lines?
- How are whistleblowers treated?
- Is the culture proactive? Do breaches in controls or unacceptable behavior have consequences?
- Are requests for increases to risk limits "rubber stamped" by the board? How often are requests for limit increases rejected?

Effective Challenge

- Do directors understand the risk reports? Have risk reports been sent back to management for simplification or clarification?
- Does the culture support constructive dissent?
- Are risk management and audit consulted before new products are introduced?
- Does risk management have the skills necessary to understand all the services and products?
- Do directors have the expertise necessary to constructively challenge business-line and risk management experts?

Incentives

- How are compensation and risk-taking behaviors linked?
- Does risk management have input into the performance reviews of risk takers?

When businesses are under intense pressure to generate more profit, because either the business model is not viable or the stakeholders are seeking higher returns, bad behavior is more likely to exist. In these cases, mechanisms to monitor behavior and the accumulation of risk, and the board's challenge of financial targets, are essential.

Behaviors are what is done—not what is thought, felt, or believed. Value statements from the board and management are important, but employees tend to follow actions more than words. If directors and management regularly choose the path of greatest profit, then the culture will view profit as the primary objective.[63]

Irrespective of the strength of the risk culture, there is always the possibility of a rogue employee underwriting a transaction that puts the institution at risk. In addition, the existence and impact of subcultures need to be understood. Sometimes, subcultures may help an institution be more agile in response to a changing business environment, making it easier to solve problems, share information, and serve customers. However, subcultures can also promote rogue risk-taking behavior that can cause harm to the culture and threaten the institution's values.

Cultures are less challenging to instill in a business that has grown as one institution than, say, an institution that has been built on multiple mergers with different cultures.[64] "The blending and integration of cultures and risk taking in mergers and acquisitions pose special problems for directors and management. Cultural differences in these environments sometimes can take years to comfortably blend," noted Cary K. Hyden, partner, Latham & Watkins.

A strong culture needs to be nurtured by both directors and management. Promoting a thiefdom or warrior culture, fostering a "star system" with little or no accountability, shooting the bearers of bad news, ignoring the warning signs escalated by the risk management function, and making decisions inconsistent with the defined risk culture all send the wrong messages and need to be avoided.

Cultures have a way of turning directors and management into conformists. Generally, those who challenge conventional thinking are not well liked; therefore, cultures reject a "nonconformist" the same way our bodies reject a foreign organ. To avoid being rejected, some individuals shy away from conflict, deflect accountability, and go along with the group. Directors need to recognize that success is predicated on a culture that truly values challenge and debate.[65]

Directors also need to pay particular attention in the boardroom to internal attributes that drive risk culture. These characteristics include the attitudes, belief systems, and core values that embody behavior and guide daily activities and decision making. Behaviors around risk management and internal control accountabilities often become apparent in how audit issues and control deficiencies are addressed and in how matters are escalated to management and the board for resolution. The timeliness in carrying out these activities is evidence of the risk culture's strength, as well as management's reaction to warning signs raised by the independent internal auditors or risk managers.[66]

Risk culture is not static and should be monitored to encourage continuous improvement. Directors must gain an understanding of the risk culture that exists, define the

---

[63] "Understanding Risk Culture and Its Challenges," by Patricia Jackson, Ernst & Young, Second Quarter, 2015.

[64] "The New York Chapter's CRO Roundtable: 2015," by Frank Devlin, *The RMA Journal*, October 2015.

[65] "Barriers to Achieving Credible Challenge," by Robert A. Prentice and Yousef A. Valine, *The RMA Journal*, July-August 2015.

[66] "Establishing and Nurturing an Effective Risk Culture," 2014.

desired behaviors, and, to the extent improvements are required, direct management to develop and execute a plan for making improvements. "Tone at the top," accountability, effective challenge, and incentives are essential indicators of a strong risk culture and should be carefully established and monitored by directors as these will determine the intensity of regulatory scrutiny.

Ultimately, the enigma that is risk culture requires the board to adopt a thoughtful approach and steady leadership. The board's oversight of the behaviors, choices, and values of management and employees is a demanding job—much more demanding than overseeing financial thresholds or other quantifiable metrics. "Tone at the top" is synonymous with "buy-in at the top," meaning the voyage begins with directors and management acknowledging the need and supporting best practices in the areas of risk culture and governance.

Risk Appetite Framework

"Risk is like fire. If controlled it will help you; if uncontrolled it will rise up and destroy you."

— THEODORE ROOSEVELT

R isk oversight begins with understanding the risk appetite. Risk appetite, which manifests itself through behavior over time, is the mutual understanding between management and the board regarding the drivers of, and parameters around, opportunity-seeking behavior. It is a high-level view of how much performance variability the institution is willing to accept. A balanced approach to value creation means boards and management accept only those risks that are believed prudent to take and able to be managed successfully.

An ongoing dialogue around risk appetite is as much about making the best bets in pursuit of value-creation opportunities as it is about avoiding and hedging bets. It opens up consideration to the full range of risk response options: avoid, accept, reduce, transfer, or exploit.[67]

An institution's risk appetite reflects both its capacity to bear risk as well as a broader understanding of the level of risk that it can safely assume and successfully manage over a given period. It reflects management's "view of the world" inherent in the strategy and in the execution of the strategy, in the form of both risks taken and risks avoided.[68]

Developing an effective risk management program and aligning it with corporate strategy is a challenging imperative. An integral component of this process, and the foundation of good risk management, is the design of a risk appetite framework. "The metaphor of risk 'appetite' is actually quite apt. How hungry is the institution? How much and, importantly, what should it eat? How does it know when to slow down and go on a diet?" said Til Schuermann, partner, Oliver Wyman.

Determining the risk appetite starts by assessing the risk capacity. The risk capacity is the institution's ability to withstand risk when it materializes into actuality, while avoiding unwanted effects such as canceled projects, postponed maintenance, damage to the institution's reputation, ratings downgrades, and, of course, default and insolvency. Once such constraints are quantified, the board is able to determine how much of that capac-

---

[67] The Risk Appetite Dialogue," Protiviti, 2010.
[68] Ibid.

ity the institution should expend (that is, how much risk should be assumed) and how much of a cushion should be maintained.

The risk appetite framework sets a forward-looking view of the desired risk profile in a variety of scenarios and establishes a process for achieving that profile. The framework defines roles and responsibilities in the areas of monitoring and assessment. It also sets forth practices that link the board's objectives with management's actions, ensuring that the risk profile remains within established parameters. The elements of the risk appetite framework should be applied at the business line and legal entity levels in a manner commensurate with the size of the exposures, complexity, and materiality of the risks.

Establishing an effective risk appetite framework helps to reinforce a strong risk culture, which in turn is critical to sound risk management.

When risk appetite is properly understood and clearly defined, it becomes a powerful tool, not only for managing risk but also for enhancing overall business performance. "The process of developing the risk appetite has been a catalyst for constructive debate about what is important to us as an institution. Our risk appetite is not intended to be just about what we do not want to have happen. It is also about understanding the businesses we should be pursuing and the risks we need to be accepting," commented Joseph E. Celentano, senior vice president and chief risk officer, Pacific Life Insurance Company.

The Trade-offs in Determining the Risk Appetite

Ability	**Willingness**
(Based on strength of financial position)	*(Function of tolerance for uncertainty)*
• Projected financials under various market scenarios	• Acceptable earnings variance in a given quarter or year for risk taking
• Additional affordable risks	• Risks to be taken and risks to avoid
• Cost versus benefit of reducing (or adding) risk	• Areas in which to place capital investment bets

Source: "The Board and Long-Term Value Creation," Report of the NACD Blue Ribbon Commission, National Association of Corporate Directors, 2015.

Expectations of the FSB and Regulators

The oversight of the risk appetite framework is not intended to be a regulatory compliance exercise. The objective is to ensure the institution is staying within its risk parameters while pursuing its strategic objectives.

Historically, there has been little formal rule-making or exacting guidance from the regulators regarding the board's oversight of the risk appetite framework or the appetite statement itself. There has been no uncertainty, however, about the regulators expecting directors not only to know the level of the risk appetite, but to approve it in line with the strategy and risk-taking activities and provide frequent monitoring thereafter.

In the Basel II Framework, issued in July 2009, the Basel Committee on Banking Supervision states it is the responsibility of the board and management to define the institution's risk appetite and to ensure that the risk management framework includes detailed policies that set specific firm-wide limits on activities that are consistent with risk-taking appetite and capacity. The Basel Committee says the board's responsibilities include being familiar with all material risks, having an understanding of the business lines and capital markets, and ensuring that accountability and lines of authority are clearly delineated for identifying, measuring, and managing risk.

Meanwhile, in December 2012, the Federal Reserve Board issued a supervisory letter that outlines its supervisory framework for the boards of large financial institutions and their committees so that they, with the support of management, can clearly articulate strategy and the risk appetite.

Financial Stability Board

The Financial Stability Board enhances the regulatory guidance on the risk management framework generally, and the risk appetite framework in particular, in the following three publications: "Thematic Review on Risk Governance" (February 12, 2013), "Principles for an Effective Risk Appetite Framework" (November 18, 2013), and "Guidance on Supervisory Interaction with Financial Institutions on Risk Culture" (November 18, 2013).

The principles establish, among other matters, key terms and definitions and minimum expectations for the board, including the following:

- *Risk appetite* is the aggregate level and types of risk an institution is willing to assume within its risk capacity to achieve its strategic objectives and business plan.
- *Risk capacity* is the maximum level of risk that can be assumed before breaching constraints determined by regulatory capital, liquidity needs, and obligations.
- The *risk profile* is a point-in-time assessment of the net risk exposures, after taking into account mitigants aggregated within and across each relevant risk category based on forward-looking assumptions.
- *Risk limits* are quantitative measures based on forward-looking assumptions that allocate the aggregate risk statement to business lines, legal entities, specific risk categories, concentrations, and other levels.
- The *risk appetite framework* is the overall approach, including policies, processes, controls, and systems, through which risk appetite is established, communicated, and monitored. It includes a risk appetite statement, risk limits, and an outline of the roles and responsibilities of those overseeing the framework's implementation and monitoring. The framework does not include the processes to establish the strategy, business plan, models, and systems to measure and aggregate risk. But it should provide a common framework and comparable measures across the institution for management and the board to communicate, understand, and assess the level of risk it is prepared to accept.
- The *risk appetite statement* defines the aggregate level and types of risk that an institution is willing to accept. It includes qualitative statements as well as quantita-

tive measures expressed relative to earnings, capital, risk measures, liquidity, etc. It should also address risks that are more difficult to quantify, such as those related to reputation, business ethics, and conduct.

"The risk appetite statement is directly linked to the institution's strategy, addresses material risks under both normal and stressed market and macroeconomic conditions, enforces the risk culture, and sets clear boundaries and expectations," noted Mark W. Midkiff, chief risk officer, GE Capital.

The FSB principles indicate the following as responsibilities of the board:

- Approving the risk appetite framework, developed in collaboration with management, and ensuring it remains consistent with strategy, business and capital plans, risk capacity, and compensation programs.
- Holding management accountable for the integrity of the risk appetite framework, including the timely identification and management of material risk exposures and risk-limit breaches.
- Ensuring that annual business plans are in line with the approved risk appetite and that incentives and disincentives are included in the compensation programs to facilitate adherence to risk appetite.
- Assessing risk appetite in strategic discussions regarding mergers, acquisitions, and growth in business lines or products.
- Regularly reviewing and monitoring actual versus approved risk limits by business line, legal entity, product, and risk category, etc., including qualitative measures of conduct risk.
- Discussing and determining actions to be taken, if any, regarding breaches in risk limits.
- Questioning management about any activities outside the board-approved risk appetite statement.
- Obtaining an independent assessment, through internal assessors, third parties, or both, of the design and effectiveness of the risk appetite framework and its alignment with the regulators' expectations.
- Satisfying itself that there are mechanisms in place to ensure management can act in a timely manner to effectively manage and, where necessary, mitigate adverse risk exposures, in particular those that are close to or exceed the approved risk appetite statement or risk limits.
- Discussing with the regulators decisions regarding the establishment and ongoing monitoring of risk appetite as well as any material changes in the elements of the risk appetite framework, current risk appetite levels, or regulatory expectations regarding risk appetite.
- Ensuring that adequate resources and expertise are dedicated to risk management as well as internal audit in order to provide independent assurances to the board and management that they are operating within the approved risk appetite framework. This includes the use of third parties to supplement existing resources where appropriate.
- Ensuring risk management is supported by adequate and robust technology and reporting systems to enable identification, measurement, assessment, and reporting of risk in a timely and accurate manner.

Office of the Comptroller of the Currency

The OCC's *Handbook on Large Bank Supervision* indicates that the board must establish the strategic direction and risk tolerances and, in carrying out these responsibilities, approve policies that establish operational standards and risk limits. In addition, in its Fall 2013 "Semiannual Risk Perspective," which examines key risks facing national banks, the OCC notes that it will focus on the board's willingness to define and communicate risk appetite across the institution.

Reference is also made to the OCC's "Heightened Expectations FAQ" issued in October 2013, which suggests examiners determine whether there is board approval of a risk appetite statement that expresses boundaries for risk taking using quantitative measures and qualitative statements, collectively covering all material risks.

The OCC's minimum standards indicate that the institution should have a comprehensive written statement that articulates the risk appetite and serves as the basis for the risk governance framework. The intent is for directors to be able to understand the risks being taken and ensure that those risks are properly managed.

The minimum standards also echo the view that a risk appetite statement should include both qualitative components and quantitative limits. The qualitative components should describe a safe and sound risk culture and how the institution will assess and accept risks, including those that are difficult to quantify. Quantitative limits should incorporate sound stress-testing processes, as appropriate, and address the earnings, capital, and liquidity positions.

The minimum standards indicate that the institution should establish limits at levels that take into account appropriate capital and liquidity buffers and that prompt management and the board to reduce risk before the risk profile jeopardizes the adequacy of earnings, liquidity, and capital.

The minimum standards also suggest the risk governance framework should include the following:

- Review and approval of the risk appetite statement by the directors, or the board's risk committee, at least annually or more frequently, as necessary, based on the size and volatility of risks and any material changes in the business model, strategy, risk profile, or market conditions.
- Communicating and reinforcing the risk appetite statement throughout the institution so all employees align their risk-taking decisions with the risk appetite statement.
- Monitoring by independent risk management of the risk profile relative to risk appetite and compliance with concentration risk limits; reporting on monitoring to the board or its risk committee at least quarterly.
- When necessary due to the level and type of risk, monitoring by independent risk management of front line units' compliance with front line unit risk limits, ongoing communication with front line units regarding adherence to these limits, and reporting of concerns to management and the board or its risk committee, all at least quarterly.[69]

---

[69] "OCC Final Guidelines Establishing Heightened Standards for Certain Large Insured Banking Institutions," KPMG, 2014.

Expectations of Other Constituents

The Securities and Exchange Commission requires institutions to publicly disclose details about how their boards are discharging their risk oversight responsibilities. Meanwhile, major credit-rating agencies include detailed questions about board risk oversight in their credit-rating reviews, and institutional investors often include an evaluation of corporate governance and the board's risk oversight in their due diligence when making investment decisions.

Equally challenging is how the increased authoritative guidance on the board's risk oversight is influencing judicial views about what constitutes the director's "duty of care" standard. The specific requirements for the board in regard to overseeing the risk appetite framework are also established, at least in broad principles, in many board charters and the charters of their committees. These expectations of other constituents suggest significantly greater scrutiny of board risk oversight, including the criticality of overseeing the risk appetite framework.

Charting Strategy Within the Risk Appetite

The risk appetite and the risk appetite framework, including the board's oversight role, need to support the institution's strategic objectives.

Setting strategy, establishing and monitoring risk limits including stress testing, and receiving reports from management are fundamental if directors are to provide a credible challenge to the risk appetite framework. The risk appetite statement, as mentioned, needs to be closely aligned with the business strategy, so that a clear understanding of the institution's risk appetite, with matching strategic levers, becomes an essential component of the strategic planning process.

From a director's perspective, the board is responsible for approving and overseeing the risk appetite of the products and services that the institution will or will not pursue as part of the strategy. As management contemplates expanding existing businesses or pursuing new products and services, the board should assist in shaping the level of risk appetite. Although the board is not expected to monitor day-to-day risk limits once they are established, it needs to assess breaches in the risk limits and determine if the risk appetite is aligned with the strategy.

"The risk appetite and risk parameters need to be defined and integrated into strategic considerations such as major investment decisions and portfolio risk exposure levels. It is important that the goals and tolerance levels for both risk and reward are communicated by the board and management, establishing a 'tone from the top' which guides decisions throughout the institution," commented Bjorn Borgen, partner, Deloitte & Touche.

It is not unusual to see tension or conflict between the strategic goals and the risk appetite thresholds. For example, in order to establish growth goals and return-on-equity targets, the institution may decide to pursue riskier products or services. In contrast, the risk appetite statement may point toward more "quality earnings" by reducing the riskier businesses and limiting exposure to credit losses. It is critical for directors and management to agree on strategic plans and the risk appetite in tandem to balance the goals for growth and returns with the need to properly manage risks.

The board and management need to ensure that the operations, risk, and finance organizations collaborate and coordinate closely in developing and linking the strategic plan and risk appetite statement, to avoid the perception or reality that either is owned or controlled by a specific or narrowly defined group.

"Risk appetite is considerably more than key performance indicators. A comprehensive risk appetite framework is the cornerstone of risk management and the core instrument for aligning corporate strategy, capital allocations, and risks," noted Theodore A. Wilm, partner, PricewaterhouseCoopers.

Operating in the New Normal

Survey Question: How challenging is each of the following in defining and implementing the risk appetite statement?

Defining risk appetite for strategic risk	55%
Defining risk appetite for reputational risk	55%
Defining risk appetite for operational risk	38%
Allocating risk appetite among different business units	37%

Note: 100% means "most challenging."

Source: "Global Risk Management Survey: Operating in the New Normal," Deloitte, 2015.

Approval of Changes

When considering the strategic goals, and as a tool for establishing boundaries around risk taking, the board and management should make the risk appetite framework, including both the risk tolerance levels and overall risk appetite levels, flexible enough to allow for changes as conditions and opportunities require.

As an illustration of ingrained flexibility, the OCC reported in 2013 that many large institutions relaxed the criteria for businesses and consumers to obtain credit during the previous 18-month period. Drivers of the looser credit standards, at the time, were an improved economic landscape, competition for a limited pool of loans, and a sustained low-interest-rate environment that had banks reaching for returns. Rather than incurring breaches to the risk appetite, institutions granted approval of changes to the risk limits by relaxing their credit criteria. This required sufficient elasticity in the risk appetite to enable changes in risk tolerance and overall risk appetite levels at midyear or in mid-cycle.

In approving changes in risk tolerances and associated changes to risk appetite, the board normally should take the following actions:

- Determine the nature and magnitude of the changes that occurred between the time when the risk appetite was approved and when the new opportunity or threat presented itself.
- Clarify the profit opportunity in terms of the expected risk-return trade-offs, or the potential impact on profit of the change to the expected risk-return trade-off.
- Assess whether potential losses associated with any additional risks are acceptable.

- Clarify that the rationale for the change is linked to dynamic market conditions and not short-term profit objectives.
- Understand the likely reactions of regulators, credit-rating agencies, and institutional investors.
- Assess potential reputational concerns and any other considerations.

The aforementioned recommendations notwithstanding, if a risk appetite statement is constantly altered to accommodate every emerging opportunity or to rationalize violations of risk tolerances and limits, it will lose its value as a rudder for navigating through unpredictable and rough waters.[70]

A Practical Approach to Defining the Risk Appetite

	Draft risk appetite statement and assess current risk profile		Assess completeness of risks	Establish consistency between risk appetite and operating limits	Update risk monitoring and reporting to align with risk appetite
Top-down approach ↓	Identify strategic objectives	Draft risk appetite			
			Connect risk appetite statement with risk profile	Confirm risk appetite statement and calibrate operating parameters	Confirm risk monitoring reporting and processes
Bottom-up approach ↑	Inventory risk measurement tools	Assess current risk profile, exposures, and limits			

Source: "Recover, Adapt, Advance: A Survey of the World's Largest Banks," Ernst & Young, 2011.

Board 'Best Practices'

Regulators' increased enforcement actions in response to compliance failures are driving directors to follow best practices in assessing and monitoring risk appetite. Although institutions continue to develop customized approaches to risk appetite, directors should be familiar with the essential attributes of board "best practices."

The risk appetite statement should:

- Be easy to understand and communicate.
- Be forward-looking and closely linked to the strategy.

---

[70] "How Risk Appetite Should Impact Behavior," Protiviti, 2014.

- Be established so that there is an adequate buffer between risk appetite and risk capacity, even in stress scenarios.
- Embody all risks, both quantitative and qualitative, and link directly to other statements that define specific risks, such as credit, market, operational, and reputation.

The risk appetite framework should:

- Offer guidance on how to respond to risk and ensure it is at the center of the broader risk framework.
- Provide the risk parameters to govern decision-making across all businesses and risk types.
- Enable the allocation of the institution-wide risk appetite to specific risk categories, lines of business, legal entities, and geographical regions.
- Influence decisions directly on strategy, annual business planning, capital allocation, budgeting, and new products and services.
- Include parameters that protect the institution from actions that grossly exceed its risk appetite.
- Enable risks to be aggregated and disaggregated with sufficient precision and granularity so that directors are comfortable that aggregate risk does not exceed the overall risk appetite.
- Provide rigorous monitoring and reporting mechanisms that transmit information about risk taking and business objectives to the board and throughout the institution.
- Include mechanisms to escalate responses in the event of potential risk breaches.
- Require documentation that risk appetite is given proper consideration in key decisions.
- Link risk appetite to performance assessments, advancement, and compensation.
- Include mechanisms to change and adjust risk parameters in response to market and economic conditions.[71]

Since market conditions over time cannot be forecast with any certainty, the risk appetite statement must be dynamic. That is, it must establish boundaries without becoming excessively rigid, and be flexible enough to respond to changes in the business environment. At the same time, the risk appetite statement must be viewed as a series of benchmarks that have been vetted and approved by the directors. Any movement away from the core risk strategy should be recognized as a deliberate decision to move outside of established boundaries.[72]

---

[71] These attributes were highlighted by the Bank Governance Leadership Network, Tapestry Networks, September 30, 2013.
[72] "How Risk Appetite Should Impact Behavior," 2014.

Questions Directors Should Ask About the Risk Appetite Framework

- What is the projected financial capacity for risk taking under various market scenarios? How much additional risk is affordable? What is the cost versus benefit of adding or reducing risk?
- How much earnings variance is acceptable in a given quarter or year? Which risks are acceptable and which risks are not? Where should capital be deployed?
- What are the strategic objectives? Which mechanisms are in place to ensure that the risk appetite framework is consistent with strategy, business and capital plans, and risk capacity?
- How do performance and compensation programs facilitate adherence to the risk appetite?
- To what extent is risk appetite included in important strategic discussions and decisions, including business and capital plans, mergers and acquisitions, and growth or contraction in new and existing services and products?
- Which mechanisms and metrics are in place to hold management accountable for the integrity of the risk appetite framework, including the timely identification, management, and escalation of issues relating to breaches in risk limits and material risk exposures? Are mitigation strategies or contingency plans in place and working effectively?
- How is the risk appetite communicated to promote a stronger risk culture?
- Do the board and management regularly review and monitor actual versus approved risk limits by business line, by legal entity, by products, and by risk categories, including qualitative risks?
- How are scenario analyses and stress tests used in establishing and monitoring risk appetite measures?
- What is the process to determine activities or initiatives outside the board-approved risk appetite statement?
- How are changes made to the risk appetite limits and the design of the risk appetite framework? Are proposed changes previewed with the regulators?
- Which independent assessments by internal audit or third parties are made of the design and effectiveness of the risk appetite framework and its alignment with regulatory expectations? What are the results?
- How does management determine that adequate resources and expertise are dedicated to risk management, including the use of internal audit and third-party resources, if required, to ensure compliance with the approved risk appetite framework?
- What assurances exist that risk management is supported by adequate and sufficient IT resources to enable the identification, measurement, assessment, and reporting of risk promptly and accurately?

Strong risk appetite frameworks help withstand shocks and create sustainable value by balancing management's willingness to take risks with the institution's ability to do so, thereby bringing discipline to major decisions. Management should take the lead in preparing the framework, and the board should provide input and oversight. In addition, directors will want to know that the framework is strong enough to support strategic planning, performance management, and risk-governance activities.[73]

---

[73] "The Board and Long-Term Value Creation," Report of the NACD Blue Ribbon Commission, National Association of Corporate Directors, 2015.

The regulators expect that the board, in addition to its ongoing monitoring, will at least annually (or after significant events) approve the risk appetite statement, conduct an assessment of the effectiveness of the risk appetite framework, and perform an evaluation of its own effectiveness in meeting oversight responsibilities.

The entire board needs to be engaged in assessing the effectiveness of the risk appetite framework, although compliance with risk appetite and tolerance levels and changes to the framework are often delegated to the risk committee and, in some cases, the audit committee.

The regulators will review the risk appetite process within the institution's overall risk governance framework. This review will include an assessment of the organizational structure, roles and responsibilities, policies and procedures, and escalation protocols in the event of breaches.

Clarifying objectives, expectations, and the key components of an effective risk appetite framework is imperative in fulfilling board responsibilities, taking them beyond high-level statements to practical applications. The formation, measurement, and changes to the policies and procedures associated with the risk appetite, which form a basic building block of the framework and provide a means to understanding the risk appetite, are also critical. These tools guide day-to-day decisions.

The board needs to be comfortable that both the directors and management are able to adequately describe the risk appetite and the risk appetite framework, as well as determine the institution is operating within its risk appetite and risk capacity, even in stress scenarios. The board also should be able to demonstrate that it seeks multiple views on potential deviations from the normal course by challenging assumptions in stress scenarios.

Directors should ensure that the risk appetite discussions are used in important decision-making processes, including planning and budgeting, target setting, performance management, and product and service approvals. The risk appetite framework needs to define appropriate limits and tolerance measures and be able to cascade these measures down to the various lines of business, the business units, and different geographies in an effective and transparent manner. Risk appetite discussions need to be integral to decisions on budgets, capital and funding, liquidity, and new and existing business opportunities.

Directors also should ensure that the risk appetite is forward looking and that information on risk appetite is communicated throughout the institution. The risk appetite framework needs to be embedded in the culture so that risk is everyone's business. As part of their evaluation of the risk appetite framework, the regulators will examine the risk appetite documents, metrics, reporting, and other activities to ensure the directors understand how management interprets and applies the risk appetite and risk limits. For some institutions, a useful tool for the board is a "dashboard" listing each of the risk areas along with comments from management as to the status of each.

Moreover, the board needs to determine that the risk appetite framework is adequately resourced with qualified personnel and that the technology and management information reporting systems support and facilitate the regulators' enhanced expectations.

Aligning Strategy and Risk Tolerances

Strategy

Maximum acceptable level of loss
- Earnings per share
- Cash flow
- Gross margin
- Portfolio value
- Economic and/or regulatory capital

Specific policy prohibitions
- Contractual arrangements
- Restricted services or products
- Maximum customer concentrations
- Markets and customers to avoid

Target services and operating parameters
- Debt ratings
- Growth
- Earnings volatility
- Diversification
- Liquidity
- Regulations

Risk appetite

Alternative risk responses
- Avoid/accept/reduce/transfer/exploit

Risk tolerances

Loss limit structures
- Specific products and services
- Designated businesses
- Trading activities

Acceptable level of variations
- Strategic vendors
- Operating processes
- Customer service levels
- Customer satisfaction targets
- Operation of key controls

Source: "The Risk Appetite Dialogue," Protiviti, 2010.

It is important that the work of the board and its required discussions and determinations are documented in appropriate detail, balancing the need to maintain an adequate record with the need to avoid inhibiting debate among directors.

"Directors may find the minimum standards of their oversight of the risk appetite framework particularly challenging and perhaps even perplexing. The task can be more onerous with an institution having a global footprint, multiple regulatory jurisdictions, and complex products and services," commented Jim Negus, partner, KPMG.

Director Expertise

The Financial Stability Board noted that, during the financial crisis, many boards of financial institutions were populated with directors who had little financial or industry experience and only a limited understanding of the complexity of the institutions they were leading. Moreover, the FSB indicated that directors were sometimes unable to dedicate sufficient time to understanding the business model and were too often deferential to management.

This deficiency of skills and the willingness to accept management recommendations without sufficient challenge can become particularly critical with regard to the board's oversight of the risk appetite framework. The FSB indicated that not only do directors collectively bear this oversight responsibility, but their individual reputations are at risk, as are those of the institutions they oversee.[74]

There is an expectation that the board is comprised of highly experienced directors who together have the knowledge, skills, and abilities to challenge management and to assess and monitor the strategy and the risks. It is also important that directors be able to dedicate ample time to reviewing information and developing an understanding of the key issues.

"To be able to credibly challenge the risk appetite framework, the board must have knowledge of the industry, an understanding of the strategy and associated risks, and a sufficiently detailed perspective of the institution's products and services. No doubt some directors and even boards will find it difficult, at times, to meet these standards," commented Patrick S. Brown, partner, Sullivan & Cromwell.

---

[74] "Thematic Review on Risk Governance," Financial Stability Board, February 2013.

Strategic Risk Calls for 'Thinking Outside of the Box'

"However beautiful the strategy, you should occasionally look at the results."
—WINSTON S. CHURCHILL

Overseeing and managing risk effectively is a hallmark of successful institutions. But in today's dynamic environment, it is difficult for directors and management to have confidence that plans and strategies will be executed as anticipated. A major factor is that strategic risks, those that either affect or are created by strategy decisions, can surface quickly, hastened by lightning-fast trends and technology and stimulated by social media, cloud computing, mobile devices, and big data. Institutions that fall behind become prey to disruption.[75]

Enterprise risk management encompasses a wide range of risks. Many boards and management do well in identifying, modeling, and mitigating knowable risks, such as the potential for natural catastrophes. But they face prodigious challenges dealing with more ambiguous strategic threats, many of which evolve over time and seem highly uncertain due to unexpected fact patterns. These risks can arise from internal process issues as well as forces in the external environment caused by competitors' activities, changes in client and customer preferences, technological advances, movements in the financial markets and the economy, and the actions of regulators.[76]

Some risks reflect exposures that, although harmful, will not threaten the well-being of an institution or its ability to ultimately meet its objectives. For example, a data-center outage can result in a short-term crisis or customer dissatisfaction, but the institution, once recovered, can quickly be back on track. Other events can result in losses that not only impair the ability to meet objectives, but threaten the institution's survival. Technology advancement is an illustration of this type of risk. The process used to identify these risks sometimes requires "thinking outside of the box" using a variety of disparate pieces of information. These more elusive risk exposures are elevating the importance of strategic risks and strategic risk management.[77]

---

[75] "Exploring Strategic Risk," Deloitte, 2013.
[76] "Risk Oversight: To Manage Disruption, Understand Strategic Assumptions," *Board Perspectives,* Protiviti, 2014.
[77] "Strategic Risk Management: A Primer for Directors," by Matteo Tonello, The Conference Board, August 23, 2012.

Risks to the Business

- Competitive actions
- Demand shortfall
- Customer retention issues
- Integration problems
- Pricing pressures
- Regulatory actions
- Industry downturn
- Technology advances
- Stakeholder pressures

Strategic

Operational

- Cost overruns
- Operating controls
- Poor capacity management
- Supply-chain issues
- Employee bad behaviors
- Regulations
- Commodity prices
- Bribery and corruption

- Political issues
- Legal issues
- Terrorism
- Natural disasters

Hazard

Financial

- Debt and interest rates
- Financial mismanagement
- Asset losses
- Goodwill and amortization
- Accounting and reporting problems

Source: "Sharpening Strategic Risk Management," by Mohammed Armoghan and Richard Sykes, Pricewaterhouse-Coopers, 2015.

According to Deloitte's global survey on exploring strategic risk, executives say their view of strategic risk is changing. They note the following:

- Strategic risk management is a board and management priority, a clear indicator of its growing importance. Of those surveyed, 81% say strategic risks are explicitly managed.
- Many institutions are taking a broad, inclusive view of strategic risk that focuses not just on challenges that might cause a particular strategy to fail, but on any major risks that could affect longer-term positioning and performance.
- The majority of those surveyed believe technology enablers and disrupters such as social media, mobile, and big data could threaten their established business models. Ninety-one percent have changed their business strategies since these technologies began to emerge.
- More institutions are integrating strategic risk analysis into their planning processes. Among those surveyed, 61% believe their risk management programs are performing "at least adequately" in supporting the development and execution of business strategy.[78]

---

[78] "Exploring Strategic Risk," 2013.

Changing Course in a Disruptive World

Remember not so long ago, when every street corner and strip mall seemed to have a big blue Blockbuster? Although Netflix appeared in 2000 and Redbox began in 2002, Blockbuster, at the turn of the century, was the dominant, unassailable leader in home video rental, with 5,500 stores in the U.S. and other outlets overseas. Who could have predicted that just a few years later, the industry giant that took out nearly all the neighborhood mom-and-pop rental shops would itself be out of business? Blockbuster filed for bankruptcy in 2010 and ceased operations in 2013.

Source: "Blockbuster's Demise: Farewell to the Original Video-on-Demand," *The Wall Street Journal*, November 6, 2013.

Regulatory Perspectives

The regulators make it clear that the importance of strategic risk requires that the board and management understand the potential of future events, identify the mosaic of possible threats and their ambiguities, and develop plans to monitor and manage these risks.

The Basel Committee on Banking Supervision's guidelines issued in July 2015 indicate that risk identification should encompass all material risks (including the harder-to-quantify risks), which implicitly covers strategic risk.

The Federal Reserve Board's ROPE guidance offers explicit guidance on what are considered to be leading and lagging practices in capital planning. It also provides examples of those practices on the treatment of risks that are more difficult-to-quantify, including strategic, reputation, and compliance risks. The ROPE guidance suggests that the risk identification process should ensure that all risks are appropriately accounted for when assessing capital needs, by incorporating the effect of reputational and strategic risks into projections when calculating capital requirements. The guidance notes that assumptions and methods used to quantify the effect of these risks on reduced revenue, added expenses, or a management overlay on top of loss estimates should be transparent and clearly defined.

The Federal Reserve Board's SR 15-19, outlining the capital planning expectations at large and noncomplex institutions, however, somewhat lowers the expectations regarding the identification of difficult-to-quantify risks, allowing for the option to use either qualitative or quantitative risk measurement approaches for both strategic and reputation risks.

The OCC's minimum standards indicate that directors should evaluate and approve the strategic plan and monitor management's implementation efforts, and that directors and management need to incorporate reputation and strategic risks into their decision-making processes. The guidelines also indicate that the CEO, with input from front-line units, independent risk management, and internal audit, is responsible for developing a written strategic plan covering, at a minimum, a three-year period. The board needs to evaluate and approve the plan and monitor implementation at least annually. The guidelines note that the plan includes an assessment of the risks, an overall mission statement and strategic objectives, and an explanation of how the risk governance framework will be updated to account for changes to the risk profile. Additionally, the plan needs to be reviewed, updated, and approved by the board when there are changes in the institution's risk profile or operating environment that were not contemplated when the plan was developed.

The OCC's July 2015 *Semiannual Risk Perspective* notes that strategic risk remains among the top concerns. The OCC observes that the challenging environment is causing many institutions to reevaluate their business models and risk appetites, as well as the deployment of capital.

The OCC updated its guidance in December 2015 regarding the risk assessment system (OCC Bulletin 2015-48), which will be reflected in its examination handbooks. Risk was previously defined by the OCC in terms of impact to current or anticipated earnings or capital for the risk categories of credit, interest rate, liquidity, price, operational, and compliance. For strategic and reputation risks, consideration was given to potential changes in franchise or enterprise value.

The revised guidance from the OCC applies a single definition of risk to all categories. Risk is defined as "the potential that events will have an adverse effect on a bank's current or projected financial condition and resilience." Under this broader definition, financial condition includes impacts from diminished capital and liquidity. Capital in this context includes potential impacts from losses, reduced earnings, and market value of equity. Resilience recognizes the institution's ability to withstand periods of stress. The updated guidance expands strategic risk and reputation risk assessment to include both the quantity of risk and the quality of risk management. Previously, the OCC assessed only the aggregate level and direction of strategic and reputation risks. Although the OCC indicated that measuring the quantity of these risks may be difficult, the revised guidance provides a means for the OCC to better assess and communicate efforts to control these risks.

Board's Role in Strategy

Strategy is governed by the willingness of the board and management to accept risks in pursuit of value creation, as well as the capacity and willingness to bear these risks. The business model inherent in the strategy should exploit the areas in which the institution excels relative to the competition, including the assumption of risks included in the strategy execution.

Strategy-setting describes the sources of competitive advantage, as evidenced by the institution's differentiating capabilities and the infrastructure needed to successfully execute those capabilities. Strategy focuses on how value will be created for shareholders, customers and clients, employees, and other stakeholders over a stated period.

The Stanford Graduate School of Business notes that directors have four primary responsibilities regarding strategy and risk management:

1. Determine the risk tolerance in consultation with management and stakeholders.
2. Evaluate the strategy and business model in the context of the risk tolerance.
3. Ensure management's commitment to operate at the agreed upon risk level.
4. Ensure management has the requisite internal controls in the risk framework.[79]

The National Association of Corporate Directors suggests that directors should work with management to ensure the proper development, execution, monitoring, and, when

---

[79] Stanford Graduate School of Business, Center for Leadership Development and Research, 2011.

necessary, modification of the strategy. The nature and extent of the board's engagement will depend on the particular facts and circumstances. The NACD advises that the strategy must continually adapt to ever-accelerating change due to new competitors, emerging technologies, globalization, regulations, demographic trends, and economic and geopolitical volatility. As a result, the NACD recommends directors recognize that board involvement in strategy is a continuing process and that issues related to strategy should be a central focus and year-round board activity.[80]

An essential component of the board's role in strategy is its review and challenge of the strategic assumptions—or, simply, management's views regarding the environment during the strategic planning horizon. These assumptions represent the internal and external factors that are both favorable and unfavorable to achieving the desired goals of the strategy. The strategic assumptions highlight the hard and soft spots in the strategy and outline the potential disruptions and important risks that could threaten the institution. Collectively, the assumptions provide a foundation for understanding the sources of uncertainty in the strategy by identifying and testing relevant scenarios.

The aspirational objectives established in the strategy, and the protection of shareholder value through risk management, need to be aligned and integrated. On a tactical and operational level, strategic objectives need to be transformed into performance prognosis, plans, and projects, and supported by fact-based analysis of the most important risks and value drivers. Together, the two activities of strategy-setting and risk management facilitate the development of the critical assumptions underlying the strategy.

"The board's understanding of the strategic assumptions is essential. It places directors in a position to consider and, as necessary, challenge management's plans and evaluate their performance in implementing and executing the strategy," commented Samuel A. Di Piazza Jr., a board member of AT&T, Jones Lang LaSalle Inc., and ProAssurance Corporation.

According to KPMG's Global Pulse Survey, the closer linkage of strategy and risk was cited most often by respondents as a key to improving risk-related decision making. Of the institutions responding, 75% are either "satisfied" or "somewhat satisfied" with this linkage today in the boardroom.[81]

Aligning Business and IT Strategy

The increasingly critical role of technology in the direction and execution of strategic imperatives mandates that IT strategy is to be aligned with and become an integral element of the overall business strategy.

The *FFIEC Information Technology Examination Handbook* issued in November 2015 specifies that the board should set the tone and direction for an institution's use of technology. The Federal Financial Institutions Examination Council[82] suggests that the

---

[80] "Report of the NACD Blue Ribbon Commission on Strategy Development," National Association of Corporate Directors, October 2014.

[81] "Global Pulse Survey: Calibrating Strategy & Risk," KPMG, 2015.

[82] The FFIEC is a formal interagency body empowered to prescribe uniform principles, standards, and report forms for the federal examination of financial institutions by the Board of Governors of the Federal Reserve System, the Federal Deposit Insurance Corporation, the National Credit Union Administration, the Office of the Comptroller of the Currency, and the Consumer Financial Protection Bureau to make recommendations to promote uniformity in the supervision of financial institutions.

board needs to approve the information security strategic plan, the information security program, and other technology-related policies requiring directors to understand IT activities and the associated risks. The FFIEC recommends that the IT strategic plan must be linked to, and be an integral part of, the enterprise-wide strategic plan.

According to the FFIEC, management is responsible for strategic IT planning, oversight of IT performance, and aligning IT with business needs. While the board may delegate the design, implementation, and monitoring of certain IT activities to management, the FFIEC indicates that directors are to remain responsible for overseeing IT activities and should provide a credible challenge to management.

Defining Strategic Risks

The OCC's *Large Bank Supervision Comptroller's Handbook* indicates that strategic risk is the risk to current or projected financial condition and resilience arising from adverse business conditions, poor implementation of business decisions, or lack of responsiveness to changes in the industry and operating environment. This risk is a function of an institution's strategic goals, business strategies, resources, and quality of implementation. The OCC notes that the resources needed to carry out business strategies are both tangible and intangible. They include communications channels, operating systems, delivery networks, and managerial capacities and capabilities.

The OCC notes that the assessment of strategic risk focuses on opportunity costs and on how plans, systems, and implementation affect financial condition and resilience. It also incorporates how management analyzes external factors, such as economic, technological, competitive, regulatory, and other environmental changes.

As a consequence, the identification of strategic threats is much different from traditional risk management practices such as measuring operational risks, which are generally focused on near-term uncertainties related to people, processes, and technology. Operational risks may also include external events, external resources, and regulatory compliance, but only in cases where they impact operations, not overall strategy.

Risks resulting from strategic decisions can be lethal because they could threaten the institution. For example, innovation of any kind can improve quality, create new markets, reduce costs, extend a product range, replace products and services, and dramatically improve processes. However, innovation also can be seriously disruptive and life-threatening if it materially improves a competitor's products or services in unexpected ways, typically by lowering prices significantly or allowing for a product or service that transforms the way the consumer's needs are fulfilled.[83]

In setting the strategy, it is critical to define the threats, loss drivers, and incongruities that are inherent in the strategic objectives and that could materially affect performance and adversely impact execution. These are the risks—the strategic risks—that really matter.

---

[83] "Risk Oversight: To Manage Disruption, Understand the Strategic Assumptions," 2014.

Strategic risks can evolve over time. According to Michael Roberto, a professor of management at Bryant University, most breakdowns and collapses do not occur in a flash. They begin with a series of small problems, a chain of errors that often stretches back many months or even years. As time passes, the small problems balloon into larger ones. Mistakes compound over time as one small error triggers another. Once set in motion, the chain of events can be stopped. However, as time passes and momentum builds, once seemingly minor issues can spiral out of control.[84]

McKinsey & Company gives an example of a strategic threat in banking, noting that if the last epoch in retail banking was defined by a boom-to-bust expansion of consumer credit, the current one will be defined by digital. This includes the rapid innovation in payments and the broader transformation in systems enabled by digital technologies. The urgency of acting is acute. McKinsey predicts that banks have three to five years, at most, to become digitally proficient. If they fail to take action, the institutions risk entering a spiral of decline and becoming laggards.[85]

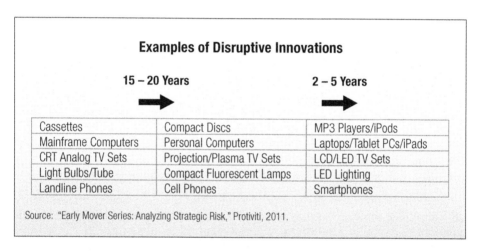

Examples of Disruptive Innovations

15 – 20 Years		2 – 5 Years
Cassettes	Compact Discs	MP3 Players/iPods
Mainframe Computers	Personal Computers	Laptops/Tablet PCs/iPads
CRT Analog TV Sets	Projection/Plasma TV Sets	LCD/LED TV Sets
Light Bulbs/Tube	Compact Fluorescent Lamps	LED Lighting
Landline Phones	Cell Phones	Smartphones

Source: "Early Mover Series: Analyzing Strategic Risk," Protiviti, 2011.

Strategic Risk Management

Strategic risk management is the process of identifying, measuring, and managing the risks in the institution's business strategy, including the responses when risks are actually realized. It focuses on the trends, future events, and circumstances embedded in the strategy, and it entails an understanding of the strategy, the risks in adopting it (or not), and the risks in executing it.

Standard & Poor's describes the attributes of strategic risk management as 1) management's view of the most consequential risks, their likelihood, and potential effect; 2)

---

[84] *Know What You Don't Know*, by Michael A. Roberto, Prentice Hall, 2009.
[85] "Strategic Choices for Banks in the Digital Age," by Henk Broeders and Somesh Khanna, McKinsey & Company, January 2015.

the frequency and extent of updating the identification of these top risks; 3) the influence of risk sensitivity on financial management and financial decisions; and 4) the role of risk management in strategic decision making.[86]

Identifying Strategic Risks

Identifying strategic risks focuses on the following key threats:

- Strategic initiatives: The risks of developing initiatives that improperly consider the operating landscape and fail as a result of factors other than execution.
- Strategic planning: A planning process that fails to meet objectives impacting stakeholders.
- Financial environment: Significant changes in the financial environment that compromise the assumptions in the strategic plan.
- Competitive environment: Changes in the environment that are not addressed with new products and/or services and that were not anticipated in developing the strategic plan.
- Regulatory environment: Changes in the environment that cause business objectives to become unattainable or result in excessively burdensome compliance costs.
- Remuneration: Practices that result in unintended, sub-optimal behavior or the inability to recruit and/or retain employees.
- Operational effectiveness: Ineffective or inefficient internal processes or technologies that hinder the implementation of strategic plans or impact funding and/or liquidity.
- Expansion: Growth initiatives that result in unexpected and unmitigated risks to existing businesses.
- Capital planning: Capital planning that fails to meet its funding objectives.

Given the ambiguity of strategic risks, identifying these risks can be extraordinarily difficult. While some of the risks may seem obvious, over time—and presented with additional facts, trends, and developments—other, more subtle threats become identifiable as they transform into very real-time risks.

Measuring Strategic Risk

"Risk identification is the first step, but before an institution can manage strategic risks, it must measure them. A commonly used metric is economic capital, or the amount of capital required to cover unexpected losses based on a predetermined solvency standard," commented James Lam, president, James Lam & Associates.

By applying a consistent measure of volatility, the economic capital required to support individual risks can be calculated and the result aggregated across all risks, taking correlation effects into account. Economic capital is a common currency in which risks can be quantified. It is the amount of capital which an institution requires to cover risks confronted as a growing concern.

---

[86] "Enterprise Risk Management: S&P to Apply Enterprise Risk Analysis to Corporate Ratings," Standard & Poor's, May 7, 2008.

For strategic risks, the calculation is forward-looking, such as, for example, the cushion required to support new product launches, undertake potential acquisitions, or withstand anticipated competitive actions.

Dividing the anticipated after-tax return on each strategic initiative by the economic capital generates RAROC (risk-adjusted return on capital). If RAROC exceeds the institution's cost of capital, the initiative is viable and will add value. If RAROC is less than the cost of capital, it will erode value.

However, the decision whether to support an initiative should not depend on a single case reflecting the expected value. The stress testing of assumptions by calculating multiple scenarios is necessary. A mapping of the probabilities and consequences of different outcomes not only provides a better perspective of the risks and rewards, but also helps identify trigger points for action if the initiative lags expectations.[87]

As also noted in regard to reputational risk, however, calculating a simple percentage of capital or using only expert judgment to quantify strategic risk without providing thoughtful analysis and support is likely to fall short of the regulators' expectations.

Managing Strategic Risk

During the strategy-setting process, the risk appetite statement is used as a critical guide in strategic discussions to manage risks. Effective strategic risk management will ensure the institution takes only those risks it is best equipped to manage within the parameters of the risk appetite, while minimizing exposures to those areas considered off-strategy. At the same time, the board and management need to ensure that the institution is not taking on too little risk.

It is essential that plans are developed and implemented to manage, mitigate, and respond to strategic risks. These plans often involve improvements in policies, processes, people, reporting, and systems to ensure that all these components are properly aligned with the strategic plan. Risk responses will involve monitoring the vital signs in the external environment to ensure continued validity of the critical strategic assumptions.

The analysis supporting strategic risk management often consists of risk dashboards or risk maps, including key performance indicators, for each key business unit or products/services, and the deployment of risk-adjusted performance measures. The strategic risk monitoring and reporting need to be embedded into the core processes for budgeting, business-performance monitoring, scoreboards, and performance-measurement systems.

An effective risk management program will facilitate an ongoing evaluation of the strategic risks, including an understanding of how taking action to mitigate one risk would affect other risks. "Strategic risk reviews" are often an integral part of ongoing strategic risk management, enforcing the criticality of linking the strategy, risks, and execution.

---

[87] "Strategic Risk Management: The Next Frontier for ERM," by James Lam, Workiva, 2015.

Questions Directors Should Ask About Strategic Risks

- How well is the strategy defined and how frequently is the strategy discussed and debated? What are the emerging threats associated with each line of business?
- What are the strategic assumptions underlying the strategy? What is the process for challenging and changing the assumptions? What are the revisions in these assumptions from prior periods?
- How much time and attention is devoted by the board and management to thinking "outside of the box"? How are these discussions facilitated?
- Which factors are considered and what are the parameters to ensure that new emerging risks are brought to the board? What emerging risks cause management the most anxiety?
- Are risks considered in all strategic discussions and how are these discussions documented?
- Are the risk management functions integrated with strategic assessment, decision making, and monitoring of strategic plans?
- What are management's capabilities for collecting data, analyzing developments and trends, and drawing meaningful conclusions?
- Are directors and management establishing the right behaviors and a risk-sensitive culture, in line with the institution's strategy?
- How do compensation rewards encourage risk-based thinking and behavior? Have the key risks been mapped to key performance and value measures?
- How much confidence do directors have in the reliability of the budgeting and forecasting processes? What improvements are necessary?
- Does the board possess directors with industry and specialist expertise capable of presenting an effective challenge to management? How will the board's capabilities gaps, if any, be addressed?

Ambiguity of Strategic Risks

Strategic risks are more about what is not known. What sets strategic risks apart from other risks is their ambiguity. They are made difficult to read by uncertainty and require ongoing monitoring of the environment to ensure strategic assumptions remain valid over time given the circumstances.[88]

A component of strategic risks is sometimes referred to as "compensated" risks because the potential for upside often is sufficient to warrant accepting the downside exposures. The risks associated with establishing operations in new markets, introducing new products, or undertaking large research and development projects, as examples, are

---

[88] "Early Mover Series: Analyzing Strategic Risks," Protiviti, 2011.

compensated risks because they are often inseparable from executing the strategy. In contrast, "uncompensated" risks, such as cybersecurity, are one-sided because they offer the potential for downside with no upside.

Monitoring and assessing strategic risks require much more than surveys and listening to customer feedback. The accepted information hierarchy, including established newspapers and media outlets, has given way to a multidimensional information matrix where no single voice dominates information, and opinions of all kinds are easier to access yet more difficult to evaluate and control.

Traditional approaches to managing strategic risks include monitoring leading financial indicators and the evolving regulatory environment. These indicators are helpful but no longer definitive. Because they are often grounded in audited financial statements, the resulting risk strategies and hedges are driven largely by prior performance and past events and do not necessarily serve to detect future strategic risks or predict future performance.[89] In response, some institutions are making deliberate efforts to improve their data collection and data analytics capabilities as part of strategic risk management.

Directors need to recognize that strategic risks are not susceptible to precise measurement and therefore the analytical framework applied to them is more qualitative compared to financial or operational risks. For example, interest-rate risk is rather straightforward to quantify in terms of its impact on the business, taking into account potential changes in the economy and market volatility. On the other hand, strategic risks arising from invalid assumptions are more about having sufficient knowledge about changes in economic trends, competitors, customers, suppliers, regulators, and other external factors. Monitoring these factors helps in evaluating whether disruptive change may be occurring or is about to occur. The change may result in a deficient strategy if one or more critical underlying assumptions are no longer valid.[90]

Monitoring of the environment often requires connecting the data of peripheral information. Although this information may not seem core or pertinent to immediate business activities or risk profiles, monitoring strategic threats involves all relevant information sources, not just mainstream data. By the time information is published in mainstream sources, it is likely no longer peripheral. The periphery is inherently blurry and incomplete; therefore, conflicts and differences in viewpoints, as well as multiple hypotheses, can help illuminate different parts of the picture. The signals emanating from this information can be opaque today and become clear only as time passes and the information is connected.[91]

"It is as difficult for directors to plan for the unthinkable as it is for management. The board should strive to anticipate every possible scenario that could materially impact shareholder value and to understand the mitigation plan for each risk," said Doreen Woo Ho, a board member of U.S. Bancorp.

---

[89] "Exploring Strategic Risk," 2013.
[90] "Early Mover Series: Analyzing Strategic Risks," 2011.
[91] "Strategic Risk Management: Facilitating Risk-based Insurance Decisions," PricewaterhouseCoopers, 2012.

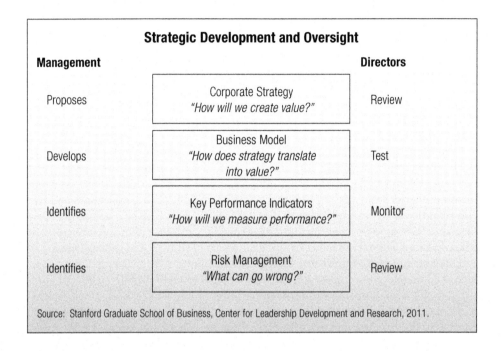

Strategic Development and Oversight

Management		Directors
Proposes	Corporate Strategy *"How will we create value?"*	Review
Develops	Business Model *"How does strategy translate into value?"*	Test
Identifies	Key Performance Indicators *"How will we measure performance?"*	Monitor
Identifies	Risk Management *"What can go wrong?"*	Review

Source: Stanford Graduate School of Business, Center for Leadership Development and Research, 2011.

Implications for Directors

The external viewpoint that directors bring to the boardroom plays an essential part in ensuring that risk taking enhances strategic thinking. Because directors are not part of the institution's day-to-day activities, they are not normally locked into a particular way of thinking or course of action. As a result, they can be more open to "thinking outside of the box" and recognizing strategic threats.

The culture plays a significant and important role in how well strategic risk is managed and must be considered as part of a strategic risk assessment. Directors need to be alert for a risk culture that enables or permits ethical lapses throughout the institution. Management can set the rules, but it is the culture that determines how employees follow them.

PricewaterhouseCoopers highlights three specific concerns of board members and trends in regard to strategic risk management practices. First, many directors are concerned that the strategic risk framework and processes currently in place are no longer giving them the level of protection they need. Second, boards are seeing rapid increases both in the speed with which risk events take place and the contagion by which they spread across different categories of risk. They are especially concerned about the escalating impact of catastrophic risks, which can threaten the very existence of the institution and even undermine entire industries. And finally, directors believe they are spending too much time and money on operating current risk management processes, rather than moving quickly and flexibly to identify and tackle new and emerging risks.

As a result, some directors are not convinced that their return on spending is fully justified by the level of protection they gain from it.[92]

Directors and management need to ensure that strategy and risk are aligned. In some cases, risk management functions separately, in a silo, from strategic assessment, decision making, and monitoring against plans. Risk management can become flawed when risks are evaluated after the strategy is formulated. The end result can be strategic objectives that are unrealistic and risk management that is simply an appendage to the operations. Consequences could include a strategy that is undeliverable, an inability to continually adapt to change, and the loss of enterprise value that took years to build.

Some boards discuss with management the strategic plan perhaps once a year. However, with the dynamic landscape and the rapid speed of technological advances, high-performing boards perform their strategic oversight regularly and make it an ongoing dialogue, consistent with the recommendations of both the regulators and the NACD. Because opportunities and threats can surface suddenly, boards that review strategy infrequently are likely not keeping pace.

According to PricewaterhouseCoopers, boards are addressing strategy and strategic risk by doing the following:

- Regularly challenging management's assumptions that underlie the strategy, considering current market activity, and understanding how prior-year assumptions have changed in the current year and whether historical assumptions and risk identification were reasonable based on business activity.
- Having each significant business unit examine the disruptive technologies that could impact its strategy and provide this insight to the board and management.
- Creating a "think tank" tasked with identifying and presenting innovative ideas, considering how the institution is changing the nature of the industry, and identifying potential disruptors.
- Gaining external and broader views on the strategy—which may include the opinions of customers, third-party advisors, and non-management employees—to understand how others perceive the institution, how they articulate the assumptions, and how they view the risks.[93]

Importantly, strategic risk assessment needs to be integrated into the performance measurement processes. Just as strategic risk management is an ongoing process, so is the need to establish an ongoing linkage with the institution's core processes in order to set and measure its strategies and performance. This would include integrating risk management into both strategic planning and performance measurement systems. The maturity and culture of the institution will dictate how this is performed.

Reliable budgeting and forecasting processes in which the board and management have confidence are crucial to the strategic planning process and risk management. The

---

[92] "Sharpening Strategic Risk Management," by Mohammed Armoghan and Richard Sykes, Pricewaterhouse-Coopers, 2015.

[93] "Boardroom Direct: Addressing the Strategic Development and Execution Gap," PricewaterhouseCoopers, May 2015.

strategic plan needs to identify metrics and measures for directors to monitor, requiring accurate budgeting and forecasting.

A challenge for boards is finding the time to regularly assess strategy. Directors need to ensure adequate time is reserved for these important discussions. Some boards make strategy an agenda item at each meeting. Another approach is allowing directors to have unstructured time for more in-depth discussions regarding strategy and strategic risks, which could be obtained through a board retreat or similar forum.

Although strategic risks can pose the greatest threat to many institutions, the development of strategic risk management programs remains a work in progress. Strategic risk identification requires directors and management to ask themselves whether their thinking is sufficiently broad, whether they are being objective, and whether there are topics not discussed in the boardroom that need to be addressed.

As a matter of reference, the debate continues among large and noncomplex financial institutions and smaller firms over the treatment of difficult-to-quantify risks such as strategic risk and reputation risk. For capital planning purposes, the regulators allow for some flexibility in addressing these risks. Regardless of the approach, however, it is evident that these risks need to be identified and considered as part of enterprise risk management.

"Being proactive in dealing with strategic risks and overseeing strategic risk programs have become imperatives for directors given the radical pace at which technologies and new competitive paradigms are disrupting businesses," said Jaynie Miller Studenmund, board member of Western Asset Funds Inc., CoreLogic Inc., LifeLock Inc., and Pinnacle Entertainment Inc.

Directors and management who understand the importance of "thinking outside of the box" when addressing strategic risks are better able to identify potential threats in time to take corrective action. This early warning is perhaps the most important consequence of strategic risk management.

Reputational Risk Requires Board Vigilance

"The way to gain a good reputation is to endeavor to be what you desire to appear."
— SOCRATES

The most reputable financial institutions are only now reemerging from the impact of the financial crisis that magnified their weaknesses and exposed significant flaws in their safeguards. Although in recovery, customer trust in large institutions has been impacted by compliance violations, civil money penalties, fraud, information security breaches, denial-of-service attacks, and inadequate reinvestments. These events, in almost all cases, are linked to distinct risk management gaps within operational silos. The resulting erosion in trust has coincided with damaged reputations.

Reputation is built on how an institution's character is perceived by its stakeholders. It is qualitative, difficult to measure, yet essential to an institution's long-term health. Successful institutions regularly identify reputation as one of their most valuable assets. Reputation drives value and key performance metrics such as sales and market share, employee recruiting, morale and turnover, credit ratings, and investor and regulator confidence.

Reputation has become a new type of asset, built on an intangible foundation and subject to a connected stakeholder market. This interactive market brings new escalating threats for managing reputational risk.[94]

Reputational risk crosses the boundaries of an institution and can result from breaches in the limits of risk appetite; fault lines in business strategy; behaviors or incidents caused by customers, suppliers, vendors, or other third parties; difficulties with new products; defects in processes; advertising issues; communication problems; regulatory actions; and media disruptions. Today, an institution's reputation is increasingly shaped by the enhanced oversight of the media, online conversations, and the regulators. The ubiquity of the 24-hour news cycle and social media gives everyone who has an opinion a platform to share it. Other movers of reputation include the rapidly changing business environment, evolving environmental and social factors, globalization, technology advances, and incidents or changes related to trademarks, tradenames, and intellectual property.[95] All of these potential disruptions, if realized, can negatively impact revenues, stock prices, and the license to operate, potentially decimating an institution.

---

[94] "Before Disaster Strikes: Proactive Monitoring Can Help Protect Your Bank's Reputation," by Kenneth J. Ramaley and Bradley W. Brooks, *The RMA Journal*, May 2013.
[95] "The Interplay Between Operational Risk and Reputation Risk or Impact," by Edward J. DeMarco Jr., The Risk Management Association, 2015.

Key Stakeholders

Stakeholders	Descriptions
Clients and customers	Individuals or entities using products and/or services
Employees	Full-time and part-time
Shareholders and others	Owners, affiliates, debtholders, funding sources, and others
Regulators	Office of the Comptroller of the Currency, Federal Reserve System, Consumer Financial Protection Bureau, Federal Deposit Insurance Corporation, Securities and Exchange Commission, and others
Public/media	Media, nonprofit organizations, special interest groups, trade associations, rating agencies, nonregulatory government officials, and others
Third parties	Vendors, suppliers, strategic partners, independent contractors, and others

The primary responsibility for overseeing and managing reputational risks resides with the board and management. Risks associated with reputation have no start date and no end date, so they require the same vigilance, intensity, and constancy the board dedicates to credit, market, and other critical risks.

"Reputation is an accumulation of the perceptions of key stakeholders like the owners, clients and customers, employees, and the regulators. Although it is built over years and decades, an institution's reputation can be destroyed by a single, high-profile incident," commented Richard K. Davis, chairman and CEO, US Bancorp.

Thomas J. Curry, the Comptroller of the Currency, said that it speaks volumes that some of the most significant losses institutions have sustained were due not to the loans they made, but to lapses in operational risk management and the ensuing legal judgments, regulatory fines, and reputational damage.[96]

Sarah Bloom Raskin, formerly a member of the Board of Governors of the Federal Reserve System and now deputy secretary of the U.S. Department of Treasury, said that the effects of the financial crisis, combined with the power of the Internet to broadly and quickly publicize information, should alert institutions to how they manage their reputations. The regulators have a duty to see that all risks are fully understood even if those risks, like reputational risk, are a challenge to quantify or have not fully emerged.

Furthermore, Raskin noted that the approach to managing reputational risk tends to be reactive rather than proactive. Institutions and the regulators regularly focus on

---

[96] Remarks by Thomas J. Curry, Comptroller of the Currency, at RMA's Governance, Compliance, and Operational Risk Conference, Cambridge, Massachusetts, May 8, 2014.

addressing reputation threats that have already surfaced. In her view, this is not risk management but crisis management, a reactive approach aimed at limiting the damage. She proposes that the regulators incentivize boards and managements to address the factors that impact the level of reputational risks before they emerge.

Finally, Raskin highlighted cybersecurity attacks as representing a very significant reputational risk beyond the potential theft of data and the disruption of service. Cyberattacks have the potential to cause dissatisfaction among customers or, even more chilling, the total loss of consumer confidence.[97]

Despite chronic threats to reputations, not all boards monitor the institution's position in the marketplace. A National Association of Corporate Directors survey indicates that while 47% of public-company directors in all industry sectors routinely oversee stakeholder relations, only 29% indicate that they do not receive ample information regarding nonfinancial risks. More than half do not stay abreast of social media activity, an important and regular point of contact between an institution and its stakeholders.[98]

"In some ways, underlying events that create reputational issues are indicators of board and management competency. This means that some events are forgiven to some extent, like a cyber breach. Stakeholders look at it and say, 'Well, it can happen anywhere and people who live in glass houses shouldn't throw stones.' Then, there are events like a significant charge-off or restatement because an account was discovered unreconciled for two or three years, and the stakeholders walk away thinking, 'Does this management have a clue what they are doing?'" said Yousef A. Valine, executive vice president and chief risk officer, First Horizon National Corporation.

Regulatory Perspectives

The guidelines issued by the Basel Committee on Banking Supervision note that the risk assessment process should include an ongoing analysis of existing risks as well as the identification of new or emerging risks, both quantitative and qualitative. Harder-to-quantify risks, such as reputation risk, should be considered and evaluated.

The Federal Reserve Board's ROPE guidance suggests that, when assessing capital needs, the risk identification process should ensure that all risks are accounted for by incorporating the effect of reputation and strategic risks into the calculations.

In addition, the OCC's guidelines on minimum standards indicate that practices for managing reputation and strategic risks are less developed than those associated with other risk categories. However, the guidelines suggest that it is important for directors and management to incorporate these risks into their decision-making processes.

---

[97] Remarks by Sarah Bloom Raskin, member of the Board of Governors of the Federal Reserve System, at the Banking Outlook Conference, Atlanta, Georgia, February 28, 2013.
[98] "2014-2015 NACD Public Company Governance Survey," National Association of Corporate Directors, 2014.

Events Giving Rise to Reputational Risk

Bad Conduct	Questionable Judgment	Operational Shortcomings	External Attacks
Disreputable exposure to controversial clients	Unexpected exposures in noncore markets	Major product or service quality failures	Collateral damage from a peer company incident
Misuse of customer data or information	Misbehavior by directors, management, and/or employees	Badly executed business strategy	Incorrect or unfounded rumors and accusations
Doing business in an unethical manner	Overly aggressive regulatory positions/ poor relations with the regulators	Poor customer relations	Negative public remarks by politicians/ public institutions
Misrepresentation of the institution's position to the market	Excessive executive compensation	Nonperformance of core infrastructure, including IT	Protest group opposition to business activities
Illegal or fraudulent activities by rogue employees	Business activities that contradict core values	Poor labor standards and approach to labor issues	
Workplace violence	Mishandled response to operational/ conduct failures	Business disruption from a natural or manmade disaster	

Note: The actual events may overlap between these categories.

Source: "Reputation Risk: A Rising C-Suite Imperative," Oliver Wyman, 2014.

Defining Reputational Risk

Reputation risk is the risk of loss to the goodwill or franchise value of an institution resulting from a decision, act, or omission. It can arise from operations, external events, or third-party relationships. A reputational risk that is not properly managed can quickly escalate into a major crisis.

The Federal Reserve System's Commercial Bank Examination Manual, originally issued in March 1994, defines reputational risk as the potential that negative publicity regarding an institution's business practices, whether true or not, will cause a decline in the customer base, costly litigation, or a reduction in revenue.

Reputation risk is also sometimes referred to as the impact on earnings or capital resulting from the loss of trust in the institution or the institution's inability to meet the expectations of stakeholders. This can expose the institution to negative public perception, which may not be factually based, and hinder its ability to achieve its objectives.

Reputation risk has clear drivers and tangible consequences. It is often characterized as a "risk of risks" that does not exist on a stand-alone basis. In fact, some view reputation risk as not a risk at all, but rather an outcome or consequence of other operational risks. For this reason, it is difficult to model. There are few threats to reputation that are not intertwined with other types of business problems or troublesome matters. As a consequence, reputational risk is an amplifier of other corporate vulnerabilities and, in many cases, provokes other risks (such as brand erosion).[99]

Irrespective of the precise definition, reputation risk is a pervasive threat that permeates the institution and, if left unchecked, can severely undermine the institution's financial performance and sustainability over both the short and longer term.

Reputational Damage

Sometimes, institutions are exposed to reputational damage even when they have done little, if anything, wrong.

A challenge in calibrating reputational damage is identifying the potential risk events. AIRMIC and the Reputation Institute[100] surveyed AIRMIC members about the areas where the greatest likelihood for future reputational risks may materialize. The leading response to the survey (at 60%) was in the area of governance and the potential for events or issues that will reduce the perception of their institutions as open, honest, and fair in the way they do business. Additionally, 56% of the respondents believed reputational issues may arise from the delivery of goods and services, and 44% were concerned about issues arising from the leadership of the institutions.[101]

Strictly speaking, reputational damage does not include operational losses, fines and penalties, and recovery or restitution costs directly associated with an incident. These are the impacts of other risks, such as conduct failures. Rather, reputational damage results in the diminution of corporate value, constrained future opportunities, and an increased cost of future business, all of which are a consequence of how the institution is perceived following an incident.[102]

Negative perceptions can destabilize the strengths of the institution, its strategic positioning, its technical competence, and its financial condition. This reevaluation often casts aspersions on the judgment of the board and management, as well as the depth of their knowledge of the business, their attention to detail, and the quality of governance.

A reputational crisis begins when an institution does not set expectations properly, fails to meet them, or a negative incident occurs. As a result, stakeholders turn on the institution and lower their expectations. The economic consequences result from how

---

[99] "Reputation Risk: A Rising C-Suite Imperative," Oliver Wyman, 2014.
[100] Based in the U.K., the Association of Insurance and Risk Managers in Industry and Commerce (AIRMIC) promotes the interests of corporate insurance buyers and those involved in enterprise risk management. Encouraging best practices, it provides support through training, research, information-sharing programs, and lobbying. The Reputation Institute is a research and advisory firm that examines reputation issues.
[101] "Defining and Managing Reputation Risk: A Framework for Risk Managers," Reputation Institute, 2015.
[102] "Reputation Risk: A Rising C-Suite Imperative," 2014.

customers respond, how effectively employees work, how third parties set borrowing rates and establish terms, and how severely regulators impose sanctions and penalties.[103]

A breakdown of trust and a loss of confidence can adversely affect the behavior of key stakeholders. Existing or future clients and customers, who are anxious about a certain product or service or who do not want to be associated with a tarnished brand, may withdraw their business, leading to a decline in market share. Suppliers may be unwilling to offer the same terms as in the past. Employee morale may drop and it could become harder to attract top talent. The regulators could tighten their expectations. Shareholders may take a dim view of all of the above, including the strength of the board and management, and decide to withdraw their capital.

The harm from these actions can be significant and will vary over different periods. In the short term, the institution might see a dip in share price, cash flow or liquidity impacts, capital constraints, and revenue losses due to clients and customers switching to competitors, either temporarily or permanently. From an operations perspective, the intermediate term might see an inability to secure major business, the need for significant relationship-building efforts with key stakeholders, or the overhaul of a major technology or processes.

Key financial indicators could come under threat, and the institution might experience reduced creditworthiness, a higher cost of capital and increased capital requirements, and the possible need for asset sales or capital redeployment.

Longer-term concerns might include a failure to recover market share, heightened regulatory scrutiny, and multiple forgone opportunities. When the reputational damage is so devastating that future operations are no longer sustainable or permissible, reputational damages, if unmitigated, can lead to the institution's eventual demise.[104]

Reputational Risk Management

Reputational risk management is, by its nature, highly dependent on the institution's unique facts and circumstances. It requires the regular and thoughtful monitoring of the underlying events and perceptions that could impact reputation. Reputational risk management focuses on changes in the operating environment and across customers, products, and services, and includes an acute awareness of the dispositions and perceptions of stakeholders.[105]

It entails the integration of enterprise risk management practices, a strong risk culture, and crisis preparedness. The effective identification and management of risk can reveal major threats to reputation and help to ensure they are reduced to an acceptable level. In addition, effective preparedness plans can also minimize reputation damage when threatening events occur.[106]

---

[103] "The Interplay between Operational Risk and Reputation Risk or Impact," 2015.
[104] "Reputation Risk: A Rising C-Suite Imperative," 2014.
[105] "The Interplay between Operational Risk and Reputation Risk or Impact," 2015.
[106] "Managing Reputation Risk," Protiviti, 2012.

The culture sets the tone for protecting the institution's reputation. A reputation-protecting culture encourages a strong control environment, a balanced incentive compensation structure, clear accountability for results, open communication, transparent reporting, continuous process improvement, and a strong commitment to ethical and responsible behaviors.

Impact of Cybersecurity

Cybersecurity breaches are a significant threat confronting business and a constant reputational threat. Breaches, which are increasingly frequent and have become almost expected, are among the usual suspects for reputational damage.

Questions Directors Should Ask About Reputational Risk

- Who are the most important stakeholders? What is their perception of the institution's strengths and weaknesses? Which metrics are used to monitor the perceptions of these stakeholders?
- How does the risk assessment process source significant threats to the institution's reputation and identify gaps requiring response plans to improve preparedness?
- As a result of a defined incident, how much would the institution's reputation be impacted among the various categories of stakeholders? Would the damage to reputation be temporary or long-lasting?
- What processes are used to timely notify the board of significant changes in the risk profile, including the identification of emerging risks?
- What are the response plans in the event of a crisis? How often are these plans updated and tested? What are the communication plans?
- Which factors are essential to ensuring that the institution's reputation is being preserved? Are directors satisfied that management is focused on the fundamentals of enhancing and preserving the reputation?
- Is there evidence that the institution listens to customers, employees, and other stakeholders? Does management seek to understand their needs and deal with them responsibly and fairly?
- Is there a statement of core values or a code of ethics that expresses the commitment to responsible business behavior? If so, is the statement supported by appropriate performance/incentive programs and reinforcement mechanisms?
- Is risk effectively integrated into strategy-setting and business planning, and is consideration given to the potential for market forces to disrupt the business model?
- Are directors providing sufficient oversight on strategy setting, policy making, performance and execution, transparent reporting, and other matters vital to effective governance?
- Is there a strong control environment in place that lays the foundations for a strong culture around establishing and maintaining effective internal controls?

The Ponemon Institute released a study sponsored by Experian Data Breach Resolution focusing on the reputational impact of data breaches. Among the findings in the study are the following:

- Reputation is one of an institution's most valuable assets.
- Reputation and brand image are inextricably linked.
- Not all data breaches are equal; some are more devastating than others. The loss or theft of customer information is viewed as the most devastating data breach.
- Reputation and brand image are almost always damaged by the negative events involving data breaches.
- When a data breach occurs, the collateral damage to reputation and the brand normally results in negative financial impacts.[107]

Evaluating Reputational Risk

Reputation risk is the sum of the perceptions of those who matter. Their perspectives impact the institution's decision making and the ability to foster long-term relationships, a prerequisite to building confidence in the institution and its reputation.

An impaired reputation can impact institutions in different ways over varying time horizons. The quantification of reputational damage needs to distinguish between the consequences on share price, earnings, and capital adequacy, as well as the less measurable longer-term impacts, such as negative external perceptions of corporate ethics and values and a degradation of the brand. Each of these considerations differs in behavior and in the time required to define the risk and monetize the damages.

A Deloitte survey on reputational risk indicates that reputation problems have the most negative impact on revenue and brand value. The respondents, who had previously experienced a negative reputation event, said the most prominent effects are lower revenues (41%), loss of brand value (41%), and more regulatory investigations (37%).[108]

The foundation of the reputational risk framework begins with identifying the key stakeholders, such as clients and customers, employees, shareholders, regulators, the media, and third parties. The framework also identifies key drivers, which are among the underlying causes that can affect the institution's reputation with stakeholders, such as 1) incidents involving financial performance, asset quality, and long-term value; 2) governance and leadership; 3) regulatory actions, 4) social responsibility; 5) culture, talent, and the workplace; 6) commitments to clients and customers; and 7) peer and industry perceptions.

The intersections between the perceptions of the key stakeholders and the key drivers formulate the critical risk indicators—that is, the direction or trend line of reputational risk. None of the intersections are considered in isolation. Rather, evaluating reputational risk requires a collective assessment across the spectrum of stakeholders and drivers. The critical risk indicators are meant to detect the perceptions at the individual

---

[107] "Reputation Impact of a Data Breach," Ponemon Institute, November 2011.
[108] "Global Survey on Reputation Risk," Deloitte, October 2014.

stakeholder level before they become too extreme or too widespread. Identifying these indicators is therefore essential.

Key Drivers	
Drivers	**Descriptions**
Financial performance, asset quality, and long-term value	Incidents causing change in the financial stability of the institution by impacting the adequacy of earnings and/or capital
Governance and leadership	Activities that reflect the direction of the institution and the proficiency of the directors and management
Regulators	Imposition of fines, penalties, and sanctions
Social responsibility	Activities that provide service to communities and strive to make meaningful and consistent contributions
Culture, talent, and the workplace	Ability to create and maintain an efficient and desirable work environment and experience
Client and customer commitments	Ability to develop and execute products and services that meet client and customer needs
Peers and industry	Perceptions of the institution's peers and others in the industry

Other prescriptions or drivers also can be used to evaluate reputational risks. For example, the Harris Interactive Reputation Quotient Poll, which measures the reputations of the leading companies as perceived by the general public, employs a reputation quotient that groups attributes or key drivers into six dimensions of reputation: 1) products and services; 2) workplace environment; 3) financial performance; 4) vision of leadership; 5) social responsibility; and 6) emotional appeal.

Evaluating reputation risk requires breaking it into specific components that are manageable and measureable. At that point it is possible to begin evaluating the threat from a reputational crisis.

Metrics often used to quantitatively calibrate changes in the perceptions of stakeholders can include changes in share price, gains/losses in market share and deposits, customer surveys, customer complaints, employee focus groups, data analytics, shifts in media reporting, and changes in the number and frequency of regulatory concerns.

Economic capital required to support individual risks, such as reputational and strategic risks, can be calculated and the result aggregated across all risks, taking correlation effects into account.

Allocating capital for reputation risk is a challenge because it is tantamount to adopting a strategy that would allow an institution to tarnish its reputation. Nevertheless, some large, complex institutions use internal capital targets to account for difficult-to-quantify risks such as reputation risk, putting in place an incremental cushion above internal targets to allow for the risks, as well as the inherent uncertainty represented by any forward-looking capital planning process. In other cases, institutions assess and calculate the impact of reputation risk in terms of some combination of reduced revenues, added costs, or a management overlay on top of loss estimates.

For those institutions that do not incorporate the potential impact of these risks into their capital targets, a clear definition of reputation risks and other difficult-to-quantify risks are sometimes addressed by adding a cushion above the capital targets and providing robust explanatory support.

"Although monetizing reputational risk is imprecise, calculating a simple percent of capital or using only expert judgment to determine a cushion above a capital target, without providing a comprehensive analysis and support, is a lagging practice," noted Daniel J. Jackett, partner, PricewaterhouseCoopers.

Crisis Preparedness

Crisis preparedness is an essential component of an effective reputational risk management program.

It helps a business react quickly and effectively when faced with unplanned interruptions, as well as anticipate and mitigate a crisis's impacts on revenue, reputation, compliance, and expense management. An ongoing process, it includes the identification of natural and manmade events that have the potential to disrupt business activities; preparation for those events (and prevention of them, where possible); mitigation of their effects to achieve operational recovery; and post-execution analysis to promote greater resilience during future events.

The development of crisis preparedness plans can improve the ability to respond to a crisis, reduce damage to the institution's brand and reputation, and minimize regulatory sanctions, penalties, and fines.[109] A quality response to a crisis is vital to an ultimate recovery from it.

Consideration should be given to having a cross-functional incident response team and an incident response plan that engages IT, compliance, corporate communications, legal, and finance to anticipate scenarios. Preventative and responsive measures should be tailored to each scenario. Responsibilities for incident response should be defined and understood, and reporting requirements should be clear, including with respect to which incidents require immediate board notification. The plan should be tested and refreshed regularly.

Crisis preparedness helps the board and management stay ahead of growing threats that have the potential to undermine reputation. "Crisis preparedness begins with identifying and preparing for the risks and includes a broad portfolio of capabilities such as simulation, monitoring, risk identification, response, and communications. All of these capabilities need to be in place before an incident occurs that could affect reputation," observed Michael E. Flynn, partner, Gibson, Dunn & Crutcher.

Implications for Directors

Reputation risk management embodies a variety of stakeholders and many different behavioral and other intangible drivers. Board oversight on matters of strategy, policy, ex-

---

[109] "Intersecting Risk Management and Crisis Management," Protiviti, 2013.

ecution, and transparent reporting is essential to effective corporate governance, which is a powerful contributor to sustaining reputation. Pursuing, achieving, and maintaining a strong reputation requires the board's vigilance and management's persistent focus on embedding the right risk practices into the institution. Directors need to support management in establishing the institutional view that the protection of reputation is a corporate necessity.

"Management needs to be able to articulate to the board which issues and incidents could impair the reputation, and which events are unlikely to impact the opinions of clients and customers, the regulators, employees, and other stakeholders. While expert advice and judgment is inherently involved, directors need to follow their own compass in determining the likelihood of the possibilities," noted Ian D. Campbell, vice chairman, Abernathy MacGregor Group Inc.

It is critical for directors to ensure that management defines, establishes, and agrees on a set of both quantitative and qualitative metrics to assess how the institution is perceived. In addition to being reinforced by management's periodic reporting to the board, these metrics also should be incorporated into executive compensation plans to motivate the proper behaviors.

Assessment Criteria

The institution:
- Offers products that are of high quality.
- Offers products and services that are of good value for money.
- Stands behind its products and services.
- Meets the needs of clients and customers.

The institution:
- Is innovative.
- Is generally the first to go to market with new products and services.
- Adapts quickly to trends and changes.

The institution:
- Offers equal opportunities in the workplace.
- Rewards employees fairly.
- Demonstrates concern for the health and well-being of its employees.

The institution:
- Is fair in the way it does business.
- Behaves ethically.
- Is open and transparent in the way it does business.

The institution:
- Is environmentally responsible.
- Supports noble social causes.
- Has a positive influence on society.

The institution:
- Is well organized.
- Has a strong and appealing leader.
- Has excellent managers.
- Has a clear vision for its future.

The institution:
- Is profitable.
- Shows strong prospects for future growth.
- Shows better results than expected.

Source: "Defining and Managing Reputation Risk: A Framework for Risk Managers," Reputation Institute, 2015.

Boardroom culture can have an important impact on reputation. While the institution's reputation rests heavily on management and individual employees, who are part of day-to-day operations, directors can impact reputation in two important areas: promoting longer-term thinking and creating an open culture. Pressure to meet quarterly earnings targets, achieve budget goals, or meet scheduling deadlines can deflect attention from important issues such as quality of services and products, or lead to unacceptable risk taking, thereby placing the institution's reputation at much greater risk. Moreover, support for escalating less-than-positive information, including risk areas, should start in the boardroom. By setting an example, directors can help address the threat that if fear of penalties or even job loss discourages communication about risks, they may not be reported at all.[110]

Not infrequently, customer complaints are warning signs of a systemic problem or an operational risk in people, processes, or systems. If not properly and timely addressed, these signals can morph into litigation, civil money penalties, and regulatory actions that can damage an institution's creditability, profitability, and reputation. As a consequence, directors need to be alert to these warning signs and closely monitor the timeliness and effectiveness of management's follow-up processes to these complaints.

Strategy discussions between the board and management should establish a shared understanding of potential risks (including reputational risk), their likelihood, and damage potentials. Boards need to look for connectors between reputational risk management, the risk assessment, and an emphasis on crisis preparedness planning, including the following:

- *Understand that speed matters.* When events become public, stakeholders, including the media and investors, judge and draw conclusions earlier in the cycle and on the basis of fewer facts.
- *Designate spokespeople and keep communications training fresh.* While the CEO will usually speak on behalf of the institution, in some cases the nonexecutive chair or lead director may voice the board's support of decisions. That said, communications during a crisis should be delivered by as few spokespersons as possible, particularly during the early stages, when the board and management may still be determining facts and assessing potential losses.
- *Regularly test crisis preparedness plans.* The crisis response plans need to be tested regularly. Forecasting possible reactions from stakeholders can help refine the response plans. Also, directors can assist management in evaluating the role of social media in responding to a reputational issue.[111]

The board and management also need to establish the appropriate tone in building resilience to reputation risks. Directors must demonstrate visible leadership in a crisis and commit the institution to putting things right. "It is important for the board to understand that a mishandled response to a crisis can generate more reputation damage and spur greater financial consequences than the incident itself. This is especially true

---

[110] "Mitigating Board Information Risk," National Association of Corporate Directors, 2013.
[111] "Board Oversight of Reputation Risk," National Association of Corporate Directors, December 2014.

Seven Dimensions Driving Reputation	
Dimension	**Expectations**
(1) Products and services	Institution can deliver high-quality products and services at an acceptable value
(2) Innovation	Institution is innovative and brings new products to market
(3) Workplace	Institution treats its employees well
(4) Governance	Institution is open and honest in the way it does business
(5) Citizenship	Institution is a good corporate citizen and takes responsibility for its actions
(6) Leadership	Institution has a clear vision for the future as well as its industry
(7) Performance	Institution delivers strong financial results that will ensure that it is around for years to come

when the response appears to undermine the institution's core values," commented Dennis B. Parrott, partner, KPMG.

In addition to the risk mitigants and crisis preparedness, directors need to appreciate the many important benefits resulting from a strong reputation. For example, in July 2013 the *American Banker Magazine*, a leading industry publication, surveyed customers about which institution has the best reputation among the top 30 bank holding companies in the United States. Union Bank was selected as the leading institution,[112] a significant and noteworthy recognition. This served to elevate, in ways both noticeable and undefined, the institution, its directors, management, and the employees. Although the recognition represents only one data point, it enhanced the institution's acquisition of new clients and customers, the recruitment of talent, perceptions in the communities, and relations with the regulators. Some of these benefits were immediate and could be quantified, while others are expected to be realized over a longer horizon.

"This achievement resulted from a great deal of focused attention by our board and management on the fundamental importance of reputation and risk management and

---

[112] Fourth Annual American Banker Magazine/Reputation Institute of Bank Reputations Survey, *American Banker Magazine*, July 2013.

on an emphasis in doing the right thing, every day," commented Masashi Oka, president and CEO, Union Bank.

Good corporate behavior and sound practices are the best safeguards against reputational problems. Establishing a culture that is ethical and mindful of risk requires the committed leadership of directors and management, as well as processes and structures that allow less tangible values to flourish.

Ultimately, the directors and management own the responsibility to protect the institution's reputation. They need to be vigilant to ensure that those conducting risk assessments and monitoring the perceptions of stakeholders understand the environment, the business, and the temperatures of stakeholders.

Escalating Perils with Information Technology

"Our technological powers increase, but the side effects and potential hazards also escalate."

—ALVIN TOFFLER

I nformation technology[113] has a balance sheet that is perhaps one of the most important summaries and analyses of an institution. Are boards overseeing IT with the discipline they would apply to a financial balance sheet? Who are the sources of independent oversight and jurisdiction? Which metrics and ongoing monitoring are directors relying on? Board members today are dealing with unknowns they never have dealt with before, and many do not know whom to rely on for guidance.

Most directors recognize the asset side of the IT balance sheet—that is, the power of technology both strategically to transform the business and operationally to improve services and performance. "Even for businesses which are not viewed as technology companies, technology is the lifeblood of their abilities to connect with and serve customers, run complex analytics that provide unique insights, manage projects and people, meet regulatory requirements, and perform a host of other mission-critical functions. With very few exceptions, every business now has, or will have, IT as its foundation," said Bernard F. Mathaisel, the former CIO of the Walt Disney Company, Ford Motor Company, and Solectron Corporation.

On the liability side, the perils or the risks with information technology are escalating, both in terms of strategic or operational disruption. Strategic disruption can emanate from nontraditional entrants leveraging IT in new businesses (such as in lodging, ground transportation, retail, fintech, and social media) and thus have the advantages of process innovation through technology and lower costs. The long list of potential operational disruption includes 1) security issues like compromises of intellectual property, customer lists, privacy, and protected personal information, hostage-taking of critical operational systems, and the denial of service; and 2) systems or networks imploding or

---

[113] Technology usually refers to the infrastructure of big hardware, operating systems, application software, data, and networks. Information technology (IT) refers to the application of computers and the Internet to store, retrieve, transmit, and manipulate data or information. It is commonly used as a synonym for computers and computer networks, but it also encompasses other information distribution technologies such as hand-held devices, telephones, etc. The terms technology and IT are used interchangeably in this book.

Board Oversight of Information Technology Risks

Data security	Understand the level of security risk, the comprehensive security strategy, and the controls designed to mitigate the risk.
	Determine how management tests resistance to attacks.
	Ask management about the IT security resources and whether the security spend level is appropriate.
Mobile computing	Understand the role mobile is playing and evaluate the appropriateness of the strategy.
	Understand the policy for allowing employee use of personal mobile devices to access corporate data.
	Discuss how the mobile policy is communicated to employees and how they are trained in its implementation.
Data privacy	Understand how sensitive data is protected from the risk of theft.
	Understand the internal and external data privacy policies.
	Ask management about privacy policies related to any data exchanges with third parties.
Social media	Take interest in how the institution and its competitors use social media to engage customers, develop markets, and recruit talent.
	Understand whether the institution knows what is being said about it on social media platforms.
	Discuss how employees use social media at work and what safeguards exist to protect the brand.
Cloud services and software	Ask management about the pursuit of cloud strategies and cost/ benefit considerations.
	Discuss security and privacy risks associated with using the cloud, including backup and recovery.
	Inquire about existing regulations and the compliance risks of cloud computing.
Big data and other digital means	Ask how management is leveraging IT to enhance communications.
	Understand the use of big data and advanced analytics to give the institution a competitive edge.

Source: "Directors and IT: What Works Best," PricewaterhouseCoopers, 2012.

failing to work properly and efficiently. Moreover, the prodigious use of digital devices by employees poses hazards to both privacy and confidentiality.

A classic example of the implications of operational disruption is Knight Capital, which was engaged in market and electronic execution of financial products. On August 1, 2012, a technology error occurred while the firm was installing a new version of its trading system. The mistake resulted in major price moves in almost 150 stocks traded on the New York Stock Exchange. The glitch caused Knight Capital to buy and sell millions of shares of more than 100 stocks in less than 45 minutes. Selling and covering those positions cost Knight Capital over $450 million, which was four times its prior year's profits. The company's share price declined 73% in two days, and its IT issues invoked class action litigation, increased regulatory oversight, and prompted a substantial payment to the SEC to settle charges.[114]

Directors are as accountable for overseeing IT risk as they are for all other risks. However, many board members are inexperienced with technology, and even if they were to pose insightful questions, it is dubious whether they would fully digest a good answer from a bad one. While some management teams have kept pace with rapidly changing technologies, it is the exceptional board that has been able to provide the sufficient governance and leadership that is so desperately needed in this area.

According to an NACD survey on public company governance, information technology is the area boards are most concerned about in terms of both quality and quantity of information received from management.[115] A survey of public companies in all industries conducted by PricewaterhouseCoopers indicates that 65% of directors would like to devote more board time to IT risks, but their experience and competence in this area are said to be "weak." PwC's findings support that only 25% of directors think their institution's IT strategy and risk mitigation approach is supported by a sufficient understanding of technology in the boardroom. Less than a third of directors "very much" believe the institution's approach to managing IT provides them with adequate information to exercise the proper board oversight.[116]

Unlike other areas of managed risk, IT has no established or equivalent audit processes or disciplines. Even if the directors hire a third-party consultant to conduct an assessment, how will they ensure that the recommended and approved changes are put in place? And given the dynamics of IT, how are board "best practices" identified and kept relevant?

Profiling IT Risks

As a matter of good governance, directors are expected to oversee the threats imposed by information technology and to understand the risk mitigations. Cybersecurity attacks in the form of data theft, compromised accounts, destroyed files, and disabled or degraded systems continue to occupy significant boardroom attention and media exposure. However, cyber is not the only IT risk. "The threats associated with information technology

---

[114] "Technology: It's Not Just About Cyber," by Jane Chwick, *Directors & Boards,* Second Quarter 2015.

[115] "2015-2016 NACD Public Company Governance Survey," National Association of Corporate Directors, 2015.

[116] "Directors and IT: A User-friendly Board Guide for Effective Information Technology Oversight," PricewaterhouseCoopers, 2016.

are not restricted to cybersecurity. Major investments in systems and process upgrades, operating model transformations, and data management all have significant IT components that can imperil the business if something goes seriously wrong," said Chris Perretta, chief information officer, MUFG Union Bank.

Among the most prevalent and formidable IT risks are cybersecurity and incident response risks, competitive risks, portfolio risks, execution risks, third-party risks, data management risks, resiliency and continuity risks, compliance risks, and failures in risk management.

Cybersecurity and Incident Response Risks

Cybersecurity and data privacy are at the top of most board agendas. Some directors wish for a single means of addressing all cybersecurity threats, but the perpetrators are creative and there is no "silver bullet." Regardless of the nature and source of cyber attacks, directors and management should not expect that all cyber attacks can be eliminated. There is too much money and value in intellectual property and other sensitive information for the perpetrators to patently ignore. Nor is it practical to protect all assets equally. Some stratification of assets and risks, from the most to the least critical, is necessary, paired with the best mitigations against those risks.

The companion of prevention is incident response. In the event of a cybersecurity incident, the institution must have, and test, the ability to recover. Cyber incident response is activated when cybersecurity fails. The high probability, if not certainty, of a cyber incident dictates that management assure the board that it maintains solid, well-tested response plans ready to launch when an incident is detected. Responses should be proportionate to the incident and cover technical, forensic, communications, and compliance protocols. Priorities include securing the digital evidence, restoring operations, and notifying the board, management, affected stakeholders, and perhaps law enforcement and the regulatory authorities.[117]

An important component of incident response planning is how the institution intends to communicate in a crisis. Directors should inquire whether the communications plan embraces social media as a critical means of reacting when a negative event arises. This can ensure that the institution's version of the story is quickly and accurately disseminated.

The good news for directors is that the IT industry itself is improving prevention, detection, and response capabilities. There are now professional certifications for those who become experts in prevention and recovery, and these should be part of the requisite skill set of the institution. Boards should ensure the capabilities are up-to-date and be prepared to regularly invest. The costs of cybersecurity weakness in terms of recovery, litigation, and reputational damage can be far greater than the investments needed to minimize the likelihood and severity of an incident.

Competitive Risks

New business models are often enabled through the introduction of new technologies. Information technology can change the channel to the end-consumer and strengthen

---

[117] "Information Technology Risks in Financial Services," Deloitte, 2016.

customer relationships, dramatically alter the economics of a business, or eliminate altogether the need for the institution's products and services. "Innovative technology can be a real disrupter and/or pose significant risks. Technology advances are taking business models and industries that historically have not been viewed as dependent on technology to now being transformed by it," highlighted Kimberly Alexy, a board member of Microsemi Corporation, FireEye, Inc., Five9 Inc., and CalAmp Corp.

Board members estimate that almost one-third of their institution's revenues are threatened by digital disruption, according to research conducted by the Massachusetts Institute of Technology. Most boards report feeling unprepared for this challenge. Much of the governance focus on digital disruption has been on cybersecurity, data privacy, compliance, and spending on IT. Less than 40% of board members report discussing the impact of digitalization on their business models.[118]

Boards and management must balance the risk of adopting new technologies against that of ignoring them or waiting for things to settle. Technology solutions and digital transformation hold both immense promise and significant hazards. Financial technology, or fintech, a focus of much innovation in financial services, is an example of a consequential threat disrupting the status quo. Although some predict that digital disruption can help them create better, faster, and cheaper services that will make banks an even more essential component of everyday life, others believe that digital disruption has the potential to shrink the role and relevance of today's banks.[119]

Operating in a Digital World: What Is New?

- "Smart" devices and services can result in unintended consequences and a mass of data, increasing vulnerabilities for exploitation. Humans are often removed from decision-making processes.
- Social media and "bring your own device" are creating issues. Employees, customers, and citizens are "always on" and sharing information, not fully appreciating the implications for privacy and confidentiality.
- Institutions are putting more data in the cloud and with third parties. While attractive, this has a dangerous side, including loss of control, increased threats, and unexpected connectivity.
- Human behaviors are changing, in both positive and negative ways.
- Rafts of new legislation and regulations are forcing a change in processes. These changes are creating vulnerabilities, which further change the threat landscape (often widening it, not reducing it) and the attack surface of an institution.

(Note: The digital world generally refers to the Internet of Things, mobile, 3D printing, cloud, cyber, sensors, analytics, social, and artificial intelligence.)

Source: "Creating Trust in the Digital World," E&Y's Global Information Security Survey, Ernst & Young, 2015.

An illustration of assertively getting ahead to mitigate competitive risks is Toyota Motor North America, which took a leadership role in introducing digital innovation into the company's products and services. To instill a culture of innovation, beyond its longstand-

---

[118] "Becoming Better Prepared for Digital Disruption," by Peter Weill and Stephanie L. Woerner, *NACD Directorship,* March/April 2016.

[119] "The Future of Fintech and Banking: Digitally Disrupted or Reimagined," Accenture, 2015.

ing Kaizen practices management, Toyota first encouraged innovation within IT. As those efforts blossomed, IT was able to reach out to other parts of the company. Toyota wanted to be ready to seize the opportunities presented by technology disruptions such as autonomous driving, social analytics, and the Internet of Things, thereby addressing the risks imposed by fast-moving competitors.[120]

It is critical for directors to understand how management is dealing with competitive threats. Boards have a responsibility to assess the risk that the disruptive use of IT could alter the value proposition of core businesses and enhance the capabilities of competitors. In response, some institutions are establishing start-ups that are free from the normal protocols and free to invent new businesses. While the reaction to these challenges is unique to each institution, boards should ask management for a comprehensive, fact-driven evaluation of the risks across all product and business lines.

Portfolio Risks

Portfolio risk refers to the danger of overspending on basic operational expenses instead of making transformational investments, or investing in "moonbeam" projects that will be written off and distract from core operations. Since IT is so diffused, the portfolio can involve hundreds, if not thousands, of independent projects. Many of these investments are dedicated to business-as-usual operations, such as messaging, transactional, and financial systems. While these projects are important and necessary, they are unlikely to fundamentally alter the institution. IT and the business lines must agree on the appropriate portfolio of investments, how much to spend to maintain the status quo versus investing in new technology and capabilities, and on which specific technologies will be required. Overspending on maintenance can crowd out opportunities to adopt new technologies and develop new capabilities.

Barriers to Effective Challenge

What are the main obstacles challenging the information security operation's contribution to the institution?

Budget constraints	62%
Lack of skilled resources	57%
Lack of executive awareness or support	32%
Lack of quality tools for managing information security	28%
Management and governance issues	28%
Fragmentation of compliance/regulation	23%

Source: "Creating Trust in the Digital World," E&Y's Global Information Security Survey, Ernst & Young, 2015.

A related portfolio risk is the failure to integrate IT and business strategies. The IT strategy must support evolving business priorities and operating models, as well as enable agile responses to market developments. This requires a convergence of priorities.

---

[120] "Digital Innovation at Toyota Motor North America: Revamping the Role of IT," by Paul Betancourt, John G. Mooney, and Jeanne W. Ross, Center for Information Systems Research, Massachusetts Institute of Technology, October 6, 2015.

Many institutions struggle to phase out or decommission outmoded technologies, including data centers, platforms, and applications. Often, technology retained to support select geographies, specific products, or unique processes results in excess complexity and higher costs. When this occurs over thousands of applications, management can find itself impeded by its own technology.[121]

Given the significance, virtually all boards are involved in the review and approval of the information technology budget. It is important for directors to consider how management prioritizes the portfolio and allocates the IT budget to achieve efficient risks/returns. Directors with a high awareness of IT issues look for a structured and well-documented process for making budget decisions, monitoring performance, and reviewing the overall shape and size of the portfolio. Management should be able to clearly explain the trade-offs, which would demonstrate they are making thoughtful and measured decisions, optimizing capital and resources, and taming the risks with information technology.[122]

Execution Risks

Execution risk is the inability to deliver critical capabilities on time and within budget. Execution threats include programs misaligned with strategic objectives, program charters that fail to address the risks, lack of program governance, uneven execution, misallocation of resources, and the failure to communicate. Boards and management that have not experienced at least some of these deployment failures are rare. Sometimes, the technology does not work as planned or does not properly integrate, slows down business processes, or implodes completely. Major enterprise resource planning deployments are notorious for these shortcomings, sometimes resulting in cost overruns, litigation, regulatory scrutiny, and reputational damage. At any given time, institutions will have multiple IT programs in development across functions and geographic regions. Not infrequently, these same teams are involved in leading multiple programs, stretching resource capacity beyond acceptable limits.

The growing trend is for institutions to use third-party-provided cloud services, as an integral component of execution, to replace their proprietary data centers. No longer considered an emerging technology, cloud computing has entered the mainstream. The use of the cloud is both an asset and a liability. The asset side is consistent with the benefits of the shared economy—that is, the efficiency, reliability, and economics of renting computing services, rather than owning dedicated equipment, facilities, and associated services, all of which depreciate quickly and have high maintenance costs. However, there are risks associated with cloud computing. Some boards and management fear that communicating data over a public network increases vulnerability to cyber attacks. Others worry that cloud service providers offering the same infrastructure to multiple clients across varying locations will not be able to maintain segregated confidentiality. Still others express concern that transmitting data across borders will result in exposure to diverse legal and regulatory requirements in other jurisdictions.[123]

---

[121] "Information Technology Risks in Financial Services," 2016.

[122] "Taming Information Technology Risk: A New Framework for Boards of Directors," National Association of Corporate Directors, 2011.

[123] "Building Trust in the Cloud," Ernst & Young, 2014.

Risks with Cloud Computing

- *Disruptive force:* Facilitating innovation and the cost-savings aspects of cloud computing can themselves be viewed as risk events. By lowering the barriers of entry for new competitors, cloud computing could threaten or disrupt business models, rendering them obsolete.
- *Residing in the same risk ecosystem:* When an institution adopts third-party-managed cloud solutions, new relationships with the cloud service provider and other tenants of the cloud are created with respect to legal liability, the risk universe, incident escalation, incident response, and other areas.
- *Lack of transparency:* A cloud service provider may not always provide complete information about its processes, operations, controls, and methodologies.
- *Reliability and performance issues:* Systems failure is a risk event that can occur in any computing environment, but poses unique challenges with cloud computing.
- *Vendor lock-in and lack of application portability or interoperability:* Some cloud service providers offer application software development tools with their cloud solutions. When these tools are proprietary, they can create applications that work only within the cloud service provider's specific solution architecture. In addition, the more applications developed with these proprietary tools and the more data that's stored in a specific cloud solution, the more difficult it becomes to change providers.
- *Security and compliance concerns:* Depending on the processes cloud computing is supporting, security and retention issues can arise with respect to complying with regulations and laws, as well as the various data privacy and protection regulations enacted in different countries.
- *High-value cyber attacks:* Multiple institutions operating on a cloud service provider's infrastructure present a more attractive target than a single institution, increasing the likelihood of attacks.
- *Risk of data leakage:* A multi-tenant cloud environment in which user institutions and applications share resources presents a risk of data leakage that does not exist when dedicated servers and resources are used exclusively by one institution.
- *IT organizational changes:* If cloud computing is adopted to a significant degree, an institution needs fewer internal IT personnel in the areas of infrastructure management, technology deployment, application development, and maintenance. The morale and dedication of remaining IT staff members could be at risk as a result.
- *Cloud service provider viability:* Some cloud service providers are relatively young companies, or the cloud computing business line may be a new one for a well-established company. Hence, the projected longevity and sustainability of cloud service providers cannot be verified.

Source: "Enterprise Risk Management for Cloud Computing," Committee of Sponsoring Organizations of the Treadway Commission, June 2012.

Proficient operational processes are required to protect the integrity of the technology environment and ensure effective execution. IT should deliver services at levels agreed upon with the business, manage capacity, understand and manage its assets, comply with software license agreements, and manage incidents and problems. Nonstandard and complex architectures can hinder the ability to meet service performance objectives.[124]

---

[124] "Information Technology Risks in Financial Services," 2016.

A seemingly regular execution failure is the release of a change in the IT environment that renders a technology unusable. Changes to technology need to be tested, released appropriately, and handled with extreme care. Effective change management discipline, led by expert program managers, can help mitigate risks. Change management focuses on the people/process/technology compatibility and integration. The industry has black-belt certifications for change managers, and these talented people will earn their keep if left to do their jobs. Their skill is a combination of data and analytics, experience, and personal insights. Data-driven decision-making methods can supplement or replace the anecdote-driven approach that often prevails in project planning and likely result in fewer surprises.

Third-Party Risks

As arrangements proliferate with vendors, service providers, joint venture partners, and other third parties, so do the risks, particularly those related to data security and privacy. In fact, third parties' own technology risk can generate operational, financial, reputational, and other risks to the institutions that use their services. Directors need to know that these threats sometimes can be obscured by management's enthusiasm for the relationships, by standard forms of assurance provided by third parties, and by check-the-box due diligence processes.[125]

Management must develop and implement proper due diligence, contracting, and monitoring procedures for significant third parties engaged by IT. Due diligence should be performed on the third party's reputation, strategic alignment, financial viability, compliance, and other attributes. And when acquisitions, strategic alliances, or partnerships are considered, the board and management should understand the potential hazards of integrating the other institution's IT systems.[126] This often is a significant challenge and can be an integral component of deal negotiations.

Data Management Risks

Boards, management, and the regulators are all intensely focused on data management and the quality of data, given that risk and capital depend heavily on reliable and timely information. In addition, all institutions are increasingly combining external data with internal data, adding both new layers of complexity to data management and new threats. Ineffective data management can lead to financial irregularities, regulatory penalties, and the loss of stakeholders' trust.

Rigorous data management capabilities depend on governance and policies that support the accuracy of data and clarify data ownership and uses. Controlled creation, transformation, storage, and disposal of information are central to the concept of data integrity. When institutions retain unnecessary data, they face additional costs, complexity, and risks of a breach. Institutions should have policies and standards supporting the

---

[125] Ibid.
[126] "Directors and IT: A User-friendly Board Guide for Effective Information Technology Oversight," 2016.

sound disposal of data, as well as assurance that the policies are put into practice and being followed regularly and consistently.[127]

Big data and the use of advanced analytics is one of the fastest growing areas of information technology. Directors need to explore with management the particulars about what big data is being collected, how it is being processed, how it is analyzed, and how the risks metastasize when the data is used. Data science skills and tools are evolving, so many institutions are recruiting new talent to supplement current capabilities. This is an area where regulations are expected to increase, especially in regard to privacy and confidentiality, so boards need to be kept current on emerging developments and pronouncements.

Resiliency and Continuity Risks

With technology enabling virtually every activity, information technology must be resilient to disruptions and outages. Poor service levels and public security breaches of sensitive information can alienate customers, employees, regulators, and other stakeholders, as well as seriously damage an institution's reputation. An institution should have standards so that investments in resiliency capabilities go toward the technology that supports its most critical business assets and processes. Recovery testing, especially for critical technology, must be rigorous and validate that recovery plans will work.

Institutions need an end-to-end view of all technology required to support a particular product or process to ensure that all components can recover from a disruption. Sometimes, institutions perform one-off testing of a particular technology application, rather than comprehensively testing all technologies required to support an end-to-end process such as clearings or settlements. Directors should recognize that one-off testing rarely achieves objectives. Moreover, institutions relying on third-party providers for critical technology services must understand the third party's resiliency and continuity plans as if the technology were internally owned and operated.[128]

Compliance Risks

Today, there are a number of existing laws, both in the U.S. and internationally, related to e-commerce, data security, privacy, and data transfers to third parties. Regulations applicable to IT issues continue to evolve, so compliance risks can be expected to expand. Noncompliance with regulatory requirements, including e-discovery requirements, can have severe consequences, and in this domain IT is the essential means of ensuring compliance. Regulations can result in broad changes to operations, business processes, employee training programs, and IT systems. Directors must stay informed and ask management about existing compliance issues and potential regulations that might impact the institution and its industry. Corporate counsel often plays a key role in tracking and interpreting the risk implications on compliance.[129]

---

[127] "Information Technology Risks in Financial Services," 2016.
[128] Ibid.
[129] "Directors and IT: A User-friendly Board Guide for Effective Information Technology Oversight," 2016.

The OCC's Perspectives on Responsible Innovation

The Office of the Comptroller of the Currency observes that the financial services industry is undergoing rapid technological change aimed at meeting evolving consumer and business expectations and needs. The OCC notes that mobile payment services and mobile wallets are changing the way consumers make retail payments. New distributed ledger technology has the potential to transform how transactions are processed and settled. New technology services offer the prospect of a banking relationship that exists only on a smartphone, tablet, or personal computer. Marketplace lending has the potential to change how laws are underwritten and funded. In addition, automated systems are competing with traditional financial advisors.

The OCC emphasizes effective risk management and corporate governance. As learned in the financial crisis, not all innovation is positive. The OCC notes that the financial crisis was fueled in part by innovations such as option adjustable rate mortgages, structured investment vehicles, and a variety of complex securities that ultimately resulted in significant losses and threatened the entire financial system.

"At the OCC, we are making certain that institutions have a regulatory framework that is receptive to responsible innovation along with the supervision that supports it," said Thomas J. Curry, Comptroller of the Currency.

Source: "Supporting Responsible Innovation in the Federal Banking System: An OCC Perspective," Office of the Comptroller of the Currency, March 2016.

Failures in Risk Management

Establishing and building a risk management framework for information technology requires prioritization, investment, and agility in a rapidly changing technology environment. The failure to implement and maintain adequate IT risk processes, and dedicate skilled IT talent to risk management, can result in serious deficiencies in management and failures in the board's oversight.

The traits of ineffective IT risk management that need to be avoided can include a failure to understand the important role of IT within the institution and recognize associated threats, a noticeable lack of IT responsiveness to business priorities, a poor alignment of the IT strategy with business goals, an outdated technology infrastructure, a lack of visibility and transparency into IT's performance, and inadequate staffing of the IT risk function.

Financial institutions traditionally pursue "three lines of defense" to address risk. The first line of defense—product and process owners—identifies and manages risk. The second line—frequently executed by risk and compliance functions—provides a risk management structure and independent oversight of the first line. The third line—usually internal audit—provides independent assurance to the board and management on the effectiveness of the first two lines of defense.

Finding the right model to enable effective technology risk management presents oversight challenges. The risk function may have the risk management expertise, but lack the IT knowledge that would enable it to provide sound insights on the IT environment. Conversely, the IT function may have the knowledge of technology, but lack the independence needed to provide an unbiased view of risk.[130] Boards and management need to ensure that, in an extremely competitive environment for resources, there is a priority on recruiting, training, and retaining skilled IT risk talent in sufficient numbers to enable effective risk management.

Overseeing IT

Overseeing information technology is an integral component of the board's risk responsibilities. Boards are comprised of thoughtful, competent people who often can assess an institution's IT efficiency, effectiveness, and competitiveness without concerning themselves with the details of the technology. However, information technology is complicated. It is unrealistic to expect directors with backgrounds in other disciplines to be sufficiently proficient in IT to provide governance on their own as the technology advances.

"Directors need to be able to question management about the IT strategy, how that strategy is enabled, what opportunities have been identified, and what are the significant threats. Boards should ask about IT trends in the industry and what key competitors are doing or could do. Boardroom discussions also should focus on what innovations could change the industry and undermine business models," noted Frank E. Quinlan, a board member of the Irvine Company, Encore Capital Group, and Santa Fe Trust.

PricewaterhouseCoopers reports that 54% of the respondents to its survey indicate that the audit committee is primarily responsible for IT oversight, 27% report that it is a full board responsibility, and 10% note that it is the responsibility of either the risk committee or a separate IT committee. PwC finds that the audit committee is traditionally responsible for overseeing financial reporting, related controls, and the external audit, but it often oversees the risk management process and IT is usually discussed from a risk perspective. PwC's survey also suggests that the rather small percentage using a separate board-level risk committee to oversee IT is perhaps because only a small number actually have a separate risk committee,[131] except, of course, those regulated institutions such as large banks, which are required by regulation to put in place separate risk committees.

In order to enhance the board's perspective of the opportunities and risks, directors sometimes consider forming a board-level technology committee, or subcommittee, to facilitate their understanding and provide greater comfort in the boardroom. This committee should not be limited to risk but also oversee IT strategy, technology decisions, contracts, staffing, and budgets. This committee would interact with the IT and risk functions, management, and the board and often includes directors and members of management with expertise in information technology. Beyond the benefits of better oversight, the committee also sends a message to stakeholders that the board and management set a priority on IT and risk management.

If the board and management do not view a board-level IT committee or a subcommittee as feasible, they may consider establishing an IT advisory committee. The advisory committee could include members of management with IT expertise, and perhaps

---

[130] "Information Technology Risks in Financial Services," 2016.
[131] "Directors and IT: A User-friendly Board Guide for Effective Information Technology Oversight, 2016.

Information Technology Risk Management Framework

(1) Key Drivers and Objectives	Enabling business growth	Achieving innovation and agility	Promoting cost reduction	Supporting a customer and client focus	Solidifying effective risk and compliance management	
(2) Operating Model Components	Governance and oversight	Policies and standards	Management processes	Tools and technology	Risk metrics and reporting	Risk culture
	Organizational structure, committees, roles, and responsibilities to manage IT risk	*Management expectations for managing technology and IT risk*	*Processes to manage IT risk*	*Tools and technology to support risk management and the integration of risk with IT domains*	*Reports identifying risks and performance across IT domains*	*"Tone at the top"; clarity on risk appetite; training and awareness*
(3) IT Management Domains	IT strategy	Program management	Information/ cyber-security	Service delivery and operations	Vendor/ third-party management	
	Data management	Systems development	Service continuity management	Financial management	Talent management	

(Note: IT risks can emanate from any of the three layers within the framework.)

Source: "Information Technology Risks in Financial Services," Deloitte, 2016.

one or two external experts, to provide guidance to the board, the board's risk committee and/or audit committee, and management.

Some boards designate a specific director to take a greater role in the oversight of technology. The designated director meets regularly with IT management and can ask probing questions, solicit more detail, and gain a greater level of understanding that can be shared with the board.

Another way to broaden the board's expertise is to add a director with technology skills and experience. Many boards today are seeking new directors with "digital" experience— that is, candidates who are experienced in leading digital disruptions, possess knowledge about advances in technology, or are well versed in the area of big data and analytics. The new director could join the board when a vacancy arises, during the next director nomination process, or even when a new member is added to the current board.

Adhering to Best Practices

While there is no guaranteed path or template for preventing technology-related problems, the following 11 best practices can help directors enhance their oversight.

(1) Recognize the Importance

Recognizing the critical importance of IT and the perils in all facets of strategy and operations is an essential grounding for directors. The significance of IT and its oversight should be memorialized in board and committee charters. Overseeing and managing IT risks go far beyond ensuring proper cybersecurity controls. Board members need to grasp the technology-related opportunities, as well as the risks, that may exist within the industry and the institution. There can be great peril in standing still in a digitalized world.

The board should ensure that technology and IT risks are regular topics in board and committee agendas. In shaping the agendas, it is important for directors to define thresholds for risk incidents that are required to come to the boardroom, including IT investments, proposed third-party contracts with significant risks, and other events like cyber breaches, deployment failures, or other matters triggering regulatory notification.

(2) Use an Integrated Approach

IT risk is both an integral component of business execution and an area of specific risk that requires separate evaluation. Rather than deal with IT as an appendage of the board's agenda, the board oversight process should integrate IT risks into all strategy and risk discussions. For example, strategic and financial risks should include technological innovation, resource allocations, and project management risks. Meanwhile, operational and compliance risks should include the integrity and relevance of data, security and privacy, availability of IT resources, efficient allocation of costs to IT services, and infrastructure risks.[132]

(3) Remain Alert for Change

Directors need to recognize that, in today's environment, rapid and constant change is the norm. Accordingly, policies, processes, people, and technology must be adaptable. Critical resource decisions are involved in implementing infrastructure changes, which require broader assessments than those typically given by the IT function such as in-sourcing, outsourcing, and co-sourcing portions of infrastructure changes through the cloud.

The challenge for boards and management is to allow IT to adapt to the changing environment and keep pace with user expectations—but not to the point of permitting new systems and architectures to be replaced before realizing the full value expected from existing investments.[133]

---

[132] "Oversight of IT Risk Management," Protiviti, 2014.
[133] Ibid.

IT Oversight Guidelines for Directors

- Review and approve an IT strategic plan that aligns with the business strategy and includes an information security strategy to protect the institution from ongoing and emerging threats, including those related to cybersecurity.
- Promote effective IT governance.
- Oversee processes for approving the institution's third-party providers, including the third parties' financial condition, business resilience, and IT security posture.
- Oversee and receive updates on major IT projects, budgets, priorities, and overall performance. Approve critical projects and activities, such as expanding the institution's product lines, to include mobile services.
- Oversee the adequacy and allocation of IT resources for funding and personnel.
- Approve policies to escalate and report significant security incidents to the board, its committee, government agencies, and law enforcement, as appropriate.
- Hold management accountable for identifying, measuring, and mitigating IT risks
- Provide for independent, comprehensive, and effective audit coverage of IT controls.

Source: *FFIEC Information Technology Examination Handbook*, Federal Financial Institutions Examination Council, November 2015.

---

(4) Request Specific Information

Directors need to be specific about the information they would like to receive from management in order to oversee the IT and risk management process. Board members need insightful, fact-based reports from management. Although there is no standard level of detail, these reports should address a range of topics, such as the following:

- Data of key performance IT indicators and mitigating internal controls.
- Reports on cyber and IT security breaches, mitigations, and response plans.
- Project updates and budget reviews.
- Scope of internal audit plans and related audit findings.
- Assessment of disruptive technologies and competitive developments.
- Reports from external advisors and consultants.
- IT laws and developing regulations.
- Updates on IT governance matters.
- Reports on enterprise data management.
- Usage and strategies of cloud computing.
- Updates on the technology infrastructure.

(5) Engage the Chief Information Officer

Elevating the role of the CIO within the institution can enhance engagement and facilitate greater board awareness of technology's importance and threats. The CIO is in a unique position to help directors gain a deeper understanding of IT issues and concerns. By shaping the dialogue, acting as a technology advisor, and creating regular IT reports, the CIO can greatly assist directors in performing their oversight role. The board should ensure that the CIO has a prominent seat at the table both with management and in the boardroom and board committee meetings. [134]

(6) Use Internal Audit

An important expectation of internal audit is to be the eyes and ears of the audit committee and, more broadly, the board. Internal audit can be particularly helpful to directors by reporting on the IT landscape and evaluating IT risk management. Technology assessments by internal audit often include 1) evaluating the management of risks; 2) examining the level of compliance with internal policies and procedures as well as external technology regulatory requirements; and 3) benchmarking against leading IT risk management practices. [135]

Directors should ensure that internal audit has the talent and skill sets required to independently evaluate in some granularity the technology environment. A useful best practice is to rotate IT and internal audit talent between those two organizations. It can be a value-added experience for both, although guaranteeing a round-trip ticket may be important to those who are rotating. In addition, if technical skills are deficient, external third parties can be brought in to augment the capabilities of internal audit and conduct independent reviews of select technology areas.

(7) Request an 'IT Health Check'

The age, reliability, and efficiency of the current IT infrastructure are significant considerations in overseeing technology and the associated risks. Like other fixed assets, an institution's IT infrastructure needs regular and ongoing maintenance. Because of budget or other constraints, institutions may have deferred discretionary maintenance costs, creating backlogs. This deferred IT maintenance can include postponing system upgrades and new investments in more efficient technologies for the sake of saving current-period costs or meeting budgets. Backlogs can build up year after year, causing the IT infrastructure to fall behind the rest of the business, thereby heightening threat levels.

Deferred IT maintenance can lead to impaired systems and system failures, resulting in higher IT costs to catch up. The institution's current IT environment may also be operating at suboptimal levels that negatively impact the business if a patchwork approach to fixing problems has been pursued. The result often can be hardware and software platforms that do not work together seamlessly because they are bolted to one another, often to the point where a diagram of the IT environment can almost resemble a kaleidoscope. [136]

An understanding of the institution's IT health can help directors and management prioritize areas for special and ongoing attention, serve as a stimulant, rejuvenate IT systems, and identify and mitigate risks.

---

[134] "The Proactive CIO: Three Strategies for Engaging with the Board," by Sachpreet Chandhoke, Ralf Dreischmeier, Benjamin Rehberg, and Filippo L. Scognamiglio Pasini, The Boston Consulting Group, May 22, 2015.
[135] "Directors and IT: Effective IT Oversight and Role of Internal Audit," PricewaterhouseCoopers, 2016.
[136] "Directors and IT: A User-friendly Board Guide for Effective Information Technology Oversight," 2016.

(8) Assess the IT Budget

There seems to be an almost insatiable appetite for spending on information technology, often to the extent that budget requests far exceed normal parameters and accepted expectations. Directors often are challenged in assessing and approving the appropriate level of spending. McKinsey & Company's benchmarking study of 41 banks worldwide concludes that there is no magic formula when it comes to efficiently managing IT spending.[137]

Outsourcing of IT functions and procedures, while often necessary for critical specialty areas, is not necessarily a panacea for budget woes. Although some banks outsource IT services to limit infrastructure costs, McKinsey notes that, while outsourcing IT tasks and projects can help banks optimize their use of internal resources, it will not necessarily reduce costs in the long term.[138]

Directors need to know how much of the IT budget is dedicated to maintaining existing systems and how much is spent on supporting new projects committed to cost reductions or growing the business. In many cases, the cost of maintaining or supporting existing systems consumes a significant portion of the total budget, resulting in smaller allocations for investments in innovation and transformative initiatives.

Directors should ensure there is an accountable governance process for determining which projects are staffed and funded. Boards should ask management how projects are aligned to corporate strategies and what expected benefits are to be derived from the IT investments.[139]

Creating an IT Report for Directors

The chief information officer of a large global insurer took a savvy approach to preparing a report for the board—an approach that became the model for quarterly CIO updates. He created four simple dashboards, each devoted to a category of IT metrics:

1. Financials (to demonstrate the value and costs associated with IT).
2. Technology risks (to show the status of patching server software and the status of testing and validating business continuity plans, among other things).
3. Customer satisfaction.
4. Major IT projects.

The dashboards were supported by a 15-page memorandum. Although the dashboards gave directors a quick view of IT's performance, the memorandum provided more detail, discussing important trends that had surfaced since the previous report, comparing the institution with the competitors using industry benchmarks, and making projections for these metrics in the months or years ahead.

Source: "The Proactive CIO: Three Strategies for Engaging the Board," by Sashpreet Chandhoke, Ralf Dreischmeier, Benjamin Rehberg, and Filippo L. Scognamiglio Pasini, The Boston Consulting Group, May 22, 2015.

---

[137] "Capabilities, Not Costs, Should Inform Banks' IT-Outsourcing Strategies," by Mattias Horne, McKinsey & Company, June 2016.
[138] Ibid.
[139] "Why Your Board of Directors Can't Sleep on IT," by Larry Tiemon, *CFO*, November 14, 2011.

(9) Assess the IT Talent

A potentially significant element of portfolio and execution risk is the failure to properly staff IT functions and risk management. It is essential that the institution possess the IT capabilities needed to derive full value from technology investments and to oversee and mitigate the risks. A shortage of IT-literate talent can create bottlenecks. If there are significant gaps, a boardroom discussion should be initiated about the plans for upgrading capabilities.

Management should have programs in place to ensure that staff resources have the expertise necessary to perform their jobs and achieve the goals and objectives. Professional certifications are possible in IT security, program management, privacy, and other technical areas.

The board and management should consider appropriate retention and transition strategies for key IT managers and staff. Strategies can include the use of employment contracts, professional development plans, and contingency plans for interim staffing of key management positions. Management should have succession plans for key positions and should cross-train additional personnel. The objective is to provide for a smooth transition in the event of turnover in vital IT management or IT operations.

(10) Pursue Education

Oversight of IT risk typically requires specialized education for directors, particularly in areas such as cybersecurity and advances in new technologies. Some boards consider "technology boot camp" education sessions that are similar to the accounting or finance modules that boards conduct for audit committee members. Although these sessions will not convert directors into specialists, they can provide for enhanced IT oversight.[140]

Among the possible topics for director education in the boardroom are 1) an introduction to the IT organization; 2) IT governance; 3) project portfolio management; 4) state of the systems portfolio; 5) status of the technology infrastructure; 6) enterprise data management; 7) business process quality engineering; 8) cybersecurity; 9) data loss prevention / access control / and systems monitoring; 10) new financial technology trends and developments; and 11) staffing.

Additionally, the use of external experts can assist the board with an independent view of the IT risk landscape and provide insights into what other institutions are doing, how the institution compares, and where new capabilities or investments may be needed. Almost half of the boards responding to PwC's survey pursue outside advice on IT.[141]

(11) Remain Vigilant to Social Media

Directors need to follow social media closely for at least three reasons. First, it is an important way to advertise and promote products and services. Second, it is a valuable communications tool. And third, it is helpful in learning what is being said about the in-

---

[140] "Elevating Technology on the Boardroom Agenda," by Michael Bloch, Brad Brown, and Johnson Sikes, McKinsey & Company, 2012.
[141] "Directors and IT: A User-friendly Board Guide for Effective Information Technology Oversight," 2016.

stitution, its leadership, and its products and services. Although not specific to IT, there are inherent risks in all of these areas. Plans must be in place to identify and respond to threats to people, processes, facilities, and reputation. "Directors need to have an appreciation of the power of social media and the use of digital communications—what is being said and how, the safeguards around communications, and the monitoring—because there is so much potential risk," commented Bob Zukis, a senior fellow with the Conference Board Governance Center and the author of the book *Social, Inc.*

Board members should consider the broader role of digital communications, determine whether management is aware of what is being said on the Internet, and understand how employees may be using it in ways that impact the business. The inappropriate use of social media can indelibly affect the institution's brand and can impact its reputation in sudden and dramatic ways.

Guiding a Tiger by the Tail

The board's oversight of IT is an important responsibility and unique challenge. It can sometimes make directors feel particularly dismayed, like guiding a tiger by the tail. Getting comfortable with technology and IT risk can take time and effort for directors lacking IT experience. However, taking a thoughtful approach and having an inquiring intellect can help directors cut through the jargon and present a credible challenge to management.

The board's oversight of technology is intended to be a safety net for ensuring that a comprehensive IT program is being followed and that existing and emerging threats are sufficiently identified and properly addressed. "Given the dynamics of the environment and the rapid pace of technological advances, directors will want regular communications and updates from management on changes to plans impacting business strategies, information technology, and the IT risk mitigations," said Michelle C. Kerrick, a partner at Deloitte & Touche.

Directors need not be IT specialists to exercise good governance. But they do need to know how to assess the IT balance sheet, which areas to probe and challenge, how to surround themselves with the requisite talent, and when to seek advice.

Questions Directors Should Ask About Risks with Information Technology

- What is the IT strategy as it relates to supporting the business, products and services, customers, third parties, and other stakeholders?
- How does the business strategy reflect the full potential of technology and improve strategic and operational agility? How will information technology change the basis of competition?
- What is the IT risk identification process? What are the most significant IT risks and how are the levels of risk measured? Are the IT risks aligned with the risk appetite?
- Are the most critical IT risks being mitigated to acceptable levels? What controls are in place?
- How has IT been integrated into the risk management processes? How comprehensive and effective is the IT risk management program?
- Has the board evaluated the adequacy of current IT risk reporting and communicated to management what specific information the directors require?
- What is the budget for information technology? Is the budget aligned with the strategy?
- What are the greatest vulnerabilities for cyber attacks and the mitigations? What are the incident response plans?
- What are management's plans to use technology for crisis communications? What is the digital response strategy?
- What are the most crucial business processes, technology assets and applications, infrastructures, and third parties? What are the backup plans in the event of failures?
- How are IT compliance risks addressed?
- How are the IT risks and other risks related to using third parties being addressed?
- How effective are the data management standards and policies? How is data governance integrated with IT processes?
- How is management mitigating risks resulting from reliance on cloud service providers?
- What is the pattern of down times for critical technologies? Which technologies are most threatened? What upcoming process or application changes could result in an outage?
- Is the talent sufficient to both deliver the appropriate value from IT and properly manage the risks?
- How does the board remain current with its knowledge and understanding of technology and IT risks as they relate to the institution and the industry? How effective are boardroom discussions of IT?

Cybersecurity Represents an Existential Threat

"The single biggest existential threat that is out there, I think, is cyber."

— MICHAEL GLENN MULLEN, FORMER CHAIRMAN OF THE JOINT CHIEFS OF STAFF

Boards and management are fighting and some are losing the cyber war with yesterday's tools and approaches. The issue is that the prevalent information security model assumes a small, cohesive, and easily defensible repository of core data—when, in fact, institutions today have multiple data repositories, broad information and process flows, and a web of internal and external relationships that make the perimeter notion as senseless as trying to apply the medieval gated-city model to a modern nation-state. Mobile devices, social media, the Internet of Things, connected devices, and cloud computing are extensions of the institution beyond the walled fortress and are new areas of vulnerability.

Without cyber knowledge or resources, many directors and management are at a loss to combat highly skilled and aggressive cyber criminals, who are increasingly more sophisticated in their methods. "A defining characteristic of today's attacks is that the institutions' perimeter defense systems, such as firewalls and intrusion detection systems, are breachable. No one and nothing is safe," said Gary Loveland, principal, PricewaterhouseCoopers.

Boards rely on a variety of cyber risk monitoring and reporting mechanisms, including risk and control self-assessments, internal audits, and crisis management simulation exercises. Yet, there seems to be a lack of clarity in the boardroom on the role directors need to play to address cyber threats. Moreover, there is no agreed-upon approach for reporting on cyber risk management and the related controls.

Security incidents, which are any events that compromise the confidentiality, integrity, or availability of an information asset, often leave behind a broad spectrum of financial, operational, and reputational damage. Attacks routinely attempt to steal corporate data, including personal information, credit data, business plans, trade secrets, and intellectual property. As recently as a few years ago, cyber attacks were largely instigated by hackers and a few highly sophisticated and motivated individuals. Although troubling, many institutions chalked up these transactions as simply an incremental, albeit frustrating, cost of doing business.

Recent cyber attacks on Target Corporation, JPMorgan Chase, Citibank, and Sony Pictures have compromised trade secrets and millions of confidential customer records.

Today, data breaches, which are incidences that result in confirmed disclosures to an unauthorized third party or parties, result in high recovery costs, including regulatory intervention and legal costs, and a possible loss of business due to customer mistrust. Cyber issues can no longer be viewed merely as a cost of doing business. Instead, an information security mind-set must permeate the business and create a more robust security-enabled business. It represents the new normal.

Sources and Costs of Breaches

According to Verizon's report on data breach investigations, the motives for attacks are multiple and varied. Attackers may be looking to steal payment-card data or sensitive commercial information, or simply to disrupt the business. And the methods of attack are becoming increasingly sophisticated, often involving a combination of phishing, hacking, or malware. Moreover, attackers can break defenses with staggering speed. It can take only a few seconds.[142]

Financial institutions remain one of the largest targets for data breaches and cyber attacks. Almost 40% of data breaches affect financial institutions. This is largely due to the type of information maintained by the institutions and the sizable financial gains from intercepting this information successfully. These institutions also have additional access points for breaches that go beyond traditional computers and phones, such as debit and credit cards, ATM machines, online banking services, and mobile banking. Obtaining intellectual property, disrupting operations, and conducting other forms of espionage are also significant motives.[143]

Cyber criminals are not just targeting the large financial institutions. Increasingly, smaller institutions are being targeted because hackers seem to believe that they are easier to penetrate. Standard & Poor's views cybersecurity as a huge risk to financial services firms, noting that cyber attacks may not be discovered immediately, owing in part to the complexity of the business. It may take weeks or months before an intrusion is discovered.[144]

Cyber attacks often appear random, but they can be highly correlated as a result of contagion caused by global interconnectivity, which exists among banks, merchants, data owners (health care providers, telecom companies, etc.), and other sources (vendors, distributors, and suppliers). Disturbingly, data breaches have been going on long enough for cyber criminals to have collected substantial data on a large number of institutions and individuals. Hackers use these insights to establish clever methods for breaching data and disrupting business operations.

The Verizon report concludes that a common denominator across the major causations of cyber breaches, accounting for 90% of all incidents, is people. That is, major causes are people "goofing up, getting infected, behaving badly, or losing stuff."[145] In many cases, current and former employees are culprits or the sources of security inci-

---

[142] "Data Breach Investigations Report," Verizon, 2015.

[143] "Cybersecurity: Risk Assessment, Management, Response & Mitigation Strategies," by Edward J. DeMarco Jr. and Annmarie Giblin, The Risk Management Association, 2015.

[144] "U.S. Financial Services Credit Ratings Are Resilient to Cybersecurity – For Now," Standard & Poor's Ratings Services, June 9, 2015.

[145] "Data Breach Investigations Report," 2015.

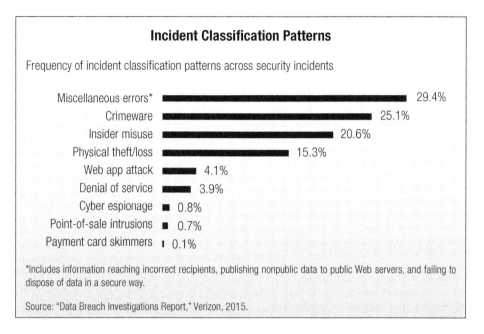

Incident Classification Patterns

Frequency of incident classification patterns across security incidents

Miscellaneous errors*	29.4%
Crimeware	25.1%
Insider misuse	20.6%
Physical theft/loss	15.3%
Web app attack	4.1%
Denial of service	3.9%
Cyber espionage	0.8%
Point-of-sale intrusions	0.7%
Payment card skimmers	0.1%

*Includes information reaching incorrect recipients, publishing nonpublic data to public Web servers, and failing to dispose of data in a secure way.

Source: "Data Breach Investigations Report," Verizon, 2015.

dents. Employees may unintentionally compromise data by losing mobile devices or by unknowingly responding to targeted schemes. It is estimated that over three-quarters of employees are unable to detect even the most common and frequent methods of attacks, such as phishing.

Employees are not the only source of inside threats. Third parties—including current and former service providers, consultants, and contractors who have trusted access to networks and data—are also potential culprits.

Although most boards and management are rightly concerned about the immediate, negative financial impact of cyber attacks, sometimes the longer-term implications are even more troubling. "The implications of attacks, in addition to the immediate potential for financial loss and system down-time, are the loss of customer confidence, harm to reputation, loss of proprietary information and intellectual property, impact on share price, possible regulatory actions, and likely litigation," said Stephen D. Alexander, partner, Morgan, Lewis & Bockius.

Legal Framework

There are no federal laws that deal specifically with cyber attacks or mandate the reporting of such attacks. The Gramm-Leach-Bliley Act generally requires financial institutions to ensure the security and confidentiality of customers' personal information. The Fair Credit Reporting Act requires federal banking agencies, the National Credit Union Association, and the Federal Trade Commission to prescribe regulations and guidelines for financial institutions and creditors regarding identify theft. Currently a number of states have laws requiring notification of security breaches involving personally identifiable information. These laws are varied and have different definitions of personal information, as well as different requirements for notification.

The Federal Trade Commission has brought numerous actions against institutions for failure to prevent unauthorized access to consumers' personal information, calling these failures "unfair or deceptive acts." Settlements involve consent decrees requiring improved information security programs and annual independent audits for as long as 20 years. Further, state laws addressing unfair and deceptive trade practices can lead to private rights of action. Institutions also need to be concerned with state and federal data breach notification laws and the risk of lawsuits for alleged failure to promptly notify affected persons of security breaches that involve exposure of personally identifiable information. In addition, depending on the facts of the situation, cybersecurity failure can give rise to negligence and breach-of-contract claims.[146]

Despite these enforcement efforts, successful prosecution of the perpetrators is virtually nonexistent. It is estimated that less than 1% of cyber criminals are successfully prosecuted.[147]

Board's Oversight Role

Cybersecurity has become a boardroom conversation on an unprecedented scale. Boards and management are challenged to balance the protection of assets and the mitigation of losses with maintaining profitability and growth in a competitive environment. Directors have an obligation to protect corporate assets, including confidential and proprietary information, reputation, and goodwill. This includes overseeing the systems that management has put in place to identify, manage, and mitigate risks.

Directors' confidence about their board's understanding of cyber risk remains low. A survey by the NYSE Governance Services, in partnership with a leading cybersecurity firm, finds that cybersecurity is regularly discussed at 81% of board meetings. However, the same survey reveals that only 34% of directors are confident about their ability to defend the institution against a cyber attack. The survey also indicates that directors view cybersecurity through a financial lens. Brand damage, breach cleanup costs, and the theft of intellectual property are the top concerns of board members.[148]

More troubling, the National Association of Corporate Directors finds that only 14% of respondents to their survey believe their boards truly understand the risks associated with cybersecurity, and 31% of responding directors are either "dissatisfied" or "very dissatisfied" with the quality of information they receive from management on this topic.[149]

The NACD notes that leading institutions are viewing cyber risks in the same way as other critical risks in terms of risk versus reward. That is, they are not considered in isolation. The NACD identifies the following areas to consider in order to enhance the board's oversight of cyber risks:

- Directors should approach cybersecurity as an enterprise-wide risk management issue, not just an IT issue.
- Directors should understand the legal implications of cyber risk as they apply in the institution's specific circumstances.

[146] "Board Oversight of Cybersecurity Risks," by Holly J. Gregory, *The Practical Law Journal*, March 2014.
[147] "Exploring Criminal Justice: The Essentials," by Robert M. Regoli, Jones & Bartlett Learning, 2011.
[148] "Cyber Security in the Boardroom," NYSE Governance Series, New York Stock Exchange, 2015.
[149] "NACD Public Company Governance Survey," National Association of Corporate Directors, 2015.

- The board should have adequate access to cybersecurity expertise, and discussions about cyber risk management should be given regular and adequate time on board and committee meeting agendas.
- Directors should set the expectation that management will establish an enterprise-wide cyber risk management framework with adequate staffing and budget.
- Discussions of cyber risks should include identification of which risks to avoid, which to accept, and which to mitigate or transfer through insurance, as well as specific plans associated with each approach.[150]

According to the Global State of Information Security Survey conducted by PricewaterhouseCoopers and the *CIO* and *CSO* publications, respondents declare cyber as the risk that is defining this generation. Many boards are addressing cybersecurity as a serious risk oversight issue that has strategic, cross-functional, legal, and financial implications. The survey suggests that boards are seeking more regular and comprehensive reporting and less fear-factor reports from management.[151]

Questions Directors Should Ask About Cybersecurity Risks

- Which data requires protection? What are the institution's most valuable assets? Where do these assets reside?
- Why is the institution a likely target for cyber attacks? What are the major points of vulnerability?
- Where are the leadership and the responsibilities for cybersecurity within the institution?
- How many cyber breaches or incidents have been experienced, in which categories, and of what magnitude? How did the institution respond to each incident?
- What are the characteristics and thresholds of cyber incidents requiring board notification? What are the protocols?
- What information is leaving the institution and how is it determined?
- What are the institution's capabilities to monitor and detect compromises of valuable assets? Which third-party services are being used to keep the institution current on the threat landscape?
- How long does it typically take to detect a cyber attack? Which containment procedures are in place? How frequent and how effective are incident response test runs?
- What is being done about internal threats to cybersecurity?
- Which resources are deployed and what is the budget for cybersecurity? How do the staffing and budget compare with those of peers?
- What are the plans to regularly update the board and its committees on cyber risk and the mitigations?
- What are the directors' experiences and capabilities for providing oversight of cybersecurity?

"Boards are very interested in information on cybersecurity. It is essential for directors to directly hear from management about the risks of cyber on a regular basis," noted Barbara T. Alexander, a board member of Allied World Assurance, Choice Hotels International, and Qualcomm, Inc.

---

[150] "Cyber Risk Oversight: Directors Handbook Series," National Association of Corporate Directors, June 2014.
[151] "Global State of Information Security Survey," PricewaterhouseCoopers and the *CIO* and *CSO* publications, 2015.

NIST's Framework

There are no compulsory data security frameworks, but rather a mix of data and privacy laws. Two notable voluntary frameworks have been promulgated to provide guidance: NIST's Cybersecurity Framework and the FFIEC's Cybersecurity Assessment Tool.

In February 2014, the U.S. Department of Commerce, through its National Institute of Standards and Technology,[152] issued a set of standards and best practices to help reduce cybersecurity risks. This framework is being used widely within financial services and other industries.

NIST's framework is intended to be used to create, assess, and improve a cybersecurity program and provide a common framework for discussing, communicating, and evaluating cybersecurity functions. NIST's framework sets out five core functions that relate largely to risk management and oversight:

1. *Identify cybersecurity risks and vulnerabilities.* The institutional understanding to manage cybersecurity risks to organizational systems, assets, data, and capability should be developed.
2. *Protect critical infrastructure assets.* The appropriate safeguards, prioritized through the risk management process, to ensure delivery of critical infrastructure services should be developed and implemented.
3. *Detect the occurrence of a cyber event.* The appropriate activities to identify the occurrence of a cybersecurity event should be developed and implemented.
4. *Respond to a detected event.* The appropriate activities, prioritized through the institution's risk management process to take action regarding a detected cybersecurity event, need to be developed and implemented.
5. *Recover from a cyber event.* The appropriate activities, prioritized through the risk management process to restore the capabilities or critical infrastructure services that were impaired through a cybersecurity event, should be developed and implemented.

NIST's framework also includes mechanisms that can be used to assess cybersecurity compliance by categorizing practices into tiers, ranging from partial compliance to adaptive compliance, and to help identify steps to achieve a target cybersecurity profile.

While adoption of the NIST framework is voluntary, it has become an important reference for the regulators, and the plaintiffs' bar, in assessing whether a cybersecurity program is designed to reduce and manage cybersecurity risks.

FFIEC's Assessment Tool

In June 2015, the Federal Financial Institutions Examination Council issued its Cybersecurity Assessment Tool, which is intended to help directors and management of financial institutions understand the expectations of regulators, increase the awareness of cybersecurity risks, and assess and mitigate the risks faced.

---

[152] NIST is a measurement standards laboratory that promotes innovation and industrial competitiveness by advancing measurement science, standards, and technology in ways that enhance economic security.

While use of the tool also is optional, the OCC intends for it to supplement its examination work in order to gain a more complete understanding of an institution's inherent risk, risk management practices, and controls related to cybersecurity. Institutions could also follow the NIST framework or their own internally developed framework.

The Assessment Tool, which is based in part on NIST's framework, was developed to measure the inherent risk profile and the maturity of cyber controls.

The measurement of inherent risk is designed to inform management as to the level of risk exposure or the likelihood of an attack. It incorporates the type, volume, and complexity of the institution's operations and corresponding threats. The cybersecurity maturity level is a measure of the institution's preparedness for a cyber risk event based on an assessment of controls to prevent, detect, and respond to attacks.

The Assessment Tool can assist in assessing cybersecurity during the making of key decisions. It bases risk assessments on factors such as customer base, geographic footprint of operations, types of products and services, delivery channels, and communications. The Assessment Tool is meant to help institutions not only assess their current practices and controls, but also consider new markets, products, and services.

The Assessment Tool is not designed to provide a comprehensive measurement of all risks, as cyberattacks are only one avenue of risk. The cybersecurity assessment, along with a thorough fraud risk assessment, is intended to be incorporated into the existing risk management program to ensure it is integrated throughout the governance processes, information security, business continuity, and third-party management.

According to the Assessment Tool, the role of the board, or a designated committee, includes the following:

- Engage management in establishing the institution's vision, risk appetite, and overall strategic direction.
- Approve plans to use the assessment.
- Review management's analysis of the assessment results, including the reviews or opinions expressed by independent risk management or internal audit functions regarding those results.
- Review management's determination of whether the institution's cybersecurity preparedness is aligned with its risks.
- Review and approve plans to address any risk management or control weaknesses.
- Review the results of management's ongoing monitoring of the institution's exposure to and preparedness for cyber threats.

The FFIEC recommends that, in order to be effective, the assessment should be completed periodically, given that an institution's inherent risk profile and corresponding maturity levels will change over time as threats, vulnerabilities, and operations evolve. The value derived is associated with the level of management's effort in completing the assessment and the intensity of the board's credible challenge.[153]

---

[153] "New Tool Assesses Banks' Cybersecurity Readiness," *The RMA Journal*, November 2015.

FFIEC's Assessment Tool

There are two parts to the Assessment Tool: an inherent risk profile and cybersecurity maturity.

1. The *inherent risk profile* identifies the amount of risk posed to a bank by the types, volume, and complexity of the bank's technologies and connections, delivery channels, products and services, organization characteristics, and external threats, notwithstanding the bank's risk-mitigating controls.

2. *Cybersecurity maturity* is evaluated in five domains: cyber risk management and oversight, threat intelligence and collaboration, cybersecurity controls, external dependency management, and cyber incident management and resilience. Each domain has five levels of maturity: baseline, evolving, intermediate, advanced, and innovative. A bank's appropriate cybersecurity maturity levels depend on its inherent risk profile.

Source: FFIEC's Cybersecurity Assessment Tool, June 2015

Many financial institutions develop their cybersecurity programs based on a blend of the NIST and FFIEC models. Some also deploy portions of the IT security framework developed by the International Organization for Standardization (ISO) which, for many years, was the de facto banking industry standard. An additional framework sometimes used is the Control Objectives for Information and Related Technology (COBIT), which was created by the Information Systems Audit and Control Association (ISACA) for IT governance and management.

While no tool or framework is prescribed specifically, it seems as if the OCC prefers the FFIEC's Assessment Tool while the Federal Reserve prefers the NIST's framework.

Business Continuity Planning

In February 2015, the FFIEC issued an IT examination handbook, *Business Continuity Planning* (BCP), which, among other objectives, is designed to provide guidance to financial institutions regarding the implementation of their business continuity planning process. The guidance indicates that the BCP establishes the basis for institutions to recover and resume business processes when operations have been disrupted unexpectedly. Because financial institutions play a crucial role in the economy, the objective is for disruptions in service to be minimized in order to maintain public trust and confidence in the financial system.

The guidance specifies that directors and management are responsible for overseeing the business continuity planning process, which includes:

- Establishing policies by determining how the institution will manage and control identified risks.
- Allocating knowledgeable personnel and sufficient resources to properly implement the BCP.
- Ensuring that the BCP is independently reviewed and approved at least annually.
- Ensuring employees are trained and aware of their roles in the implementation of the BCP.

- Ensuring the BCP is regularly tested on an enterprise-wide basis.
- Reviewing the BCP testing program and test results on a regular basis.
- Ensuring the BCP is continually updated to reflect the current operating environment.

The guidance notes that directors and management need to incorporate BCP considerations into the overall design of the enterprise-wide business model to mitigate the risk of service disruptions.

Implications for Directors

Cyber Is Not Just an IT Issue

Directors need to understand and approach cybersecurity as a risk management issue, not just an IT issue. Compromises can develop through printed documents, overheard speech, lost or stolen devices, or other means. Cyber risks should be evaluated in the same way as the physical security of human and physical assets are assessed and the risks associated with them are monitored.

Importantly, the board should ensure that management is assessing cybersecurity not only as it relates to the institution's IT systems, but also with regard to the larger ecosystem. Securing systems associated with partners, customers, third parties, and affiliates is essential. Directors need to understand the varying levels of risks in the ecosystem and assess them in the context of the IT, cyber risk, and overall risk tolerance.

Board Processes, Composition, and Structure

The board's oversight and evaluation of both external and internal risks are critical in maintaining vigilance against cyber threats. Directors should understand what critical information needs to be secured, such as customer information, business data, employee personal and health information, and trade secrets. In addition, directors should challenge the need to store this information and understand the compliance requirements of data-storage laws in each state.[154]

The board or its delegated committee needs to oversee the policies, controls, and procedures that have been put in place to identify, manage, and mitigate the cyber risks, as well as respond to attacks. Directors should expect management to describe efforts to educate employees on cyber risks, ensure compliance with the program, and commit the required resources. If the institution is a public filer, the board and its audit committee also need to provide oversight of related disclosures, including disclosure controls and procedures.

Directors need adequate time allotted on board agendas to understand and provide the proper oversight of risks associated with the protection of confidential information and intellectual property. By allocating time to these issues, the board inherently elevates the importance of cybersecurity.

---

[154] "Cybersecurity: Risk Assessment, Management, Response & Mitigation Strategies," 2015.

Directors should receive regular reports on cyber risks, incidents, and activities so that they understand where the institution stands in relation to industry practices, as well as whether industry standards are sufficient. The board should ensure it is adequately informed about management's efforts to monitor and mitigate associated risks. This includes giving consideration to related information and reporting systems designed to keep the board informed.

In reviewing reports from management, directors should be mindful that there might be an inherent bias on the part of management to downplay the true state of the risk environment. One study found that 60% of IT departments do not report cybersecurity risks until they are urgent and more difficult to mitigate, and they acknowledged that they try to filter out negative results.[155]

Global State of Information Security Survey

Positive responses	
65%	Formally collaborate and share with others intelligence on cyber
59%	Leverage Big Data analytics for security
59%	Have purchased cybersecurity insurance
56%	Increase in intellectual property theft
45%	Board participates in the overall security strategy
38%	Increase in detected information security incidents
24%	Increase in security spending
22%	Increase in incidents attributed to third parties

Source: "Global State of Information Security Survey," PricewaterhouseCooper and the *CIO* and *CSO* publications, 2015.

The technical nature of cybersecurity issues often raises the anxiety levels of directors about whether the board has an appropriate understanding and is providing sufficient oversight. A detailed technological understanding is not required, but directors should possess more than a basic understanding and have access to technology expertise.

According to an Accenture survey, only 6% of board members and 3% of CEOs at the world's largest banks have professional technology experience.[156] The board should consider whether it needs one or more directors with a sophisticated understanding of technology. Not all boards will require a director with deep expertise, but as institutions become ever more dependent on technologies and the risks of cybersecurity breaches grow, many boards could benefit from having at least one director who is sufficiently

---

[155] "Cyber Security: 60% of Techies Don't Tell Bosses About Breaches Unless It's Serious," *International Business Times,* April 16, 2014.
[156] "Bridging the Technology Gap in Financial Services Boardrooms," Accenture, 2016.

fluent or committed to becoming knowledgeable in these areas. Similarly, the complexity and importance of cybersecurity issues should be considered in relation to the board's work through its committee structure.

While including cybersecurity as a stand-alone item on board and/or committee meeting agendas is certainly a recommended practice, cyber should also be integrated into boardroom discussions involving new business plans and product offerings, mergers and acquisitions, new market entry, deployment of new technologies, and major capital investment decisions such as facility expansions or IT system upgrades.

Board and committee minutes should reflect that cybersecurity is included on the agenda at meetings of the full board and/or board committees, depending on the allocation of oversight responsibilities. The regulators expect these discussions to be robust and well documented. The discussions should include updates about specific risks, as well as reports about the institution's overall cybersecurity program and the integration of technology with corporate strategy, policies, and business activities.

Program Development and Staffing

Management should ensure the proper attention, resources, and leadership are dedicated to the cybersecurity program and take the lead in developing it, formulating the requisite policies and procedures, and establishing mitigations. It should tailor internal controls, compliance, and employee education initiatives to respond to its assessment of the cyber threats.

The board or its delegated committee should review the cybersecurity program for completeness, including the leadership structure and staffing. It is the board's responsibility to challenge management to ensure the proper caliber and number of dedicated resources. The appropriate staffing of the cyber program is essential, as competitive pressures to deploy increasingly cost-effective technologies can often negatively impact the allocation of sufficient human resources.

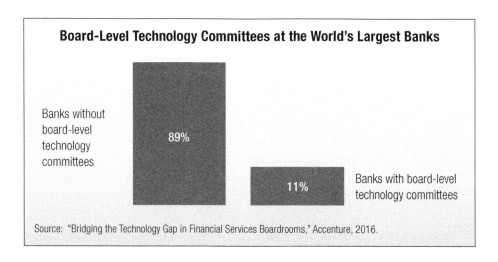

Board-Level Technology Committees at the World's Largest Banks

Banks without board-level technology committees   89%

11%   Banks with board-level technology committees

Source: "Bridging the Technology Gap in Financial Services Boardrooms," Accenture, 2016.

Budget

Directors normally are expected to approve the budget for IT, including cybersecurity. The magnitudes of amounts involved are significant and increasing, including the costs associated with people, technologies, and the use of third-party services that can provide security assessments or ongoing threat management. The budget approval process is an important opportunity for the directors to gain a full understanding of the institution's commitment to cybersecurity. It is critical to develop and adopt an enterprise-wide cyber budget aligned with the cyber program. Cybersecurity is more than IT security; thus the budget should not be tied exclusively to the IT department.

The benchmarking of the annual budget against peers, whenever possible, can be useful in calibrating the breadth and depth of the program. Benchmarking also gives the directors confidence that the budget requests are responsive to the needs of the business and the environment and that the level of budget appropriations is within reasonable parameters.

Use of Metrics

Directors often are challenged to provide a heightened level of accountability around performance measurements related to cybersecurity. Nevertheless, a focus on metrics will help the board determine whether management is appropriately adapting to potential cyber threats and responding to them properly and promptly.

Metrics associated with cyber should focus not only on the total number of breaches but also on the success of the institution's response to each breach. Among the metrics for directors to monitor are the following:

- How many breaches were inflicted?
- How deeply did hackers penetrate the system? How were businesses, products, and services impacted?
- How quickly did management address or react to the breach?
- What were the results of penetration-testing on third parties?[157]

Access to Expertise

Directors are entitled to rely on management's expertise as well as the advice of outside experts. Directors can bring knowledgeable perspectives into the boardroom by scheduling briefings from third-party experts and independent advisors, such as external auditors and outside counsel, who have multi-client and industry-wide perspectives on cyber trends. Hiring external experts to review the cybersecurity strategies and benchmarking these strategies against peers also can be very helpful. Additionally, participating in relevant director education programs focusing on cyber, whether provided in-house or externally, can be particularly useful for directors.

---

[157] "Taking Charge: How Boards Can Activate, Adapt and Anticipate to Get Ahead of Cybersecurity Risks," Ernst & Young, 2015.

Collaboration

The seriousness of cyber crime has led to greater collaboration between private businesses and public institutions, including the FBI, SEC, and the U.S. Department of Homeland Security.

Directors should encourage the fostering of relationships with government agencies, including the local FBI cyber task force, to keep informed of new and emerging trends in attack types and in the methods, tools, and techniques to deal with them beforehand. Government agencies engage in constant surveillance and are often the first to uncover and bring attention to cyber threats.

Cyber Insurance

Verizon estimates that the average loss caused by a breach is between $0.21 and $0.52 per record. Therefore, a breach affecting 10 million records costs between $2.1 million and $5.2 million.[158] In many cases, these estimates may undervalue the true cost.

Directors need to discuss with management whether cybersecurity insurance is required and, if so, whether the amount of insurance is adequate relative to the approximate costs that would result from a data breach. Commercial insurance policies typically do not cover damage associated with data theft, destruction, compromised data, or other harms resulting from cybersecurity breaches.

Cyber insurance is designed to mitigate losses from a variety of incidents, including data breaches, network damage, and cyber extortion. The following are examples:

- Event management, including notification costs, public relations expenses, and electronic data loss.
- Business interruption, including lost revenues due to network disruption.
- Cyber extortion, including the costs of investigation and reimbursement of monies paid to obtain assurance that operations will not be interrupted.
- Network security and privacy, including the costs associated with defense of claims and payment of settlement and damages.

Although it is often said that what cannot be protected can be insured, this is not necessarily the case with cyber insurance. "It is unlikely that any company can currently insure against the full risk of loss resulting from cyber incidents. While the market is rapidly evolving, it has not yet reached a point where a carrier can provide 100% comprehensive coverage for all losses associated with cyber incidents. It is a dynamic, developing market for insurers," says Priya Cherian Huskins, senior vice president, Woodruff-Sawyer & Co.

In addition to providing economic protection should a breach occur, the documentation and the audits that insurers require can provide an extra incentive or motivation to put in place appropriate prevention measures as well as loss detection and reporting systems.

---

[158] "Data Breach Investigations Report," 2015.

Crisis Preparedness

Crisis preparedness can be challenging, requiring careful consideration and planning by the board and management. Given their perceptions and interests, the many stakeholders—including customers and clients, investors, the regulators, employees, and vendors—may view a small breach through the same lens as a large and dangerous breach. As a result, the damage to corporate reputation and share price may not correspond directly to the size or severity of the event.

The board should review management's plans to address a cybersecurity breach to ensure that the institution is well prepared to respond when a problem arises. The security policy should require the prompt and timely reporting of actual and suspected breaches and significant cybersecurity incidents. There should be a hierarchy protocol for internal notifications, including communications to the board.

Management will find it virtually impossible to prevent a cyber attack, so the best alternative is to be prepared with a well-integrated, enterprise-wide plan for managing cybersecurity. The board can help move to a state of readiness against cyber threats by fostering an environment in which cyber threats are expected and proactively addressed though a focus on the future environment. Directors need to direct management in planning for the consequences of a cyber breach and confirm that management has not only adopted an enterprise-wide plan, but is also working to perfect the details of the incident response plan. This enables preventive action and response mechanisms to operate smoothly and quickly. Boards should encourage management to rehearse all incident response capabilities to gain confidence in the institution's ability to respond effectively to cyber-related threats.

Cybersecurity Leadership

Cybersecurity risks represent an existential threat. The enormity of the threat is due to its complexity and speed of evolution, the potential for significant damage, and the reality that total protection is unattainable. It is likely that the board will be challenged by regulators, or class action lawsuits, for not providing proper governance, oversight, and direction on security.

Directors should actively engage in discussions around the cybersecurity program, assessing whether it protects the most valuable assets and ensuring cybersecurity is getting the appropriate level of attention, leadership, resources, and budget. The environment is dynamic, so directors will need to accept and cope with a never-ending cycle of reevaluating the risks and improvements in the program.

"Directors must set the tone for confronting the cyber challenge. Most boards and management understand that cybersecurity is not a problem to solve but a business risk that must be managed," commented Susan G. Swenson, a board member of Wells Fargo & Company, Harmonic Inc., and Spirent Communications PLC.

Digesting the Budget with an Insatiable Appetite

"Budgets are not merely affairs of arithmetic, but in a thousand ways go to the root of prosperity of individuals, the relation of classes, and the strength of kingdoms."
—WILLIAM E. GLADSTONE

O verseeing the budget for information technology often lacks the understanding and the proper challenge from directors because the budget process can be poorly designed, take too much time, or deliver too little value. Directors need to be alert and cognizant that there are significant vulnerabilities and potential risks associated with the IT budget. In fact, there seems to be an almost insatiable appetite for spending on IT.

Institutions continue to invest in technology as the most direct path to meaningful innovation and operational efficiency. Boards and management pursue what is needed to establish a flexible and secure foundation for delivering services and experiences that will set them apart. They recognize that to move to the forefront of data-driven business-es, the less-glamorous aspects, such as infrastructure, integration, and authentication, also must be addressed.[159]

IT strategy and spending are garnering much more board-level attention. Few industries rely more on technology, or are potentially more threatened by it, than financial services, and this is reflected in board engagement. PricewaterhouseCoopers notes that directors in financial services are providing more oversight in IT budget-setting and major project implementations, and are increasing their oversight of strategies involving new technologies and channels, such as social media. Almost 70% of directors in financial services report being engaged in the oversight of the IT budget process.[160]

Nevertheless, only one-third of respondents to a Deloitte mid-market survey said that they have "mature" systems governing IT processes. At least for this level in the market, IT governance represents a serious gap.[161]

Digesting the IT budget is a critical component of a director's oversight responsibilities. Directors are responsible for overseeing IT and need to provide a challenge to management. The opportunities and threats imposed by the information age cannot be underestimated, and the associated costs are most often among the largest budget ap-

[159] "PwC's U.S. CEO Survey 2016: How Our Businesses Will Drive Growth," PricewaterhouseCoopers, 2016.
[160] "Across the Boards: Views from the Financial Services Boardroom," PricewaterhouseCoopers, May, 2016.
[161] "Technology in the Mid-Market: Perspectives and Priorities," Deloitte, 2014.

portionments. Board members who do not take the time and energy to understand the budget, ensure alignment of the budget with business priorities, and approve the allocation of IT investments between existing needs and longer-term strategies may be derelict in fulfilling their responsibilities. Moreover, the vulnerabilities of either overspending or underspending on IT can have significant immediate and long-term financial, operating, and strategic implications for the institution and its sustainability.

"Oversight in the boardroom is a significant factor in ensuring that an institution's technology spend is focused on strategic needs and aimed at improving financial and operating performance, and in responding to competitive pressures. There are serious implications and risks to the business in either over or under-spending on IT or investing in the wrong things," commented Kenny M. Smith, partner, Deloitte & Touche.

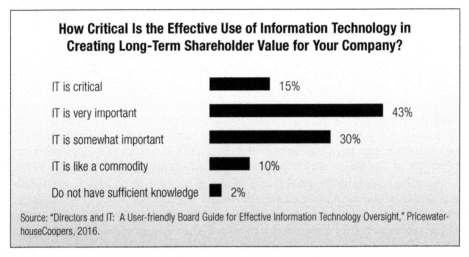

How Critical Is the Effective Use of Information Technology in Creating Long-Term Shareholder Value for Your Company?

IT is critical — 15%

IT is very important — 43%

IT is somewhat important — 30%

IT is like a commodity — 10%

Do not have sufficient knowledge — 2%

Source: "Directors and IT: A User-friendly Board Guide for Effective Information Technology Oversight," PricewaterhouseCoopers, 2016.

Alignment with Strategy

The critical role of technology in the direction and execution of strategy mandates that IT investments and the business strategy are aligned. As the major pillars of the overall business strategy are outlined and debated, directors should inquire about the dependencies on IT and the budget implications. The development of the budget is an opportunity to link IT capabilities with business performance and value.

IT oversight includes asking relevant and probing questions about the budget, which is meant to be both a financial tool for controlling how money will be spent and a management tool for helping directors and management understand how IT expenses contribute to the value of the business.

While the institution's business strategy drives the IT budget, the IT strategy sets the overall direction and provides common goals across business units and departments. Without a cohesive IT strategy, the criteria for enterprise-wide collaboration will be lacking. Moreover, driving the budget from the institution's business strategy can afford the opportunity to change the focus from IT as a cost center to IT as an important resource to help achieve strategic goals.

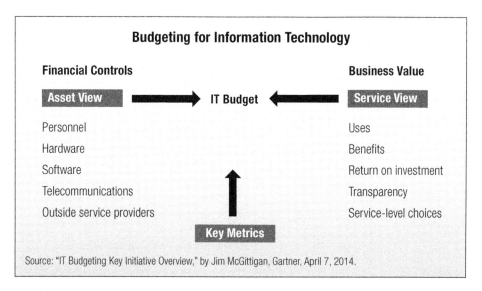

Budgeting for Information Technology

Source: "IT Budgeting Key Initiative Overview," by Jim McGittigan, Gartner, April 7, 2014.

Although the customer experience may drive competition, information technology is applied across a range of internal processes including back-end efficiencies, risk management, the use of data, and compliance. This contributes to the need for directors to take a wide view of the budget in order to understand where investments are made and ensure they contribute to the broader strategic objectives. Among the areas where technology is transforming the operations of banks, for example, are big data and advanced analytics, robotics and artificial intelligence, cloud storage, regulatory requirements, and blockchain.[162] "As technology becomes ever more central to strategic considerations, directors need to adopt a holistic approach to IT budgets and capital expenditures. The board's role in the IT budget process is critical," said Bruce G. Willison, a board member of Grandpoint Bank and SunAmerica Annuity Funds.

Some boards have introduced a "State of the Union" report on the institution's wide-ranging IT capabilities and infrastructure and how they support corporate strategy and the operations. Often done in conjunction with the annual review of the IT budget, this is essentially a review of the entire IT portfolio's alignment with corporate and business unit strategy, focusing on major IT systems and components. The review includes core business systems, as well as the IT operating model and resource strategy. The "State of the Union" review also embodies ongoing issues and projects, such as cybersecurity and major transformational efforts, which often have substantial IT components.[163]

A growing aspect of strategy and IT budget discussions in the boardroom focuses on spending to develop new technologies and align with new partners. Some banks, as an example, are strategically placing bets by investing in companies where there may be opportunities to improve their own technology, create a solution to a problem, or

---

[162] "Accelerating the Technological Transformation of Banking," Bank Governance Leadership Network, Ernst & Young, June 2016.

[163] "Elevating Technology on the Boardroom Agenda," by Michael Bloch, Brad Brown, and Johnson Sikes, McKinsey & Company, October 2012.

avoid disruption. In this space, banks have established initiatives or accelerators, and apportioned the necessary budget, to invest in and partner with fintech companies.[164]

Evaluation Criteria for IT Spend

Areas of Focus	Evaluation criteria	Description
Value	Business value	The expanded business benefits of the investment usually expressed by business value metrics, such as time to market, customer satisfaction, or product quality.
	Financial return	The expected return from the investment, usually a calculation based on the degree to which the planned benefits exceed the estimated investment cost.
Alignment	Strategic fit	Degree to which the investment supports the institution's strategic business objectives.
	Technical fit	Degree to which the investment fits with the institution's technical requirements.
Risk	Implementation risk	The risk of the implementation being more expensive, taking longer than planned, or not completing.
	Operational risk	The risk of not getting the planned benefits from the investment.
Other	Investment themes • Predetermined allocation of funds (for example, target portfolio mix) • Implementation schedule • Cash flow requirements	

Source: "Align IT Budgeting with the Enterprise Strategic Planning Process to Drive More Value," by Jim McGittigan and Barbara Gomolski, Gartner, March 9, 2016.

Budget Process

Institutions of all shapes and sizes struggle with budgeting information technology costs. Perhaps this is because IT management often does not understand the budgeting process and/or the financial management does not understand IT.

In many ways, the board's approach to IT spending needs to follow the budget process as in other areas. All institutions attempt to optimize IT spending, but those that do it best focus on cost optimization as an ongoing discipline rather than a one-off exercise.

The IT budget process represents an opportunity for directors to not only digest the amount spent on technology, but also assess management's prioritization of IT projects and the appropriation of available funds. In order to provide the proper oversight, directors need to (1) understand how the budget is developed and supported; (2)

---

[164] "Accelerating the Technological Transformation of Banking," June 2016.

calibrate the appropriateness of the spending levels and expected benefits; (3) ensure that the IT budget is aligned with the institution's business strategy and priorities and the IT strategy; and (4) determine how investments are allocated to short-term needs and longer-term transformation projects.

Directors should ensure there is an accountable governance process for determining which projects are staffed and funded. Boards should ask management how projects are aligned to corporate strategies and about the expected benefits from IT investments.

Sometimes, the IT budget is prepared in isolation, without a clear understanding of the institution's strategies and objectives. In these cases, IT budgets often focus on individual general ledger line items, rather than on ensuring that the right investments are made to support institutional goals and objectives. The IT budget not infrequently is viewed as "fixed" and lacking flexibility to fund the right things required to enable both short- and long-term success. Additionally, investment decisions are too often driven by whether the spend is classified as an operating expenditure or a capital expenditure, which speaks to accounting treatment rather than strategic priorities.[165]

Some institutions apportion the IT budget according to four categories of investment: infrastructure, transactional, informational, and strategic. Each type of investment represents a different asset class with its own unique risk-return profile. The portfolio categories underscore the importance of how management intends to use technology instead of focusing on the technology itself. Making sensible allocations requires management to be definitive about what they wish to achieve and about who will be held accountable—hardly the stuff of technical specifications.[166]

Other institutions define IT investments in a way that reflects their value to the business. Instead of type-oriented categories, they allocate their investments by the benefit horizon and strategic nature, with an emphasis on top-line business growth. In doing so, IT investments can be cast as run-the-business, grow-the-business, and transform-the-business.[167]

Additionally, some institutions specifically identify "end of service" investments, wherein a vendor of systems or software will no longer provide maintenance, troubleshooting, or other support. Such software, which is abandoned service-wise by the original developers, is also called abandonware. Sometimes, software vendors hand over software on end-of-life, end-of sale, or end-of service to the user community, to allow them to provide service and further upgrade themselves.

Whatever the method of stratification, the critical point is that the budget breakdown furnished to the directors should permit visibility into the major components of spending. Although detailed explanations and justifications need to be provided for support of large IT projects, this documentation should be given to directors normally only on an exception basis.

---

[165] "Align IT Budgeting with the Enterprise Strategic Planning Process to Drive More Value," by Jim McGittigan and Barbara Gomolski, Gartner, March 9, 2016.

[166] "Generating Premium Returns on Your IT Investments," by Peter Weill and Sinan Aral, *MIT Sloan Management Review*, Winter 2006.

[167] "IT Key Metrics Data 2015: Executive Summary," by Linda Hall, Shreya Futela and Disha Gupta, Gartner, December 15, 2014.

A difficulty confronting boards can be management's inability to summarize the total IT spend throughout the institution. The definition of what constitutes "information technology" expenses can be rather opaque, particularly in institutions that have decentralized IT operations. Given the significance of IT spend as a percentage of total costs, the inability to provide a transparent picture of the IT budget may point to inadequate management attention. "Institutions must refine the way IT budgets are developed, maintained, and presented to the board. Management needs to communicate to directors the expected value and benefits as well as the costs. This requires transparency and the linkage of IT costs to business outcomes," said Douglas S. Ingram, a board member of Endo International plc, Nemus Bioscience Inc., and Pacific Life Insurance Co.

More than a few institutions have IT expenditures that are outside the control of the IT function. These are sometimes referred to as "shadow IT costs," which are incurred directly by business units, and not infrequently procured at a lower cost than internal IT can provide. PricewaterhouseCoopers estimates that over 60% of institutions have IT spending that is incurred directly by business units.[168] Directors need to inquire about shadow IT costs in order to gain a full perspective of the budgeted costs.

Operating Expenses vs. Capex

Operating expenses include all monetized costs that affect the current-year income statement. What qualifies as an operating expense is defined by the accounting regulations and, therefore, determined by the finance department rather than IT. However, IT management does control the amount of operating expenses incurred. In fact, controlling the level of IT operating expenses incurred is a primary objective of the IT budgeting process.

Capital expenses include all monetized costs that are partially deferred to income statements in future years. What qualifies as a capital expense is defined by the accounting regulations and, again, is determined by the finance department.

Source: "IT Budgeting Fundamentals," by Michael Smith, Gartner, July 3, 2015.

Capital Expenditures

Each time management decides how best to enter new markets, reduce operating costs, expand production or extraction, speed products to market, or realign to meet changing customer expectations, the decision likely includes an underlying capital expenditure dimension of information technology.

Capital projects involving technology require that directors take a step back to assess how projects support corporate and the IT strategy, which can result in the directors assuming a more assertive stake in tracking the execution of the strategy. The intersection of capital projects and strategy can bring goal-setting into a clearer, more realistic focus.

Capital expenditures also may include plans for new systems that allow an institution to significantly enhance its efficiency and reduce costs. These types of projects often

---

[168] "Directors and IT: A User-friendly Board Guide for Effective Information Technology Oversight," PricewaterhouseCoopers, 2016.

involve significant complexity, integration issues, cost pressures, changing plans, and other challenges. By one estimate, the top 500 institutions lose $14 billion each year because of failed IT projects. In response, directors are becoming much more engaged in overseeing the status of major IT project implementations.[169]

Trends in IT Spending as a Percentage of Revenue

Technology investment and spending of institutions of all sizes

	2012	2015
Finance and insurance	7.9%	8.5%
Manufacturing	1.7%	1.7%
Retail and wholesale trade	1.3%	1.3%
Business services	3.4%	3.5%
Media, entertainment, and leisure	1.0%	1.0%
Utilities and telecom	4.5%	4.2%
Public sector	6.2%	6.5%
Total of all institutions	4.7%	4.8%

Source: "Forrester's Data Can Help CIOs Define and Improve Tech Budgets," Forrester Research Inc., January 23, 2015.

McKinsey & Company cites an organization, as an example, that rolled out a massive systems-transformation project expected to cost several hundred million dollars, which represented the institution's largest investment ever over a five-to-10-year period. Given the importance of this effort, both strategically and financially, the directors conducted regular boardroom reviews with management on progress including budget overruns.[170]

What information do directors need from management to evaluate IT capital expenditures from a strategic perspective?

To start, directors need an understanding of the business case for the expenditure. What is the rationale? How will it affect the competitive position in the marketplace? What are the key assumptions underlying execution? What major risks could impede progress? How does this project fit within the overall portfolio? What is the forecast for return on investment in both best and worst cases?

Can the same objectives be achieved by buying the technology rather than building it in-house, from the ground up? What is the difference in cost? What is the difference in return for each scenario? And, what does competitive intelligence reveal about each scenario? What about the risks? Is there less risk to buy versus build?

Directors should use their knowledge of the institution to calibrate the importance of capital expenditures and to regularly monitor results. Board oversight of key areas at pivotal stages of strategy development and execution, from concept to feasibility to implementation, can reduce the risk of capital projects missteps.

---

[169] Ibid.
[170] "Elevating Technology on the Boardroom Agenda," October 2012.

Ultimately, the fundamental question is whether or not the capital expenditure achieves a significant sustainable source of competitive value.

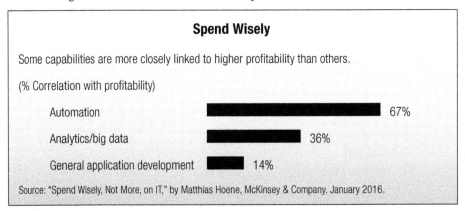

Spend Wisely

Some capabilities are more closely linked to higher profitability than others.

(% Correlation with profitability)

Automation — 67%

Analytics/big data — 36%

General application development — 14%

Source: "Spend Wisely, Not More, on IT," by Matthias Hoene, McKinsey & Company, January 2016.

How Much to Spend?

Most industries are in the midst of major transformations driven by changes in technology and dramatic shifts in consumer behavior. There is an emphasis today in boardroom discussions on innovation, new technologies, and their vast potentials. At the same time, the pressure to control costs and operate efficiently has never been more intense.

In many instances, spending on new technologies is earmarked for critical digital initiatives, building online channels, and mobile applications and services. Although management shares with the board detailed data about technology costs, operations, requirements, and outcomes, directors are challenged with approving the right areas for investment and the appropriate levels of required spending.

Directors and management face new realities about technology usage and IT performance, among them:

- *Higher stakes.* Technology is no longer just another business utility, one of many common inputs into operations. IT is shaping strategies and business models as institutions seek to meet their customers' demand for tech-enabled products and services.
- *Greater complexity.* The typical IT landscape no longer comprises collections of "island systems and applications." It is a complicated network of interlinked applications, interfaces, and databases—and many of them must be able to speak with external systems.
- *More vulnerabilities and risk.* As institutions begin to digitize, breaches of security are commonplace. Cybersecurity is a regular and even constant point of discussion in the boardroom.[171]

A variety of factors drive information technology costs. Some institutions are dealing with fragmented application landscapes. Others are burdened by high depreciation from

---

[171] "Five Questions Boards Should Ask About IT in a Digital World," by Aditya Pande and Christoph Schrey, McKinsey & Company, July 2016.

prior capital investments. Poorly structured outsourcing contracts can also lead to high costs owing to over-specified service levels, inadequate governance, or unfavorable terms and conditions. Moreover, institutions with IT resources in high-cost geographies must accommodate higher compensation costs, while those with cross-border operations may need to tackle greater complexity. As a result of these drivers, as well as shifts in consumer behavior, the increasing move to digital, and ongoing cost pressures, boards and management need to make difficult and sometimes imponderable choices about IT spend.[172]

"It can be challenging for directors to differentiate between technology investments that are compulsory—because of regulatory compliance or the need to fix old, antiquated systems—and investments in innovation and new products and services that will assist the business in competing," observed Bruce G. Blakley, a board member of Cubic Corporation and Hunter Industries.

Pursuing new technology is never a one-time thing and appropriate funding is paramount. Most businesses continue to rely too heavily on organic growth to build their new-technologies capabilities, which is likely due to budget constraints. Indeed, nearly two-thirds of respondents to an Ernst & Young survey state they would be allocating no more than 10% of their capital budget to new technologies, notwithstanding that a lack of sustained financial commitment can seriously constrain progress and ignore the disruptive forces at play.[173]

Research from the banking sector suggests that more IT investment does not necessarily boost profits, but targeting investments in particular areas might. McKinsey & Company's survey conducted with regional and superregional banks in the United States supports the axiom that investing more in IT is not as important as investing smartly. The respondents covered a range of variables, including the amount banks spend on application development, the level of functionality they believed IT provided to the business, and overall profitability. The data showed no significant correlation between the amount spent on general application development and the banks' bottom lines. However, it does appear that investing in particular areas of IT functionality, such as in automation, customer analytics, and big data, is correlated with higher profitability. Investment in the automation of back-office processes or in the capability to perform sales analytics, for instance, can also yield meaningful efficiencies. As a consequence, McKinsey concludes that boards and management should spend wisely, not necessarily more, on information technologies.[174]

Create Spending Headroom

Considering the budget pressures on IT, where should the funds for investment in new technologies come from? One option is to create spending headroom within the budget by cutting costs in both day-to-day IT operations and on application development. Disciplined cost control, rigorous prioritization, advanced sourcing practices, and relentless standardization of IT infrastructure and application architecture may be opportunities

---

[172] "Navigating the New World of IT in Consumer Packaged Goods," by Ashwin Bhave, Jeff Gell, and Marc Schuuring, The Boston Consulting Group, December 29, 2015.
[173] "Dealmaking in a Digital World," Ernst & Young, 2016.
[174] "Spend Wisely, Not More, on IT," by Matthias Hoene, McKinsey & Company, January 2016.

to lower the spend. McKinsey & Company estimates that banks that manage these areas will spend, on average, 41% less on day-to-day IT operations than banks that have self-reported deficiencies in these fields.[175]

Cost-Efficient IT

As part of the firm's actions toward cost-efficient IT, Accenture's IT organization developed tools with reporting capabilities to track how costs are generated. Specifically, the firm produces reports according to four categories. The first is reporting by IT products and services. The second is by customers. The third is by IT organization structure, which shows expenses incurred by different areas within the IT organization. And, the fourth is reporting of natural expenses, which focuses on costs associated with areas such as payroll and depreciation and feeds into Accenture's corporate financial reporting. These reporting capabilities allow IT to better align and manage IT spend with business priorities while at the same time drive efficiency. Overall, Accenture's internal IT organization has, using this approach, fundamentally improved IT efficiency and effectiveness while significantly lowering IT spend.

Source: "Accenture's 12 Actions Toward Cost-Efficient IT," Accenture, 2016.

In an attempt to continue optimizing the cost of information technology, thereby creating spending headroom, Gartner outlines top ideas to reduce costs, as follows:

1. Create a shared-service organization for some or all IT services.
2. Centralize, consolidate, modernize, integrate, and standardize technologies.
3. Leverage cloud services.
4. Increase IT financial transparency to better manage both supply and demand.
5. Utilize zero-based budgeting on the right cost categories, requiring a "re-justification" of spending often through a cost-benefit analysis based on current conditions.
6. Rationalize and standardize applications.
7. Optimize software-licensing management capabilities.
8. Improve procurement and sourcing capabilities.
9. Invest in Mode 2 capabilities. ("Mode 2 capabilities" allow IT to deliver capabilities faster, reap benefits sooner, and prioritize demand.)
10. Re-examine how end-user computing is delivered. ("End-user computing" refers to systems in which non-programmers can create working applications.)

In the search to find the next big idea, however, management sometimes overlooks basic cost-optimization techniques. Gartner suggests that many institutions have not yet realized the full benefits of cost optimization, mostly due to failure in execution.[176] As a result, the opportunities for creating headroom in spending have been delayed or even thwarted.

---

[175] "How Winning Banks Re-focus Their IT Budgets for Digital," by Giuliano Caldo, Matthias Hoene, and Tunde Olanrewaju, McKinsey & Company, December 2014.
[176] "The Gartner Top 10 Recommended IT Cost Optimization Ideas," by Jim McGittigan and Sanil Solanki, Gartner, February 26, 2016.

Cybersecurity: Costs vs. Benefits

Directors and management must strike a balance between protecting the security of the institution and mitigating downside losses, while continuing to ensure profitability and growth in an extremely competitive environment. On average, it is estimated that 9% of IT budgets today are being spent on security.[177]

Many technical innovations and business practices that enhance profitability can also undermine security. For example, technologies, such as mobile technology, cloud computing, and smart devices, can yield significant cost savings and business efficiencies, but they can also create major security concerns if implemented haphazardly. Properly deployed, these technologies can increase security, but only at a cost.

Similarly, trends such as bring your own device, 24/7 access to data, and the use of extensive supply chains may be required in order for a business to remain competitive. These practices, however, can also dramatically weaken the security of the institution.[178]

Considering IT Investment as a Portfolio

Infrastructure	Business integration
	Business flexibility
	Reduced marginal cost of business unit's IT
	Reduced IT costs
	Standardization
Transactional	Cut costs
	Increase throughput
Informational	Increased control
	Better information
	Improved quality
	Faster cycle time
Strategic	Product innovation
	Process innovation
	Competitive advantage
	Renewed service delivery
	Increased sales
	Market positioning

Source: "Generating Premium Returns on Your IT Investments," by Peter Weill and Sinan Aral, MIT Sloan Management Review, Winter 2006.

---

[177] "Forrester's Data Can Help CIOs Define and Improve Tech Budgets," Forrester Research, Inc., January 23, 2015.
[178] "Cyber-Risk Oversight," National Association of Corporate Directors, 2014.

The AFCEA[179] issued a report, "The Economics of Cybersecurity: A Practical Framework for Cybersecurity Investment," which addresses the challenges related to evaluating the costs of cybersecurity and the benefits of enhanced security. The report notes that institutions can defend themselves while staying competitive and maintaining profitability. However, successful cybersecurity methods cannot simply be "bolted on" at the end of business processes. Cybersecurity needs to be woven into business processes. When done successfully, it can help build competitive advantage.

The AFCEA notes that four basic security controls are effective in preventing most cyber intrusions: (1) Restricting user installation of applications; (2) Ensuring that the operating system is patched with current updates; (3) Ensuring that software applications have current updates; and (4) Restricting administrative privileges. The AFCEA suggests that not only are these core security practices effective, they also improve business efficiency and create an immediate positive return on investment, even before considering positive economic impact of reducing cyber breaches.[180]

Cybersecurity is an area where the IT budget nurtures the notion of an insatiable appetite and, given the magnitude of the threats, perhaps rightly so. Most boards and management have been investing in cybersecurity while not necessarily realizing that this is just the start. The effort requires a strategy and a responsive approach. Cybersecurity investments can be viewed as sufficient only when the institution consistently remains within the bounds of its risk appetite. According to an Ernst & Young survey, 70% of the respondents suggest that the spend for cybersecurity will remain at the same high levels. However, as the cybersecurity preventive measures mature, it can become less onerous to demonstrate the value of these investments. Providing more accurate quantitative assessments of costs that result from cyber intrusions can assist in justifying continued investments.[181]

"Directors are circumspect in defining and monitoring the return on IT investments, particularly in cybersecurity. The board's review tends to be concentrated on the costs, not the expected benefits. Invariably, the oversight of the IT budget seems to be much more of an art than a science," commented Lester M. Sussman, a board member of East West Bancorp, Inc.

Takeaways for Directors

Insist on Transparency

The process of determining the amount of investments in information technology more often than not can lack transparency. Directors need to determine that there is an acceptable governance process identifying which initiatives are adequately funded and staffed. Board members should make inquiries of management on the alignment of IT projects

---

[179] The Armed Forces Communications and Electronics Association (AFCEA) is a non-profit membership association serving the military, government, industry, and academia as an ethical forum for advancing professional knowledge and relationships in the fields of communications, information technology, intelligence, and security.

[180] "The Economics of Cybersecurity: A Practical Framework for Cybersecurity Investment," AFCEA Cyber Committee, October, 2013.

[181] "Creating Trust in the Digital World," Global Information Security Survey, Ernst & Young, 2015.

Board Obtains an Outside Perspective

The management of a financial institution requested substantial investment to modernize legacy software platforms and develop new capabilities in advanced risk analytics across the business. In response, the board looked for an outside perspective by an external advisor and arranged a presentation and discussion rooted in an industry context. The presentation, which looked at recent trends, found that while a new type of player – large, highly tech-enabled and data-driven institutions – was emerging in the commercial market, there would still be room for a sizable number of smaller players with varying technology capabilities. The presentation also highlighted leading practices applied by other institutions and drew on developments from other sectors in using data and analytics to improve customer segmentation and risk assessment. By engaging directors with these perspectives and then debating the implications, the board and management gained a better understanding of its business-technology gaps and the investments that would be required to close the most critical deficiencies. As a result, funding was approved by the board for substantial expenditures in the next corporate investment cycle.

Source: "Elevating Technology on the Boardroom Agenda," by Michael Bloch, Brad Brown, and Johnson Sikes, McKinsey & Company, October 2012.

---

with corporate objectives, and agree on the metrics to calibrate the expected benefits. As a practical matter, management may be strained by articulating the total spent on IT and the cost drivers, and identifying where the monies are spent. Citing the expected value and benefits of the spend also can be problematic.[182]

In many institutions, there can be a significant amount of redundancy and waste in information technology, in part because it normally represents a proportionately large spend and may be encumbered by vagueness in the accounting for IT costs. Not all institutions keep an accurate inventory of applications, databases, and hardware. Fewer still can accurately map applications to computers, and applications to business owners and business processes. A large institution typically will have hundreds of servers, many underutilized and some not used at all. How many redundant systems exist? What computers are running systems, and how many programmers are supporting them? How much is being spent on maintenance and license fees for the commercial software, other technical software, and the computers themselves?[183]

Some of the system redundancy and costs are due to business units buying or building systems without knowing what other units already possess. Other costs may relate to poor practices, such as inadequate procurement oversight. And customer and employee data sometimes is replicated in hundreds of databases on different computers because that is easier than centralizing it. Boards should insist that the identification and accounting for IT assets be as transparent as possible. The total IT spend and how the monies are allocated are proxies for how efficiently the institution uses technology assets and how IT supports the business.[184]

---

[182] "Why Your Board of Directors Can't Sleep on IT," By Larry Tieman, *CFO*, November 14, 2011.
[183] Ibid.
[184] Ibid.

Assess the Budget Apportionment

Directors need to know how much of the IT budget is allocated to maintaining existing systems and how much is spent on supporting new projects. Gartner estimates that two-thirds of IT budgets are consumed by "running-the-business" costs, resulting in smaller allocations for investments in innovation and new initiatives.[185] Board members should understand whether management is sufficiently investing in the future and appropriately responding to competitive threats.

Directors should expect management to describe how much of the IT spend is dedicated to maintaining ongoing operations and maintenance, replacement or expansion of capacity, and/or new project spending committed to cost reductions or increased revenues. As noted, in many institutions the preponderance of the budget is allocated to maintaining existing systems, leaving limited resource dollars for investment in innovation and new business projects.

Monitor Benchmarking

Benchmarking the IT spend sometimes can be difficult but it is always helpful for directors. Benchmarking can include IT operational and capital budget spending levels, analysis of IT staffing levels, and IT key performance indicators (e.g., users per server and per printer and new initiative spending). If the ratio of IT spend to company revenue compares favorably with the ratio among peer companies, the board should take comfort. If not, increased attention in the boardroom may be warranted. Also, benchmarking custom/commercial software mix can provide directors with valuable insights regarding the budgeting priorities and changes, validating assumptions underlying the IT budget and business strategy.

In order to make meaningful comparisons, it may be necessary to obtain detail of the IT budget based on the nature of the costs. The ability to separate recurring and nonrecurring investments will allow for a better peer comparison.

Benchmarking of IT Costs	
Ongoing operations and maintenance	48%
Replacement or expansion of capacity	25%
New project spending	27%
Operating budget	61%
Capital budget	39%

Source: "Forrester's Data Can Help CIOs Define and Improve Tech Services," Forrester Research Inc., January 23, 2015.

Get Lean

Directors need to recognize a chronic problem in most IT organizations is the business insisting on functionality that may never be used. This often is a side effect of the long

---

[185] "IT Financial Metrics Primer: Essential Metrics for Optimizing the Business Value of IT," Apptio, Inc., 2016.

cycle times seen in traditional software projects, and it feeds a vicious cycle where many projects are bloated and/or completed late. Management will ask for more than required to protect against the fact that there is a long wait time for anything new from IT. Gartner indicates that most functionality is seldom or never used, and only about 20% is used frequently or always.[186]

Some boards and management are faced with cutting the IT budget yet challenged to get technology-driven programs implemented. IT organizations may have layers of management and large specialist organizations that are not always an integral component of the value chain. Traditional budgeting mechanisms can make prioritization difficult to change as conditions evolve, and create delays if resources are cut. Although some institutions have begun to apply lean principles to IT, resistance is sometimes imposed by elements within the business or IT units. Nevertheless, directors need to pursue whether the trimming of the IT budget can be done by getting lean.

What Is Lean IT?

Lean IT is an extension of lean manufacturing and lean principles to the development and management of information technology products and services. The premise is the reduction of costs through the elimination of waste, where elements such as legacy infrastructure and fractured processes add little or no value. Whereas lean IT initiatives can be limited in scope yet deliver results quickly, applying lean to information technology tends to be a continuing and long-term process that may take years before lean principles become embedded and intrinsic to an institution's culture. By reducing waste through the application of lean strategies, IT can be driven from the confines of a back-office support function to a central role in deriving value.

"Because of the significance of both the opportunities and threats caused by technology, board members sometimes get concerned about the risk of not spending enough on IT solutions. Allocating more money to 'new technologies' with the vague hope that it will enhance the likelihood of getting the right technology capabilities in place is nonsensical. At the same time, it is essential to avoid unnecessary or excessive spending on outdated or incompatible legacy systems which may drain resources from the future competitiveness. Finding the right budget balance for directors comes down to understanding proposals using multiple lenses to assess the situation and ensuring investments are well targeted with clear desired outcomes and accountability," said Michael D. Fraizer, a board member of MUFG Union Bank.

Understand the Cloud's Impact

Cloud computing, which can be either "private" or "public," allows the use of a network of remote services (high-end computers) and storage devices housed together and connected to the Internet. Similar to a shared services center, the cloud permits more flexibility and agility, and potentially significant cost savings.[187]

Maintaining enterprise data centers often takes up a significant portion of the IT budget, and establishing and configuring new systems and hardware can cost significant

---

[186] "Cut Costs by Getting Lean in Lean Times," by Bill Swanton and Nathan Wilson, Gartner, February 26, 2016.
[187] "Directors and IT: A User-friendly Board Guide for Effective Information Technology Oversight," 2016.

time and money. Cloud solutions often provide distinctive advantages because they use standardized platforms or a shared service center comprised of a network of remote servers and storage devices housed together and connected to the Internet.[188]

Many observers forecast that a significant number of institutions will no longer own any IT assets within 10 years, which can have dramatic implications for strategies and significant budget implications. As a result, directors need to understand management's plans for cloud computing as an important part of the oversight process.

Final Comments

The traditional "IT budget" may require a redefinition to an "Operations & Technology budget" that enables competitiveness (and hopefully competitive advantage) along with sound controllership and regulatory compliance. The investment in technology, whether built or bought, is just one aspect of such a budget that directors must probe. Equally important are where business processes should be re-thought, redesigned, or improved to enhance effectiveness, and where investments should be made in people and their capabilities to position the institution to deal with the opportunities and challenges ahead.

Questions Directors Should Ask About the IT Budget

- How much capital is available to invest in IT? How can the board get comfortable that the budget level is appropriate?
- What is the apportionment of the IT budget for innovations vs. ongoing maintenance?
- How is the II budget aligned with the business strategy and IT stategy?
- What are the IT security resources and is the security spend level appropriate given the threats?
- Is management confident that all IT costs are included in the budget? Has there been an investigation into the existence of "shadow IT costs"?
- If the IT budget increased by another 10%, how would these incremental funds be apportioned and applied (e.g., what projects to initiate, areas requiring investment, or risks to be reduced)?
- What are the payback periods for investments in new technologies?
- How does management "back-test" the values derived from IT investments? How does management assess whether prior expenditures achieved the expected objectives?
- What factors are considered in investing in cloud services? What are the cost implications of management's cloud strategy?
- Are the rationales and justifications for all significant budget requests adequately documented and supported?
- What are the results of benchmarking the IT budget vs. peers? What is the ratio of IT spend-to-revenue?
- What are the gaps in the IT portfolio and what are the plans to address them?
- What are the four or five metrics the board should monitor to derive the most value from IT investments?

---

[188] Ibid.

Risk and Capital for Banks Using Advanced Systems

"The market can remain irrational longer than most can remain solvent."
—JOHN MAYNARD KEYNES

apital requirements, liquidity, and risk mitigation are key priorities for the board. Now, rule changes, combined with the regulators' heightened expectations, have significantly increased these board responsibilities.

Capital and liquidity are central to an institution's ability to absorb unexpected losses and continue on with its business. Therefore, an institution's processes for managing and allocating its resources are critical to its financial strength and resiliency.

The Basel II final rule permits qualifying banks[189] to use an internal ratings-based (IRB) approach to calculate regulatory credit risk capital requirements, as well as advanced measurement approaches (AMA) to calculate regulatory operational risk capital requirements. Together, the IRB approach and the AMA are referred to as the "advanced approaches"[190] or "advanced systems."[191] The Basel rule, which was mandatory for some U.S. banks and optional for others, is based on a series of releases from the Basel Committee on Banking Supervision.

The U.S. capital rules issued in July 2013, referred to as the Basel III final rule, brought the Basel II rule forward to create what regulators now refer as the "standardized approach"[192] and the "advanced approaches."

---

[189] The term "bank" includes banks, savings associations, and bank holding companies. The term "bank holding company" refers only to bank holding companies regulated by the Federal Reserve and does not include savings and loan holding companies.

[190] There are three pillars of the advanced approaches: Pillar I covers minimum capital requirements, pillar 2 covers the regulatory review process, and pillar 3 covers market discipline.

[191] Advanced systems include the bank's advanced internal ratings-based systems, operational risk management processes, operational risk data and assessment systems, operational risk quantification systems, and, to the extent used, internal models methodology, advanced credit evaluation adjustment approaches, double default excessive correlation detection processes, and the internal models approach for equity exposures and market risk.

[192] The standardized approach relies on prescriptive risk-weights not necessarily reflective of the institution's own view of credit risk.

The advanced approaches, which are sophisticated and can be complex, permit an institution to calculate its regulatory capital using internal models based on internal risk variables and profiles, and not on exposure proxies. They compel an institution to develop and implement systems, processes, and programs in order to comply with extensive and intricate requirements. "For directors and management, the benefits derived from the advanced approaches generally include better information and an improved understanding of the bank's risk management practices, better risk assessments, and a clearer perspective on the potential vulnerabilities in calculating capital," said Ashwin Adarkar, senior partner and managing director, The Boston Consulting Group.

In 2015, 14 banks used the advanced approaches, which are mandatory for banks with assets of $250 billion or more. The scope of coverage will expand as additional foreign-owned banks will be required to form intermediate holding companies subject to the Comprehensive Capital Analysis and Review (CCAR)[193] framework and the advanced approaches.

Additional costs are incurred in most cases under the advanced approaches because of the technology investments required, the need to maintain data at the highest levels of granularity, and the complexity of the calculations. "Among the challenges in overseeing and managing risk and capital are having the right data and technology in place to help measure things quickly and effectively, as well as producing and monitoring MIS reporting that can help identify risks on a timely basis. Additionally, managing the very high demands for talent, which is increasingly hard to find and expensive, is a big concern," commented John C. Trohan, managing director and treasurer, MUFG Union Bank.

Advanced Approaches / Advanced Systems

The processes that are normally followed in building the advanced systems are akin to an internal control validation framework tailored for Basel qualification. Basel qualification attempts to establish risk and capital management requirements that are designed to ensure capital adequacy given the bank's risk profile.

Banks have flexibility in determining how to achieve integrity in their risk management systems. Nevertheless, they are expected to follow standard control principles such as checks and balances, separation of duties, functional independence, appropriateness of incentives, and assurance of data integrity, including that of information purchased from third parties.

Control, oversight, and validation mechanisms for advanced systems include the following requirements:

■ Management must ensure that all components of the bank's advanced systems function effectively and comply with the requirements.

---

[193] CCAR is a regulatory framework introduced by the Federal Reserve in order to assess, regulate, and supervise large banks and financial institutions. The framework consists of a comprehensive capital analysis and review and regulatory stress testing. The objective of CCAR is to assess whether the institution has adequate capital, the capital structure is stable given various stress scenarios, and planned capital distributions are visible and acceptable.

- The board, or its designated committees, must review and approve at least annually the effectiveness of the advanced systems.
- The bank must have an effective system of controls and oversight that ensures ongoing compliance with the qualification requirements; maintains the integrity, reliability, and accuracy of the advanced systems; and includes adequate governance and project management processes.
- The bank must validate, on an ongoing basis, its advanced systems. The validation process either must be independent of the advanced systems' development, implementation, and operations, or it must be subjected to an independent review of its adequacy and effectiveness. Validation should include an evaluation of the conceptual soundness of the advanced systems, an ongoing monitoring process that includes verification of processes and benchmarking, and an outcomes analysis process that includes back-testing.
- The bank must have an internal audit function independent of business-line management that assesses at least annually the effectiveness of the controls supporting the advanced systems and reports its finding to the board or a committee thereof.
- The bank must periodically stress test its advanced systems. The stress testing must include a consideration of how economic cycles, especially downturns, affect risk-based capital requirements.

"Institutions not only need to continue to improve their ability to identify risks, as part of capital planning, they also need to demonstrate that the risks are being adequately managed. The best controls in the world can be added, but it will be counterproductive if the documentation is not in place to prove the controls exist," observed Christopher J. Monteilh, partner, Deloitte & Touche.

ICAAP/CCAR

The board's oversight of capital requirements requires a fundamental understanding of the advanced approaches and the advanced systems and how they link with risk management.

A bank using the advanced approaches will design an Internal Capital Adequacy Assessment Process (ICAAP). ICAAP is foundational and a part of the CCAR framework, which, under the Federal Reserve's rules, is used to assess overall capital adequacy, based on the bank's risk profile and strategy to maintain an appropriate level of capital.

As part of its annual approval of the bank's capital plan and the effectiveness of the advanced systems, directors must review and challenge the CCAR processes. The results of this review become part of the annual capital plan submitted to the regulators.

CCAR is part of the Federal Reserve's program for assessing capital adequacy. Under CCAR, all U.S.-domiciled top-tier bank holding companies with total consolidated assets of $50 billion or more are required to develop and maintain a capital plan supported by a robust process for assessing their capital adequacy. In 2015, there were 31 CCAR banks, including all of the advanced approaches banks.

Components of the Internal Capital Adequacy Assessment Process (ICAAP)

- An institution must have a rigorous process for assessing the overall capital adequacy in relation to its risk profile and a comprehensive strategy for monitoring an appropriate level of capital.

- Each institution must conduct an internal assessment of whether its capital is adequate given its risk profile using ICAAP.

- The fundamental objectives of ICAAP are 1) identifying and measuring material risks; 2) establishing and assessing internal capital adequacy goals that relate directly to risk; and 3) ensuring the integrity of internal capital adequacy assessments.

- Each institution should have an ICAAP that is appropriate for its unique risk characteristics.

Source: "Supervisory Review Process of Capital Adequacy Related to the Implementation of the Basel II Advanced Capital Framework," Office of the Comptroller of the Currency, Federal Reserve System, Federal Deposit Insurance Corporation, and Office of Thrift Supervision, July 14, 2008.

The board has ultimate oversight responsibility and accountability under CCAR for capital planning and needs to be in a position to make informed decisions on capital adequacy and capital actions. The board or its designated committee is required to 1) review the robustness of the process for assessing capital adequacy; 2) ensure that deficiencies in the processes for assessing capital adequacy are remedied; and 3) formally approve the capital plan.

The board's review of capital adequacy should determine that, consistent with safety and soundness, the bank's capital plan takes into account all material risks.

"Best practices" for directors in the CCAR process include the following:

- Harness board expertise to evaluate the information provided by management.
- Understand the institution's risk exposures, activities, and vulnerabilities.
- Identify the major drivers of revenue and loss changes under various scenarios.
- View the results as estimates that represent a range of possibilities.
- Assess the impact of process weaknesses and mitigation controls.
- Calibrate the range of potential stress events and conditions.

Directors need to ensure that the various systems used in determining risk-based capital requirements are operating as intended. The oversight process should draw conclusions about the soundness of the components of the risk management system, identify weaknesses and limitations, and recommend corrective action as appropriate.

In addition, the oversight process should be sufficiently independent of the advanced systems' development, implementation, and operations to ensure the integrity of the component systems. The regulators suggest that an independent verification process that effectively challenges the rigor and accuracy of the bank's approach is helpful in ensuring initial and ongoing compliance.

Using the Advanced Approaches

Advanced Approaches/Advanced Systems (1)

- Internal ratings-based approach
- Advanced measurement systems

Internal Capital Adequacy Assessment Process (ICAAP) (2)

- Identification and measurement of risks
- Stress testing and sensitivity analysis
- Capital budgeting and planning
- Risk monitoring
- Capital evaluation, reporting, and data collection

Comprehensive Capital Analysis and Review (CCAR) (3)

- Capital budgeting, planning, and processes
- Capital adequacy levels
- Qualitative and quantitative assessment, including Fed-defined stress testing

Notes

(1) The board is required to approve, at least annually, the effectiveness of the bank's advanced systems.

(2) The board is required to approve annually the ICAAP and its components, as well as review its effectiveness, the appropriateness of risk tolerance levels and capital planning, and the strength of the control framework.

(3) The board is required to approve annually the capital plans to ensure robust processes exist for managing and allocating capital under stress. Moreover, the board must review and challenge the CCAR processes to ensure that processes are supported by effective risk measurement and management practices.

A bank assesses and manages capital requirements and adequacy through its Internal Capital Adequacy Assessment Process. ICAAP is integral to how CCAR is executed, although CCAR includes the important additional aspect of including the Federal Reserve's defined stress scenarios.

Although not technically an advanced system but considered part of the broader advanced approaches through the regulatory review process, ICAAP has its own set of requirements with significant overlap with CCAR. ICAAP and CCAR ensure that capital planning processes are robust, forward looking, account for unique risks, and confirm that sufficient capital is held to continue operations through periods of economic and financial stress. Because CCAR principles cover many of the ICAAP processes, the Federal Reserve effectively compels ICAAP-like processes on CCAR banks.

Because minimum risk-based capital requirements are based on certain assumptions and address only a subset of risks faced by a bank, each institution should conduct an internal assessment of whether its capital is adequate given its risk profile. A bank must conduct this assessment using the ICAAP process, in addition to its calculation of minimum risk-based capital requirements.

Banks using advanced approaches are required to have an ICAAP that is appropriate for its unique risk characteristics. The ICAAP ensures that internal capital targets and strategies for achieving them are consistent with the bank's business plans, risk profile, operating environment, and regulatory requirements.

ICAAP consists of internal procedures, systems, models, and methodologies that ensure the bank possesses adequate capital resources to cover all its material risks. It includes the identification and measurement of relevant material risks, stress testing and sensitivity analysis, capital budgeting and planning, risk-monitoring capital evaluation, reporting, and data collection activities.

Moreover, the board is required to regularly review and annually approve the ICAAP and its components. This review should encompass the ICAAP's effectiveness, the appropriateness of risk tolerance levels and capital planning, and the strength of the ICAAP's control infrastructure. The annual review includes an assessment of the amounts, types, and distribution of capital that is considered adequate to cover the level and nature of the risks. The assessment should cover the major sources of risks and the institution's ability to meet its liabilities, and incorporate stress testing and scenario analysis. The capital measures need to be aligned with the institution's risk appetite and the expectations of stakeholders.

Advanced Systems Review

The advanced systems review is a regulatory mandate that supports the following ongoing requirements:

- Management is responsible for maintaining the effectiveness of the bank's advanced systems for regulatory capital.
- The board must review and approve the advanced systems annually and offer evidence of how the board has assessed their effectiveness.

The board's oversight of the advanced systems review should be aligned with and be part of the bank's board-approved strategic plan, the wider internal governance structure, and the enterprise risk management processes.

Capital requirements can result in overlapping responsibilities between and among committees, requiring close coordination and communication. Therefore, it is important to define board and committee oversight responsibilities.

To credibly challenge the advanced systems, the board must have industry-specific knowledge, an understanding of the business and associated risks, and an informed perspective on the bank's products and services.

"The board's oversight of the advanced systems review involves a number of challenging touch points requiring a thoughtful, careful, and comprehensive approach. It

Questions Directors Should Ask About Risk and Capital

- Is the capital plan aligned with the bank's strategic plan that the directors review and approve?
- Capital planning process and assumptions:
  - Has the population of risks, exposures, activities, and vulnerabilities been appropriately captured in the capital planning process?
  - What are the assumptions used in the capital planning process?
  - How has management validated its assumptions, data, scenarios, models, and tools?
  - Are the stress scenarios appropriate given the current economic outlook and the institution's risk profile, business activities, and strategic direction?
  - Has an "independent challenge team" or similar group been established? If so, what is the extent of the reviews and challenges? Are the appropriate cross-functional skills, knowledge, and stature present in the challenge team?
- Capital planning process results:
  - How has management documented the capital process results and related validations of the advanced systems?
  - What are management's key limitations and uncertainties with its advanced systems?
  - What findings of the advanced systems review could jeopardize the bank's capital plan, capital adequacy, capital actions, or standing with the regulators?
  - Has the bank's advanced systems review program been reviewed with the regulators? What were their key findings or recommendations and have these been incorporated in the current capital plan and process?
  - What is the assessment of the independent review of the capital planning process, assumptions, results, and management's remediation plan?
  - What was the scope of the review by internal audit and the nature of its testing for compliance with the qualification requirements? What are the findings of internal audit's annual assessment of the controls supporting the advanced systems?
  - For identified gaps or weaknesses identified either by management or through validation processes or internal audit, what are the processes and time frames for remediation?
- Directors' "credible challenge":
  - What points have the directors raised regarding the capital planning process and the assumptions, and the qualitative and quantitative results of the capital plan?
  - How will these matters be evidenced and documented and what follow-up will management provide to the directors? How will the directors be informed of progress?

is linked with the risk management processes. Passivity in this area by directors and/or management could well be criticized by the regulators," noted Rodney R. Peck.

The advanced systems review provides directors with an independent verification mechanism for gaining comfort that the systems and processes fortifying the advanced approaches are operating effectively. The advanced systems review will center, as a primary focus, on attestations of effectiveness by those who own the systems and processes and on separate challenges from other independent existing functions. The system or framework is intended to ensure regular assessments and reporting on the advanced approaches.

All of these components should be executed with the goal of supporting the board's annual review and approval.

The advanced systems review can be structured in a variety of ways, but it should address the required capabilities, including exposure classification and risk identification, risk measurement and assessment, models and methodologies, data management, risk-weighted asset calculations and capital reporting, validation and verification mechanisms, and governance and reporting. The process areas, which often go beyond the formerly defined advanced systems, may include credit risk, liquidity risk, operational risk, market risk, interest-rate risk, and others.

The advanced systems review often voyages through multiple levels of scrutiny. Assessments at the most granular level are performed by individuals who are close to the process and who have relevant subject-matter expertise. These self-assessments are, in turn, reviewed and incorporated into higher-level assessments.

Although many approaches are employed, some banks establish, though not specifically require, an "independent challenge team" or a similar group to provide an independent view and challenge to management's self-assessment results. The independent challenge team should review the results of management's self-assessments, question and challenge the rationale supporting the pre-challenge assessments, and sign off on the final results.

The independent challenge team typically comprises individuals who understand the bank's products and services, possess requisite subject-matter knowledge, and hold sufficient stature within the bank to conduct an independent challenge.

Upon completion, the self-assessment reports and the findings of the independent challenge team are presented to the board or its designated committee. Key conclusions, highlights of the assessments, and commentary on common themes emerging from the assessments are reviewed. Summaries indicating the effectiveness of important capabilities and associated process areas are examined, and assessment outcomes and summaries are presented and subject to board approval.

All material aspects of the advanced systems need to be sufficiently documented, including the nature and extent of board oversight. "Best practices" suggest that board materials and board minutes should describe the information provided to the board, the extent of the board's review and challenge, and details on how results or conclusions were reached.

"The advanced systems review provides a critical and independent verification mechanism, separate from other existing functions such as internal audit, to assure that the bank's advanced systems and processes are working as expected," noted Jennifer O'Reilly, vice president and director of Enterprise Risk Management, First Republic Bank.

Federal Reserve's SR 15-18 and 15-19

On December 18, 2015, the Federal Reserve published two guidance letters on capital planning intended to clarify differences in capital planning expectations, consistent with the broad expectations set forth in SR 12-17 issued in December 2012 and the Supervisory Expectations and Range of Current Practice (ROPE) Guidance issued in August 2013.

SR 15-18 generally applies to U.S. bank holding companies and intermediate holding companies of foreign banks that have consolidated assets of $250 million or more ("large and complex"). SR 15-19 generally applies to those institutions that have consolidated assets of at least $50 billion but less than $250 billion ("large and noncomplex"). SR 15-18/19 consolidate many CCAR-related rules that inform the regulatory requirements and expectations, but for the most part do not replace prior regulatory guidelines.

SR 15-18 and SR 15-19 reaffirm that the board is ultimately responsible and accountable for the institution's capital-related decisions and for capital planning. The capital planning should be consistent with the strategy and risk appetite set by the board and with the risk levels, including how risks may emerge and evolve. Both guidance letters reaffirm that the board annually review and approve the capital plan.

In addition, the board should direct management to provide a briefing on its assessment of capital adequacy at least quarterly and whenever economic, financial, or other conditions warrant a more frequent update. Management's briefing should describe whether current capital levels and planned capital distributions remain appropriate and consistent with capital goals.

SR 15-18 and SR 15-19 also note that the board should hold management accountable for providing sufficient information on material risks and exposures to inform board decisions on capital adequacy and actions, including capital distributions. Information provided to directors should be clear, accurate, and timely.

The guidance letters indicate that the following information should be provided by management to the board:

- Macro-economic conditions and relevant market events.
- Current capital levels relative to budgets and forecast.
- Capital goals and targeted real-time capital levels.
- Enterprise-wide and line-of-business performance.
- Expectations from stakeholders.
- Potential sources of stress to operating performance.
- Risks that may emerge under stressful conditions.

Moreover, the guidance letters suggest that the board should direct management to provide information about the institution's capital estimation approaches. The board should also receive information about uncertainties around projections of capital needs or limitations within the capital planning process, in order to understand the impact of these weaknesses. This information should include key assumptions and an analysis of the projections' sensitivity to changes in the assumptions. The board should incorporate uncertainties related to projections and limitations in the capital planning process into its decisions on capital adequacy and capital actions. Directors should also review and approve mitigating steps to address weaknesses in the capital planning process.

Finally, SR 15-18 and SR 15-19 suggest that the board direct management to establish sound controls for the entire capital planning process. Directors should approve policies related to capital planning and review these policies annually. The board should also approve capital planning activities and strategies, as well as maintain an accurate record of its meetings pertaining to the capital planning process.

Failure to Comply

If the regulators determine that an institution using the advanced systems has fallen out of compliance with one or more of the qualification requirements, the regulators will notify the bank of its failure to comply, potentially impacting the regulator's non-objection to the bank's capital plan. After receiving this notice, the institution must develop and submit a satisfactory remediation plan for returning to compliance. If the regulators determine that the advanced systems are not commensurate with the bank's risk profile, the regulators will require corrective actions. Additionally, the regulators may require public disclosure if noncompliance is significant, which undoubtedly would invite reputational risk.

Takeaways for Directors

Among the Federal Reserve's capital planning priorities for boards and management are meeting the expectations under SR 15 - 18/19 and providing that sound capital planning is an ongoing, year-round process. The regulators are focused on the level of board engagement and on ensuring that management provides directors with enough information for them to be effective in their governance processes.

The OCC's guidelines establishing minimum standards describe the board's basic duties of oversight. These guidelines suggest, among other matters, that the board must actively oversee the risk-taking activities, acquire a thorough understanding of the bank's risk profile, and hold management accountable for adhering to the framework, including questioning, challenging, and opposing decisions that could cause the risk profile to exceed the bank's risk appetite or that could jeopardize bank safety and soundness. The linkage of the board's risk oversight and capital is critical.

It is essential that a director understand the expectations of the regulators regarding the advanced systems review and capital planning. It is not the board's responsibility to become involved in day-to-day management but the regulators do expect the directors to understand the risks and capital needs and be engaged. The board's oversight in this area is intended to be a dynamic and evolving process supporting management's proposition that capital is adequate given the bank's risk profile.

In addition, the regulators suggest that internal audit should have a comprehensive understanding of the control environment supporting the advanced approaches framework, including associated policies and procedures that document how the bank achieves initial and ongoing compliance. Internal audit is expected to regularly share its views with the board and to give opinions on the systems.

The regulators generally anticipate that a designated group within the bank would be primarily responsible for providing data for the board's review and approval. This group would be tasked with gathering and collating relevant information and coordinating activities. Evidence of how the board ensures that the systems and processes are effective is imperative. This documentation should also demonstrate attestations of not only the workstream owners but also, in some cases, the independent challenge team apart from internal audit.

An institution using the advanced approaches must meet the qualification requirements on an ongoing basis. Institutions are expected to improve their advanced systems as their business-data-gathering capabilities improve and as industry practices evolve.

Because the Basel rules and the regulations have a high governance requirement for the independent validation of the advanced systems' quantitative elements, these high governance thresholds are most likely required also for the qualitative aspects.

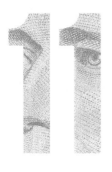

Model Risk Management Is a Challenging Imperative

"All models are wrong, but some models are useful."
— George E.P. Box

T he deployment of mathematical models is growing exponentially, given the proliferation of financial instruments and advances in quantitative computing methods. There is not a single financial institution in the U.S. that does not make use of models in some form, and often extensive use.

An important gap in the enterprise risk management practices at financial institutions, highlighted during the financial crisis, is the management of complex financial models used for business and risk management. The misunderstanding of the strengths and weaknesses of models during the period leading up to the crisis likely contributed to boards and management becoming overconfident and too reliant on models and their related outputs. The financial models that calibrate and measure an institution's risk lie very near the core of regulatory reform measures in the industry.[194]

Institutions have been using models for decision making, for risk management, and for financial and reporting purposes. Scores of new models have been developed and are being used to manage businesses and meet regulatory and reporting requirements. Information provided to the board for review and decisions is increasingly influenced by the hundreds or thousands of models used by many institutions. The use and complexity of these models continue to increase with the ever-changing market and business conditions, resulting in increased model risk.

Computing power has facilitated the evolution of modern finance and the creation of complex models. That evolution, and the dependence on models to help determine where funds should be invested and which risks to take, has forced institutions to take a closer look at their models to make sure they are functioning properly and for the purpose intended.[195]

Model failures can arise from poor management of assumptions, inputs, or implementation. How a model is developed and managed impacts its susceptibility to failure. While many situations of modeling error remain innocuous or unreported, institutions have incurred significant losses from the use of untested or improperly

---

[194]"Bank Regulation – The Risk Beyond: A Special Report," Thomson Reuters, 2014.
[195]"Model Validation: Managing Model Risk," KPMG, 2012.

validated models. The reported losses, in some cases, do not necessarily provide an indication of the collateral impacts of poor decisions based on failed models and damage to reputations.

As an illustration, one large U.S. bank had losses of $6 billion, which were partially due to value-at-risk model risk (that is, lack of modeling experience by the operator, no back testing, and operational problems in the model). In another example, a large Asia-Pacific bank lost $4 billion when it falsely applied interest rate models through incorrect assumptions, data-entry errors, and breakdowns in the models.[196]

The ultimate goal of model risk management is to reduce model risk to an acceptable level, consistent with the institution's overall risk appetite. Although the model risk management process needs to have parameters and a mechanism for escalating and reporting to the board, oversight of model risk is neither widely understood nor appreciated.

Boards are now increasingly seeking a better perspective on the soundness of models. Directors need a sensible, structured approach to the oversight of model risk, given the sheer volume, wide usage, and complexities surrounding their utility.

"The financial ecosystem has seen a metastasis of statistical and economic modeling. This clearly is a positive development but creates hurdles for both directors and management in providing the proper oversight," noted Sanjeev Mankotia, managing director - Managing and Analytic Solutions lead, KPMG.

Model Applications

The use of models has exploded because they have helped reduce uncertainties. Models are specifically designed to facilitate better decision-making in complicated environments.

Financial services firms use complex models to manage and hedge financial portfolios, value assets and liabilities, and determine regulatory capital. Large corporate treasuries use complex models to manage their debt, derivative, and foreign-currency positions. Middle market institutions use homegrown models to forecast cash and funding needs. Many model applications are being driven by regulatory requirements, such as CCAR and the Basel qualification prescriptions. In fact, more than 200 line items in the Comprehensive Capital Analysis and Review forms require some type of modeled output.[197] As institutions have learned, without periodic validation and proper oversight, the tools used to measure risk may themselves become an unintended source of risk.

Financial models are an accepted and valued tool for estimating earnings, assessing values, and evaluating risks. Models have become indispensable and practical necessities in an increasingly complex financial world. Nevertheless, an overlooked calculation error or data-integrity issue can compromise the results of these models and jeopardize the original modeling objectives while also costing time and expense to fix.[198]

---

[196] "The Future of Bank Risk Management," by Phillip Hans, Andras Havas, Andreas Kermer, Daniel Rona, and Hamid Samandari, McKinsey & Company, December 2015.
[197] "Model Risk and the Great Financial Crisis: The Rise of Modern Risk Management," by Jeffrey A. Brown, Brad McGourty, and Til Schuermann, Oliver Wyman, January 7, 2015.
[198] "Model Validation: Mitigating Model Risk," 2012.

Defining a Model

Every model provides some level of intelligence. That is, models are simplified representations of real-world relationships among observed characteristics, values, and events. They are a rough approximation of reality.

The term "model," as articulated by the regulators in their guidance on model risk management (OCC 2011-12 from the Office of the Comptroller of the Currency and SR 11-7 from the Federal Reserve), is quite broad and refers to a quantitative method, system, or approach that applies statistical, economic, financial, or mathematical theories, techniques, and assumptions to process input data into quantitative estimates. These models can take the form of "black box" third-party models, custom implementations of third-party applications, or internally developed tools, including Excel® spreadsheets.

Although definitions of what constitutes a model vary, a model typically has three components:

1. *Inputs,* which may take the form of data (either "hard data" or opinions of subject-matter experts), hypotheses, or assumptions.
2. *Processing apparatus,* which is a method, technique, system, or algorithm for transforming model inputs into outputs. It can be statistical, mathematical, or judgmental.
3. *Reporting component,* which is the system for converting model outputs into a form that is useful for decision making.

Regulatory guidance indicates that a model encompasses quantitative approaches in which the inputs can be partially or completely qualitative or specialist-based, although the output is quantitative in nature.[199]

While defining a model may seem like a straightforward exercise, it can be a challenging process inundated with conflicting views and debate. Some institutions apply a fairly objective set of rules, whereas others introduce subjectivity to make this determination. Institutions need to decide for themselves what is within the scope of a model and what is subject to model risk and affected by model risk policies and regulatory guidance. A precise definition of this scope will not usually be available, so subjective judgment is an important part of the process. The regulatory guidance requires policies and processes to define a model that is subject to validation, versus tools and calculations that may be catalogued but not subject to validation.[200]

Model Risk

Business processes such as product pricing, asset valuation, and asset/liability management take external and internal information, including data and assumptions, and feed it into models, which transform the inputs into metrics used by management to evaluate expected future performance and make decisions. Because they tend to simplify complex realities, models are subject to estimation error. In addition, models are sometimes

---

[199] "Emerging Trends in Model Risk Management," by Luther Klein, Michael Jacobs Jr., and Akber Merchant, Accenture, 2015.
[200] Ibid.

used for purposes other than what they were intended, resulting in a model misapplication or misuse. Collectively, these two general phenomena are referred to as "model risk."

Model risk is a by-product of knowing and understanding risk-taking activities, rather than an element used to define the institution's risk appetite.

The range of model risk includes the possibility of incurring a financial loss, making incorrect business decisions, misstating external financial disclosures, or damaging the institution's reputation. These risks can arise from the following:

- Errors in the model design and development process, such as errors in the data, theory, statistical analysis, assumptions, or computer code underlying a model, or in the model developer's judgment.
- Errors that occur as the model is implemented and deployed into a production environment.
- Errors in model operation once in production, including unauthorized and incorrect changes to the models.
- Misuse of or overreliance on models (or model results) by users.
- Use of models whose performance has deteriorated over time as a result of market conditions.

Defining the materiality or significance of model risk can be elusive, as some models impact net income directly while others have a strategic impact. A model should therefore be assessed based on the magnitude or size of its potential impact and its intended use. For example, the results of a credit model used to determine capital adequacy requires, in relative terms, less accuracy than the same model used to price an individual loan.

The larger and more complex the institution, the greater is its exposure to model risk. While the range of model risks can be rather broad, models do nevertheless facilitate a much more informed view than would be available without them.

Model Risk Management

As with all risk management activities, model risk management requires a framework that comprises appropriate infrastructure, management attention, and attentive board oversight. The key elements of the framework are as follows:

- An expression of an acceptable degree of model risk as part of the risk appetite statement, as well as a general level of awareness of and respect for model risk.
- Policy and procedures that assign clear responsibilities, accountabilities, and controls.
- Management demonstrating responsibility and accountability for the framework by the appropriate allocation of resources and attention to model risk and its management.
- The board demonstrating oversight of the risk management framework, commensurate with its importance to the institution.[201]

---

[201] "Model Risk and the Great Financial Crisis: The Rise of Modern Risk Management," 2015.

Questions Directors Should Ask About Model Risk

For All Models

- What is the institution's approach to model risk management? Does the framework include standards for model development, implementation, use, and validation? Is independence ensured between the ones validating the models and those who develop, implement, and use them?
- Does model risk management encompass model risk in aggregate and not merely that of individual models?
- Are all relevant areas covered by models? Are there new areas requiring a model? Are there overlaps across models?
- Have all models undergone an agreed-upon model risk governance process? Have problem areas or deficiencies been identified? Is there an up-to-date summary of models in use that lists their purpose, validation status (including the resolution of significant issues), and regulatory approval?
- Have the models been segmented or prioritized by management and the rankings reviewed? Which criteria were used?
- Are the findings from internal audit properly reported to the board? What is internal audit's evaluation as to whether model risk management is comprehensive, rigorous, and effective? Does internal audit verify that acceptable policies are in place and that model owners and control groups comply with these policies?

For High-Risk, High-Impact Models Only

- Is the purpose of the model understood and documented? What are the model's key assumptions and limitations? Are the assumptions consistent? How sensitive are the results?
- How do the current results compare to the historical results? To peers? To challenger models?
- What is the range of reasonable outputs given the scenario? Do the end-users of the model have a clear understanding of the accuracy and reliability of the outputs?
- Do the model results require adjustment using expert judgment?
- Is this a new model requiring greater scrutiny? Have all changes been through the governance process? How are the models operating with "temporary validation approvals" assessed?
- Do model performance reports exist and are they well documented? Are all results within tolerance? Are changes initiated where appropriate?
- Is the model subject to review by internal audit? What are the internal controls, including access protocols?

Although independent model validation has been a longstanding focus of regulated institutions such as commercial banks and thrifts, in recent years institutions have grown the function into a more comprehensive model risk management discipline, including oversight, governance, and risk-mitigation processes and reporting. Model risk should be governed and managed like other types of risk so that model risk management is an ongoing process, not a periodic activity.

Understanding the value of model governance and its role in effective risk management provides a way for directors and management to be assertive in managing model risks. This includes identifying high-risk models and prioritizing model-related risk and compliance initiatives within business practices such as model validations, assumption reviews, and data-integrity analysis. Proactively and effectively managing model risk can provide management with a significant competitive advantage if the model is used properly and its outputs instill confidence.[202]

Model risk management includes the identification of key business processes (such as pricing, valuations, estimation of risk, and forecasting) that rely on models and the implementation of internal controls to identify, measure, and control model risk across the model's life cycle. Like other risks, model risk requires sound risk management practices. Organizational nuances such as size, complexity, staffing, and accountabilities are sufficiently idiosyncratic to make any model risk management process unique.

Banks are generally further along than other financial institutions in establishing model risk management practices, owing largely to regulatory requirements and guidance such as OCC 2011-12 and SR 11-7. This guidance formalizes regulatory expectations. The guidance is far more comprehensive than the regulators' previous communications on model risk and appears to impose a heavy burden on small and medium-sized institutions. But if broken down into manageable components and focused on areas that institutions have not paid a great deal of attention to, compliance can be both manageable and highly beneficial.[203]

OCC 2011-12 and SR 11-7 recommend that model risk be addressed at the highest level—that is, by the board and management. As part of their overall responsibilities, the board and management should establish a strong model risk management framework that fits into the broader risk management of the institution. That framework should be grounded in an understanding of model risk, not just for individual models but also in the aggregate. The framework should include standards for model development, implementation, use, and validation.

While the board is ultimately responsible for managing model risk, it delegates to management the execution and maintenance of an effective model risk management framework. Just as it does for other major areas of risk, the regulatory guidance holds management responsible for reporting regularly to the board on significant model risk, from both individual models and in the aggregate, and on compliance with policy.

Moreover, the OCC's guidance suggests that the duties of management include establishing adequate policies and procedures and ensuring compliance, assigning competent staff, overseeing model development and implementation, evaluating model results, ensuring effective challenge, reviewing validation and internal audit findings, and taking prompt remedial action when necessary. From the board's perspective, the effective management of model risk not only will help meet the expectations of the regulators, but will provide for an important control in the highest levels of the decision-making and governance process.

---

[202] "Model Governance and Effective Risk Management," Protiviti, 2012.
[203] "Complying with the New Supervisory Guidance on Model Risk," by Shaheen Dil, *The RMA Journal,* February 2012.

While these guidelines have been applied primarily to regulated financial institutions such as banks, many of the key components have been adopted as "best practices" by nonbanks, especially those that are exposed to significant amounts of market or credit risk that must be monitored and managed with sophisticated models. This group includes insurance companies, money managers, and hedge funds.

Model governance needs to be rooted in the strategic thinking and risk culture of the institution. Although model governance is often viewed as a necessary evil related to compliance with regulatory requirements rather than as a value-added activity, a robust model governance structure and framework can enhance the institution's overall risk management effectiveness.[204]

"The heightened expectations around governance and controls imposed by the regulators must be addressed by the board. The costs of noncompliance can be significant and are increasing in ways both tangible and intangible," commented Til Schuermann, partner, Oliver Wyman.

Use of Models by Insurers

Many of the models used by insurance companies are actuarial in nature. It is not uncommon for one-half or more of an insurer's inventory to consist of models that actuaries have created and maintain to fulfill an actuarial function. Not only are these models critical in developing financial information about an insurer, but they also provide input into other activities such as risk management, capital planning, and regulatory compliance.

The actuarial profession has long recognized the importance of models in its work and the need to bring structure, control, and oversight to the modeling process. The American Academy of Actuaries is developing a standard of practice for insurance enterprise risk management, which includes guidance on models and model risk. The Casualty Actuarial Society and the Society of Actuaries also have devoted considerable attention and effort to this area.[205]

Since actuaries play little or no modeling role in the banking sector, it is not surprising that SR 11-7 makes no reference to actuaries or actuarial modeling. However, at a minimum, a risk management program suitable for the insurance industry would benefit from including the experience and expertise that actuaries have developed.[206]

An argument could be made that models are almost more critical for insurers than banks. Insurers require models to accurately report liabilities and value assets, and be based largely on actuarial assumptions that are subject to review by external audit and regulators. This results in increased scrutiny by these third parties. Stress testing the capital requirements of insurers and meeting regulatory requirements also involve models. Banks, on the other hand, do not rely heavily on models when preparing the financial statements. Banks use models as tools in stress testing capital requirements, valuing assets, and other decision-making activities.

---

[204] "Model Governance and Effective Risk Management," 2012.
[205] "Model Risk Management: The Next Generation for Insurers," PricewaterhouseCoopers, August 2015.
[206] Ibid.

Board's Credible Challenge

Board and management oversight of model risk remains in the early stages of maturity and continues to undergo evolutionary change.

As with other major areas of risk, management is responsible for reporting regularly to the board on significant model risk, both from the individual models and in the aggregate, and on compliance with the institution's policies. Directors should ensure that the level of model risk is within their tolerance and then direct changes where appropriate. These actions will establish the tone in regard to the importance of model risk and the need for active model risk management.[207]

How best can directors ask the proper questions and make the correct assessments, and do so without having to be modelers themselves?

It is the board's responsibility to ensure an enterprise-wide approach to model risk management fits into the institution's broader risk management structure, including standards for model development, implementation, use, and validation. The board needs to ensure that model risk management embodies model risk in aggregate, not merely by individual model.

Management's assertions in this regard should be evaluated by the board, which needs confirmation of independence between the groups that validate the models and those that develop, implement, and use them.

Annually, and as needed, the scope and coverage of all models and an assessment of the overlaps across models should be summarized by management for review with the board. The assessment normally includes a determination whether there are new areas requiring a model. Management should determine that all models have undergone an agreed-upon model risk governance process, identifying any problem areas or deficiencies. The board should confirm compliance with policies regarding model identification, model ranking, model approval, inventory administration, risk reporting, and validation execution, including model validation scheduling and frequency and regulatory approval.

Given their high volume and complexity, not all models can be subjected to rigorous board oversight, so management needs to segment or prioritize the models based on both the degree of risk and the significance of the model's impact. A framework or methodology should be established that manages the ranking of models and differentiates between model types in terms of importance. This mechanism would allow models to be classified across a spectrum from lowest to highest risk and impact, making the management and oversight processes manageable.

The criteria used in the segmentation needs to be understood and agreed to by directors. Materiality is often a principal driver for segmenting models. Other criteria by which to rank models include the underlying complexity and structure of the model, the importance of the decisions being made with the model, and the speed with which the model affects profit and loss. Also useful is a history of model error or some measure of estimated model volatility to quantify risk for individual models. In the segmentation,

---

[207] "New Supervisory Guidance on Model Risk Management: Overview, Analysis, and Next Steps," PricewaterhouseCoopers, 2011.

the relevance and importance of the model to the institution's CCAR and Advanced Systems should be taken into account.

Models determined to be high risk and high impact require a more detailed review and challenge by the board, as follows:

1. Directors should examine the purpose of the model, as well as the key assumptions and limitations for reasonableness and consistency both between and among models and between periods.
2. Model fit and variable selection should be reviewed, especially for a model relying on limited reference data.
3. The sensitivity of the results should be compared to prior periods and also to peer and other challenger models.
4. Management should present a range of acceptable results to the board, including assessments of the impact that expert judgment has on the outcomes.
5. Management needs to make directors comfortable that the end-users of the model have a clear understanding of the accuracy and reliability of the outputs.
6. A more detailed review of both the process and governance of each high-risk and high-impact model should be reviewed by directors.

New models also require greater scrutiny. Management needs to confirm to the directors that all model changes have been through the model risk governance process. Model performance reports should be presented by management for board review to ensure that the results are within the agreed-upon tolerances. A review of models operating with "temporary validation approvals" (for example, a model implemented before the model validation process is completed) should be conducted to restrict usage and impose and monitor limits. It is essential that management confirm internal audit's involvement with the governance of the models and internal controls, including access protocols.

The regulatory guidance requires that models undergo some sort of review annually, but the scope of the review can vary, depending on the segmentation or prioritization of the models. If a model has not been changed significantly, a more limited review in some years may be appropriate.

Even in the absence of changes, however, models are subject to the risks of degradation. At some point they will no longer adequately fulfill their intended business purposes. An annual model review and oversight by the board can help address those potential risks.

Directors need to be comfortable that the findings of the annual model review are properly documented by management and that they address the following, at a minimum:

- Compliance with imposed limits or conditions placed on the model as part of its approval.
- New applications or developments in regard to internally developed or commercially available models.
- Changes in the way a model is used or will be used that may affect the risk ranking of the model (for example, business volume and risks).
- Performance of the models.

- Changes in the features of the product or customer base that the model is used to evaluate.
- Changes in the market for the product.

Given the importance of model risk to the foundation of enterprise risk management, the board's oversight responsibility of model risk is not insignificant. Directors sometimes fall into the trap of managing model risk themselves, or they stand too far away and allow a vacuum to develop. The rules of engagement must be established, drawing a distinction between the role of the board in providing oversight and the role of management, which is responsible for driving day-to-day model risk management.

Board's Oversight of Stress Testing

The financial crisis highlighted the high degree of correlation of multiple risks, particularly in a deteriorating economic environment. Most institutions experienced an inability to anticipate the degree of concentrated risks and the connection between seemingly unrelated events.

In response to the crisis, the use of stress testing has gained in importance as boards and management, as well as the regulators, grapple with the outcomes of interrelated effects. The modeling of stress scenarios has emerged as a critical tool.

More than three-quarters of the U.S. banking system is required to perform stress testing at least twice annually. Stress testing uses models representing an institution's balance sheet and portfolio to simulate assumed stressful scenarios. The models proxy the portfolio and provide an assessment of the institution's financial condition under various circumstances, simulating alternative future outcomes.

Unlike the typical modeling approach, where data is used to develop a model based on the agreed-upon specifications, stress testing requires much more thoughtful input that is able to capture portfolio dynamics under abnormal or extreme conditions. The most effective approach represents a close collaboration of the modelers, management, and the board—a shared experience rather than the work of a select group of experts or practitioners.

In stress testing, directors are expected to play an assertive role by challenging the assumptions, comparing the results, and assessing the reasonableness of the outputs. Board oversight requires creative thinking. The most compelling challenges to model assumptions are frequently presented by directors from different industries and nonspecialists who develop views based on an outsider's perspective. Accordingly, an engaged board, comprising different types of experiences and skills, can be an important ingredient for challenging the reasonableness and appropriateness of model outputs.

Evolution of Model Risk Management

The board needs to be aware of the ways model risk management is evolving, especially its depth and breadth. There are at least two important emerging trends.

First, OCC 2011-12 and SR 11-7 emphasize the rationale for overseeing model risk on the broader end-to-end processes used to support management and decision making, including strategic decisions, as opposed to the limited veracity of embedded models within the framework. For example, economic capital covers various applications, such as capital adequacy, portfolio optimization, limits setting, pricing, and performance measurement. Each application requires varying levels of model accuracy. The guidance suggests that the end-to-end processes, including the various models and assumptions, need to be understood to properly assess the aggregate model risk within the framework.

Second, there is a trend toward the quantification of residual model risk (for example, the risk remaining post-mitigating controls) and, potentially, the estimation and assignment of economic capital to model risk. Quantifying model risk, however imperfect, would represent a new frontier for virtually all institutions and a significant challenge for directors and management.

Enhancing Boardroom Knowledge

Models have proven to be tremendously helpful. But as the use of models accelerates, so does the level of risk. This is an area where the potential impact of flawed modeling can be great, and it also is a field receiving greater regulatory attention and scrutiny. Boards and management benefit when structured approaches to model risk are deployed and incorporate both a framework for developing and testing models as well as effective governance.

Model risk management is a challenging discipline evolving from an earlier narrow focus on model validation. Although the regulators exhibit increased expectations for the board to provide proper oversight of model risk, directors must be realistic and practical about their role given the volume of models, their wide scope, and the complexities of their usage. A sensible, structured approach should be developed by the board and its delegated committees to ensure the proper oversight. The board, through its regular review and credible challenge, can gain insights into the risks and limitations of models, thereby developing comfort and confidence in the model outputs.

Third-Party Risk Management

"We are what we repeatedly do; excellence, then, is not an act but a habit."
—ARISTOTLE

Virtually all businesses are now extending into the virtual economy, which, by design, has created an increased reliance on third parties. Correspondingly, there is an intensification of the regulatory scrutiny of third-party risk management, especially with regard to financial institutions. Both the regulators and major stakeholders are requesting or requiring disclosure of the approach used to manage and mitigate third-party risks. For some institutions and boards, this is a natural extension of risk management. For others, it is a new challenge.

The movement toward greater reliance on third parties is an evolution of traditional business models, a trend driven largely by the need to pursue growth and innovation. Institutions choose third parties to gain specialization in products and services, to enhance customer service, to fill gaps in resources, and sometimes to lend their name or status to activities. In some cases, institutions use third parties to pursue opportunities as a joint venture or an alliance.

With the benefits of third-party relationships come risks and costs that frequently are not completely factored into the decision to proceed with these relationships. The institution can incur costs from extra resources and processes that need to be added for administration and oversight of third parties. As an illustration, cybersecurity risks associated with third-party access to internal networks demand new approaches and incur costs to protect data assets and IP and to ensure diligence on privacy. There are also costs associated with regulatory oversight of the institution and all its third-party connections, often initially underestimated.

Directors need to ensure that strategies related to core competencies appropriately address which services to retain within the internal structure, and which services are redirected to third parties.

The largest banks and credit card companies typically have more than 20,000 third-party relationships, and some institutions might have 50,000 suppliers or more. Many relationships may not be closely managed and some carry hidden risks. The company that molds and prints credit cards, for example, is also entrusted with customer data, which poses any number of privacy and security risks. Compounding the problem

Risk Assessment of Third Parties

External Risks	Process Risks	Technology Risks
Competitor Risk: What if there is third-party consolidation or failure? How seamlessly could the business be transferred to another third party?	*Vendor Reliance:* The third party may, in turn, rely on another third party.	*Performance:* The third party may not be able to meet service obligations due to systems that were inadequately designed or evaluated.
Reputation Risk: Damage to reputation or loss of clients may be incurred because of poor customer service, errors, or processing delays.	*Competency:* The third party may not be able to retain skilled employees. Will this turnover lead to process errors or poor customer service?	*Data Security and Cloud:* The third party may fail to appropriately manage access controls or may lack controls over client and confidential data.
Technology Change: The third party may have to invest heavily in new technologies in order to remain competitive. Will the third party's business model support this investment?	*Privacy:* The third party may operate in a nonregulated environment and may not have an adequate data privacy policy and program.	*Scalability:* The third party may not be able to support growth and/or usage spikes without service failures or performance degradation.
Capital and Financing: The third party's business model may be dependent on new sources of funding. It may have to invest more slowly in infrastructure than anticipated.	*Business Continuity:* The third party may operate in a nonregulated environment, and may not have an adequate business continuity policy, program, or testing.	*Availability:* The third party's architecture may not offer sufficient redundancy or resiliency in the event of individual component failure.

Source: "Vendor Risk Management," by Edward J. DeMarco Jr., The Risk Management Association, October 28, 2012.

is the changing nature of third-party relationships. In consumer financial services, most institutions have signed agreements with marketing partners, co-branding partners, fee-based service providers, and others to gain access to assets and capabilities. These are complex arrangements in which risk sharing is sometimes poorly specified, and some risks are not properly addressed. However, as they must bear the costs of the misdeeds of third parties, institutions have a strong incentive to broaden and deepen the way they manage these relationships.[208]

Institutions are held accountable for the actions third parties take on their behalf. The consequences of improper oversight of third parties can include not only direct mone-

---

[208] "Managing Third-Party Risk in a Changing Regulatory Environment," by Dmitry Krivin, Hamid Samandari, John Walsh, and Emily Yueh, McKinsey & Company, May 2013.

tary losses, but also loss of reputation and market share, regulatory enforcement actions, and hefty regulatory fines.

There are a number of risk categories institutions need to consider when dealing with third parties. For example, a third party with most of its resources and/or operations in one location may pose a concentration risk to the institution. If a natural disaster strikes, it could prevent the third party from providing services. If neither the third party nor the institution has contingency plans in place, the institution could be exposed to significant risks. This also applies to institutions that depend heavily on a single supplier for a critical process or service. What happens if that supplier goes out of business, or if its operations are even temporarily disrupted?[209]

The Office of the Comptroller of the Currency, the Federal Reserve, the Consumer Financial Protection Bureau and others have intensified their review of risk management practices with third parties. Their concern is that the quality of risk management and oversight of third-party relationships may not be keeping pace with the increasing level of risk and complexity of these relationships. The regulators require that oversight and due diligence, including the monitoring by directors, be commensurate with the risk and complexity of the third-party relationships, particularly for critical relationships. Targeted for review are important functions such as payments, clearing, settlements, custody, and technology.

While there is no standard "one size fits all" approach to third-party risk management given the nuanced differences between different industries and institutions, program governance capabilities, as well as established policies, standards, and procedures, are fundamental steps. Yet a survey conducted by Protiviti suggests that many institutions are no more advanced in these critical areas than they are in other components of third-party risk management.[210]

"Financial institutions are encountering difficulties associated with an increase in dependence on third-party providers and the evolution of third-party risk management programs. The challenges include addressing business needs, meeting the expectations of regulators, and providing for an appropriate transfer of knowledge from third parties," commented James Fanning, a board member of MUFG Securities Americas, Inc.

What Are Third-Party Relationships?

Most institutions will have thousands of relationships to manage, and the risks associated with each arrangement tend to vary. Moreover, each relationship differs in scope and complexity. Some offer services that may be more critical than others, while other third parties may have more robust risk management processes.

A third-party relationship is any business arrangement between an institution and an outside entity by contract or other commitment. Sometimes, third parties are defined as anything other than direct employees. Examples of third parties include vendors,

---

[209] "Managing Vendor Risks: Three Lines of Defense for Banks," by John Graetz, Walter Hoogmoed, Alfred Spahitz, and Christopher Spoth, Deloitte, May 31, 2013.
[210] "Vendor Risk Management Benchmark Study," Protiviti, 2014.

suppliers, outsource providers including IT service firms, business process outsourcing providers, call center providers, HR outsourcing providers, real estate and facilities management, joint venture partners, affiliates for which the institution is deemed to have control, other professional services firms, business alliance members, contingency arrangement participants, contingent workers, and counterparties.

Third-party relationships include activities that involve outsourced products and services, independent consultants, networking arrangements, merchant payment processing services, services provided by affiliates and subsidiaries, joint ventures, and other business arrangements where the institution has an ongoing relationship or may have responsibility for the associated records. They generally do not include customer relationships.

Moreover, third parties include institutions entering into multiple supplier relationships, with their own suppliers outsourcing further to third, fourth, or even fifth parties. An understanding of third-party relationships further down the supply chain therefore becomes important as the actions of those suppliers may impact the parent organization.

OCC's Guidelines

A primary objective of the regulators' guidelines pertaining to third parties is to determine whether the institution's third-party relationships create more risk than the institution can identify, monitor, manage, or control. These risks include those to the institution's business and solvency, as well as the institution's protection of its customers from financial harm.

In part, the regulators' concerns stem from the fact that third parties themselves may not be directly subject to regulatory or financial reporting requirements. The third parties' lack of accountability to regulators, and failures in risk management, may leave regulated institutions exposed to civil or even potential criminal penalties.[211]

In October 2013, the OCC issued Bulletin 2013-29, "Third-Party Relationships: Risk Management Guidelines," which represents an important road map. These guidelines signal a fundamental shift in how institutions need to assess third-party relationships. They call for robust risk assessment and monitoring processes to be employed relative to third-party relationships, as defined—specifically those that involve "critical activities" with the potential to expose an institution to significant risk.

The regulators are shifting their focus from primarily traditional vendors to all third-party relationships, including third parties that engage directly with customers and third parties that subcontract activities to other providers. Regulators expect that an institution will develop a robust and comprehensive risk-based third-party management framework and process that is scalable, sustainable, and commensurate with the institution's size, complexity, and risk profile.

The guidelines further direct institutions to ensure directors receive adequate reporting on third-party relationships, effectively requiring third-party risk to be fully integrated into an institution's existing risk and compliance governance framework. The

---

[211] "Vendor Risk Management in the New Regulatory Environment," KPMG, 2013.

Questions Directors Should Ask About Third-Party Risk Management

- How are the oversight roles and responsibilities for directors and management relative to third-party risk management defined?
- Which processes have been deployed to ensure that risks associated with third-party relationships are consistent with strategic goals, organizational objectives, and the risk appetite? Has the board approved the risk-based policies that govern the third-party risk management process?
- How are "critical activities" defined and does the scope of the activities provide sufficient coverage of the key risks? Has the board reviewed and approved management's plans for using third parties that involve "critical activities"? Has the board considered management's exit strategies?
- What is the extent of the board's review of the due diligence results and management's recommendations to use third parties that involve "critical activities"?
- What are the board's parameters for approving contracts with third parties that involve "critical activities"? Which contracts are subject to review and what is the process?
- How does the board ensure that management takes appropriate actions to remedy significant deterioration in performance or to address changing risks or material issues identified by ongoing monitoring?
- Which frameworks and/or standards are employed for third-party cyber risk identification and mitigation processes?
- How effective is management's oversight of the key data assets in electronic form? How is access to the data managed? How is data monitored for security? What forensics information is collected for both prevention and after-the-fact resolution?
- Which processes are followed to require that all contracts with third parties insure or indemnify against losses resulting from cyber intrusions or other noncompliance events?
- How thoroughly does the board review results from the periodic independent reviews of third-party management process effectiveness?
- How is the board's oversight of third-party risk management and management's performance in this area documented?

guidelines suggest that effective third-party risk management follows a continuous process for all relationships:

- *Planning*: Before entering into a third-party relationship, management should develop a plan to manage the relationship, commensurate with the level of risk and complexity of the relationship. Moreover, the plan should outline the institution's strategy or intentions, identify the inherent risks of the activity, and describe how the institution selects, assesses, and oversees the third party.
- *Due diligence and third-party selection*: Due diligence should be conducted on all potential third parties before selecting and entering into contracts or relationships with them. An institution should not rely solely on experience with or prior knowledge of the third party as a proxy for an objective, in-depth assessment of the third party's ability to perform.

- *Contract negotiations*: Once a third party is selected, management should negotiate a contract that clearly specifies the rights and responsibilities of each party. The contract should be in writing and include the rights and responsibilities of all parties. Importantly, management should obtain board approval of the contract before its execution if a third-party relationship will involve "critical activities." (Note: The OCC later clarified this provision to provide that the board's approval of contracts for large institutions is required in some, but not all, cases involving "critical activities.")
- *Ongoing monitoring*: Ongoing monitoring for the duration of the third-party relationship is an essential component of the risk management process. More comprehensive monitoring is necessary when the third-party relationship involves "critical activities."
- *Terminations*: The guidelines suggest that relationships should terminate in an effective manner if the activities are transitioned to another third party, brought in-house, or discontinued altogether. In the event of contract default or termination, a plan should be in place to bring the service in-house if there are no alternate third parties.
- *Oversight and accountability*: The board (or a designated board committee) and management are responsible for overseeing the overall risk management processes. The board, management, and employees within the lines of business that manage the third-party relationships have distinct but interrelated responsibilities to ensure that the relationships and activities are managed effectively and commensurate with the level of risk and complexity, particularly for relationships that involve "critical activities."
- *Documentation and reporting*: An institution should properly document and report on its third-party risk management processes and specific arrangements throughout their life cycles. Proper documentation and reporting facilitates the accountability, monitoring, and risk management associated with third parties.
- *Independent reviews*: Management should ensure that periodic independent reviews are conducted on the third-party risk management processes, particularly those involving third parties in "critical activities." These reviews should allow management to determine that the process aligns with its strategy and effectively manages risk. The internal auditor or an independent third party may perform the reviews, and management should ensure that the results are reported to the board.

The guidelines specifically outline the following responsibilities for directors:

- Ensure an effective process is in place to manage risks related to third-party relationships in a manner consistent with the strategic goals, organizational objectives, and risk appetite.
- Approve the risk-based policies that govern the third-party risk management process and identify "critical activities."
- Review and approve management plans for using third parties that involve "critical activities."
- Review the summary of due diligence results and management's recommendations to use third parties that involve "critical activities."
- Approve contracts, as necessary, with third parties that involve "critical activities."

- Review the results of management's ongoing monitoring of third-party relationships involving "critical activities."
- Ensure management takes appropriate actions to remedy significant deterioration in performance or to address changing risks and material issues identified through ongoing monitoring.
- Review results of periodic independent reviews of the third-party risk management processes.

Defining 'Critical Activities'

The OCC's guidelines define "critical activities" as significant functions (for example, payments, clearing, settlements, and custody), significant shared services (such as information technology), or other activities that:

- Could cause significant risk if the third party fails to meet expectations.
- Could have significant customer impacts.
- Require significant investment in resources to implement the third-party relationship and manage risk.
- Could have a major impact on operations if an alternate third party needs to be found or if the outsourced activity has to be brought in-house.

As noted, third-party arrangements that involve "critical activities" are expected to receive more comprehensive and rigorous oversight from the board and management.

The Fed's Guidance

The Federal Reserve's Supervision and Regulation Letter 13-21, "Guidance on Managing Outsourcing Risk," issued December 5, 2013, is similar to the OCC's road map, although narrower in focus. The Fed is concerned primarily with outsourcing relationships, whereas the OCC addresses all third-party relationships. The Fed's guidance is intended to address the characteristics, governance, and operational effectiveness of a financial institution's risk management program for outsourced activities that are beyond traditional core processing and information technology services.

The guidance from both the OCC and the Fed is principles based, reflecting the evolution in regulatory thinking. The degree to which the assessment and risk management processes need to be coordinated with the risk management and compliance functions is not specifically prescribed.

Linkage with Cybersecurity

Data breaches of third parties are costly, and the number of high-profile incidents is rising. As an illustration, a customer service software provider recently suffered a data breach when hackers gained access to information stored on its system by three prominent social media sites. The hackers downloaded e-mails from users who had contacted the social media sites' support departments.[212] Meanwhile, cyber risks are spreading beyond banks and retailers to prestigious law firms such as Cravath, Swaine & Moore and Weil Gotshal & Manges, whose computer networks were broken into by hackers. The attacks on law firms are particularly disturbing because, as third-party service providers, they hold trade secrets and highly sensitive information about their clients, including details about undisclosed mergers and acquisitions that could be stolen for insider-trading motives.[213]

Risks associated with third parties that are given access to the institution's network, data, and applications are vital oversight priorities for directors and management. Vendors, suppliers, partners, customers, or any third party connected electronically can become a potential point of vulnerability for the institution. Directors need to be particularly concerned about the immense amount of interconnection among systems, some of which operate in a way that is neither visible nor normally an area of board expertise.

Most institutions are now requiring that all contracts with third parties insure or indemnify against losses resulting from cyber intrusions or other noncompliance events. However, in some cases, accurately estimating the amount of potential or incurred losses can be problematic.

It is ironic that customers, business partners, and even government agencies expect total protection of precious assets and privacy, while they themselves may be the source of the compromised data, software, and networks.

It has become evident that cybersecurity needs to move away from the simplistic notion of a guaranteed shield of internal assets to the reality that major vulnerabilities can exist in those connections the institutions have to their outside world. In fact, some of the more notable breaches have come from the outside—that is, a breach originating from third parties with trusted connections where the perpetrator hacks into the institution's network. Protecting only the institution's perimeters is a misplaced belief that the secured perimeter approach is adequate.

In March 2015, the OCC and Federal Reserve issued two related statements regarding cybersecurity that reinforce the need for a new model. These regulatory statements establish that financial institutions should:

- Design multiple layers of security controls to establish lines of defense.
- Ensure that their risk management processes also address the risk posed by third parties.
- Ensure business continuity for resiliency and rapid recovery.

A financial institution that fails to observe the regulatory guidance could be subject to regulatory sanctions, including financial penalties. In addition to the extra costs of regulatory scrutiny (which could go on for a long while) and penalties, there are other risks, such as disruption of business operations, reputational risks, investment risks, and the loss of intellectual property.

Directors need to understand the approaches being taken for cybersecurity, and they need to possess a working knowledge of how these apply both to the institution and third parties. It requires teaming with business partners to boost immune systems.

---

[212] "PwC Viewpoint on Third Party Risk Management," PricewaterhouseCoopers, November 2013.
[213] "Hackers Hit Cravath, Weil Gotshal," *Wall Street Journal*, March 30, 2016.

Directors have a variety of available sources:

- The risk committee of the board normally will include cybersecurity in its charter. Those institutions without a risk committee rely on the audit committee to serve in this capacity.
- Insurance carriers who write risk policies can also be a good source for help. Underwriters perform their own assessment before they establish the premium for the risk policy.
- Federal law enforcement agencies, such as the National Security Agency and the FBI, are good sources of information on "best practices" and for intelligence on where the bad actors may target weak defenses.
- Technology vendors are always anxious to sell cybersecurity products and services. Intrusion detection and protection, and pattern recognition, are potentially the most critical tools for third-party defenses, and they are advancing quickly as machine-learning capabilities are becoming more robust.
- Third parties may themselves be a source of cybersecurity best practices. They need to protect their own environments and avoid intrusions.
- Legal counsel is an excellent source for establishing the ground rules for third parties, such as audits of third-party defenses and the contractual provisions for failures. Some institutions establish legal counsel as the nexus of all cybersecurity programs.

Board members need to appreciate that third-party risks involving cybersecurity may require transforming the culture. The focus needs to be shifted out of the silo of the IT department and viewed as a business risk that is both managed and integrated into the institution's strategy and operations.

Directors should think of the new cybersecurity model as a security ecology of the institution and all its extensions, using a holistic perspective on risks and mitigation, multiple technology and management techniques, and broad buy-in and accountability, layered and tailored to the threats and vulnerabilities. It requires management, with board oversight, to assess, actively manage, and hold accountable managers, employees, and business partners for their actions, and it avoids deflecting responsibility for a technology failure to the IT or security departments. It fundamentally employs the power of teaming within the institution and with third parties.

Implications for Directors

Given the increased interest from regulators, the recognition that third-party risk management is important to operational safety and soundness, and the market pressures that continue to drive the use of third parties, the board's careful oversight of third-party risk management is essential. Since board oversight is on the screen of regulators, directors must be persistent in obtaining information about how well third-party relationships are being managed and whether management is fully reporting to the board on third-party costs and risks.

The good news is that oversight of the third-party risk management program can be aligned with the institution's wider internal governance program and its risk management processes, if those are a good foundation. It is not necessary to create a whole new risk management approach and infrastructure.

Raising the Bar on Third-Party Risk Management

		Traditional programs	Best-in-class programs based on regulatory requirements
Management Approach	Scope	• Focused on vendors and managed as a part of the procurement process.	• Broader scope to include all third parties (including co-brand partners, joint ventures, fee-based or add-on services).
	Segmentation	• Primarily based on vendor size, resulting in lack of appropriate oversight for some high-risk smaller vendors.	• Risk-based segmentation, driven by the nature of risk the third party poses to the institution, with suitable controls to address the risk.
	Rules-based due diligence	• Primarily focused on financial assessment, business continuity, and information security.	• Includes assessment of compliance with regulations that govern the activity performed by the third party.
	Post-contract compliance management	• Audit activities/questions not focused on vendor-specific risks. • Scorecards primarily focused on performance indicators. • Some systematic tracking or reporting of third-party-related complaints.	• Audit questions and materials based on key breakpoints for that third party. • Supplemented with compliance and quality metrics to ensure monitoring of risks in addition to performance. • End-to-end process to capture, track, and report complaints is put in place.
	Governance/ escalation	• Owned by the business or vendor management. • Decisions made typically by vendor management and/or businesses with limited oversight. • Process for third-party-related incidents not clearly defined, resulting in inconsistent or inadequate escalation of incidents.	• Involvement of independent teams (such as compliance) in oversight activities. • Decisioning by senior cross-functional team, including representatives from legal, compliance, risk, and business. • Details of escalating incidents to ensure transparency on emerging risks and management involvement where necessary.
	Technology and tools	• Focused primarily on tracking third-party production performance data, with limited or no ability to track real-time risk performance data. • Limited or no enterprise-wide workflow management tools to ensure consistent risk management ownership across business units.	• Comprehensive source of third-party performance and risk-based data with clear records of risk management owners across businesses.

Source: "Managing Third-Party Risk in a Changing Regulatory Environment," by Dmitry Krivin, Hamid Samandari, John Walsh, and Emily Yueh, McKinsey & Company, May 2013.

Some boards and management are taking a proactive approach in expanding and integrating the third-party risk management program with their risk management and compliance functions, including board oversight. Taking a more gradual approach, awaiting more prescriptive regulatory guidance, or hoping for industry practices to marinate can result in significant criticisms from the regulators as they continue to conduct target reviews of third-party risk. Stakeholders, and possibly customers, will piggyback on these assessments if they are made public.

"The lack of an effective third-party risk management program, including appropriate board oversight, in most cases will be considered a substantive gap by the regulators under the OCC's guidelines given its potential impact on financial, operational, and reputational risks," noted Toby S. Myerson, partner, Paul, Weiss, Rifkind, Wharton & Garrison and a board member of MUFG Union Bank.

It is essential to clearly define and communicate the board's roles and responsibilities associated with third-party risk management. A formal charter for third-party risk governance is useful. The process needs to include third-party policies and procedures that are comprehensive, clear, and consistent with the strategic goals, objectives, and risk appetite.

The board needs to be engaged in determining the institution's risk posture and in defining what can and cannot be outsourced and to whom. The board's review of the identification and plans for third-party "critical activities," the review of management's monitoring of third parties and changing risks, and the oversight of independent reviews of the third-party risk processes are all essential "best practices" for directors.

While regulatory scrutiny and compliance pressures may offer plenty of reasons to take a closer look at third-party risk, directors and management should understand that forging stronger and safer third-party relationships has become a business imperative. In banking, for example, some institutions franchise their names to vendors, which in turn are offering more products and services on the bank's behalf. If these joint marketing arrangements are not handled properly, the fallout from them could potentially damage an institution's reputation and significantly impact its customer base and bottom line.[214]

Although the OCC's guidelines specifically suggest board approvals in a number of areas, directors need to be wary of taking executive actions. As in other areas of concern, the board can set parameters and standards, but it should avoid assuming management's operating responsibilities, which include negotiating and contracting with third parties.

The regulators and major stakeholders have an active interest in reviewing and ensuring comprehensive and sustainable processes of third-party risk management. Having an effective set of measures and processes in place is an investment that will provide yields beyond avoiding negative results. Directors should view third-party risk management in this important context.

---

[214] "Managing Vendor Risk: Considerations for Banks," by John Graetz, Walter Hoogmoed, Alfred Spahitz, and Christopher Spoth, Deloitte, January 30, 2013.

PART III

Disruptive Global Megatrends

Introduction to Part III: Disruptive Global Megatrends

"It is not the going out of port, but the coming in, that determines the success of a voyage."

— HENRY WARD BEECHER

A dramatic transition is under way as a result of fundamental disruptive forces, according to McKinsey & Company. Any one of these megatrends by itself would probably rank among the largest economic forces the global economy has ever seen, including the industrial revolution in advanced economies. Boards and management may call megatrends by different names, but they must organize their strategies in some way, shape, or form around them.[215]

These developments can play havoc with forecasts and pro forma plans that are made by extrapolating recent experience into the near and distant future. Many of the assumptions, tendencies, and habits that historically proved so successful may have lost much of their resonance. Although vast amounts of data are now available, forecasters are routinely caught unaware. Assumptions that drive decisions on critical issues such as consumption, resources, labor, capital, and competition now need to be reassessed, likely requiring recalibration of strategies, business plans, new markets, competitors, and talent initiatives.[216]

Transformative Global Trends

Question: Which of the following global trends do you believe will transform your business the most? Below are the top three trends named by CEOs.

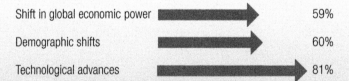

Shift in global economic power	59%
Demographic shifts	60%
Technological advances	81%

Source: "Fit for the Future: Capitalizing on Global Trends," Annual Global CEO Survey, PricewaterhouseCoopers, 2014.

In the past, directors and management typically knew their main competitors, and they often could catch up to the new competition that emerged. But competitive intensity has reached an entirely new level because technology gives an advantage to small, entrepreneurial companies over large, established businesses with huge infrastructures. Today, new competition is coming from a wave of rapidly growing newcomers that are simply not on

---

[215] *No Ordinary Disruption: The Four Global Forces Breaking All the Trends*, Richard Dobbs, James Manyika, and Jonathan Woetzel, PublicAffairs, 2015.
[216] Ibid.

the strategic radar and do not appear until they have amassed critical size. These newcomers play by a different set of rules, with lower cost bases and faster time to market.[217]

Disruption is the new normal in many industries, including financial services, which are experiencing dramatic changes in consumer behaviors, new business models, and evolving technologies. In banking, for example, new fintech disruptors are impacting the industry in significant ways across multiple business lines. To survive and remain competitive, institutions must translate the disruption and signals of change into business model strategy and operating models aimed at revenue optimization, cost reduction, and, importantly, risk reduction and mitigation.

Much as waves can amplify one another, global megatrends are gaining in strength, magnitude, and influence as they interact with, and feed upon, one another. Together, they are producing monumental change.

Three of these megatrends are described in Chapter 13. The first is the shift in economic power and dynamism to emerging markets like China and India. As recently as the year 2000, 95% of the Fortune Global 500, the world's largest industrial companies, were headquartered in developed countries. By the year 2025, when China will be home to more large companies than either the U.S. or Europe, almost half of the world's large companies, defined as those with revenues of $1 billion or more, will come from emerging-market countries.[218] Chapter 14 voyages through the risks in emerging-country markets, and Chapters 15 and 16 journey through the risks in doing business in China and India.

The second megatrend relates to changing demographics. Simply put, the human population is getting old. In many developed and some emerging-country markets, fertility is falling, and the world's population is graying dramatically. Aging and proportionally smaller workforces have been evident in developed-country markets for some time, but the demographic deficit is now spreading. Today, almost 60% of the world's population lives in countries with fertility rates below the replacement rate.[219] A smaller workforce will result in a rethinking of economic growth potentials and talent challenges. Chapter 17 sojourns through the risks associated with an aging world.

The third megatrend is the acceleration in the scope, scale, and economic impact of technology. Processing power and connectivity are only part of the story. Their impact is multiplied by the concomitant data revolution—which places unprecedented amounts of information in the hands of consumers and businesses—and the proliferation of technology-enabled business models. The furious pace of technological adoption and innovation is shortening the life cycles of companies and forcing management to make decisions and commit resources much more quickly. Chapter 18 traverses through one important aspect of this tsunami, focusing on the risks in using big data and advanced analytics.

The impacts of these disruptive forces are becoming regular topics in today's boardrooms, leading directors and managements to redirect the course of their strategies and redefine the risk profiles. They are driven by both the short-term need to enhance results and the long-term call to ensure sustainability and avoid decline or even irrelevance.

---

[217] Ibid.

[218] "Urban World: The Shifting Global Business Landscape," by Richard Dobbs, Jaana Remes, Sven Smit, James Manyika, Jonathan Woetzel, and Yaw Agyenim-Boateng, McKinsey Global Institute, October 2013.

[219] "The Global Spread of Fertility Decline: Population, Fear and Uncertainty," Jay Winter and Michael Teitelbaum, Yale University Press, 2013.

Embracing Global Megatrends

"Change is the law of life, and those who look only to the past or to the present are certain to miss the future."

— JOHN F. KENNEDY

Megatrends are not predictions but macroeconomic certainties, events with global ramifications that are already unfolding and affecting businesses. Many megatrends are global in that they have concrete and lasting impacts on businesses in multiple geographies and in various ways. And although global-scale shifts can be intimidating, they present unique and transformative opportunities for boards and management that are able to grasp the implications and adjust strategies, especially for institutions that aspire to global status. They also present sizable threats.

Many directors spend the bulk of their board time on regulatory reports, audit reviews, budgets, and compliance instead of concentrating on the longer-term and highly impactful trends crucial to the future direction and prosperity of the business. By habit, boards also tend to concentrate on the mature markets they know rather than those that are up-and-coming and far away.

But tomorrow's world will be different.

What directors face today are disruptive changes to business models and even entire industries. Whereas previously innovations might have taken a decade or more to transform an industry, the time frame continues to shrink, leaving very little time for boards and management to react. Sustaining a business model in the face of digitally enabled competition requires constant innovation to stay ahead of the change curve.

Corporate governance arguably suffers most when directors spend too much time looking in the rearview mirror and insufficient effort scanning the horizon ahead. This puts corporate survival and sustainability at a premium. The time companies spend in the S&P 500 Index is shrinking dramatically. At the current churn rate, 75% of the S&P 500 will be replaced by the year 2027, according to a prediction by the strategy consulting firm Innosight.[220]

Many boards are vigorously attempting to keep abreast. According to a survey of directors conducted by PricewaterhouseCoopers, 76% of directors say they look at long-

---

[220] "The Lifespans of Top Companies Are Shrinking," Reuters, February 13, 2012.

term, economic, geopolitical, and environmental macro-trends, and 71% of directors consider emerging technology advances when evaluating strategy. Additionally, nearly six out of 10 board members study competitor initiatives that could introduce disruptive approaches.[221]

As with most other matters, the board and its designated committees should follow management's lead in identifying and responding to trends. But many management teams are tempted, if not compelled, to adopt a short-term view, so there are times when management is the last to see big changes or disruptions on the horizon.

"While management grapples with the immediate challenges of volatile markets and day-to-day operations, it is vital that directors remain cognizant of what is coming. Boards need to spend time looking to the future, and to global megatrends, and raise red flags when necessary," said Andrew J. Policano, dean emeritus and professor, the Paul Merage School of Business, University of California, Irvine, and a board member of both Rockwell Collins and Badger Meter Inc.

The list of megatrends is long, but three global megatrends that directors should have on their radar screen are the shift in economic power, demographic changes, and the proliferation of information. The interactions between these megatrends will continue to impact businesses today and well beyond.

Country Groupings

Emerging-Country Markets	Advanced-Country Markets
Brazil	Canada
China	France
India	Germany
Indonesia	Japan
Mexico	Singapore
Poland	Taiwan
Russia	United Kingdom
South Africa	United States
United Arab Emirates	South Korea

Frontier-Country Markets
Mongolia
Morocco
Myanmar
Pakistan
Panama
Philippines
Sierra Leone

Source: Longview Global Advisors, 2015

---

[221] "Governing for the Long-term: PWC's Annual Corporate Directors Survey," PricewaterhouseCoopers, 2015.

Shift in Economic Power

The International Monetary Fund's annual forecast for 2015 indicated that emerging country markets will continue to be the primary drivers of global economic growth. While the expansion in these markets has slowed, these countries are still expected to grow in 2016 by 4.7%—compared to an average of 2.4% for advanced economies—as the relative impact of North American, Japanese, and Western European markets continues to diminish.

The world's center of economic gravity is tipping toward the east and south. Longer-term favorable trends related to urbanization, demographics, and rising income levels will continue to make rapid growth markets both an alternative source and a destination for global businesses.[222]

For boards and management, the shift in economic power is triggering major adjustments in strategic thinking. Emerging-country markets can no longer be treated as a sideshow, but making them core to the business requires some difficult shifts.

"Directors need to be vigilant. We are seeing more examples where decisions and events in one location can have a direct impact on the other side of the globe. The old world order is dissolving along with many previously safe assumptions about the business environment," noted Brian Cullinan, partner, PricewaterhouseCoopers.

A realignment of global economic and business activity is transitioning growth countries from centers of labor and production to consumption-oriented economies. This shifting center of gravity is creating a new level of complexity that boards and management must navigate.

Historical and Projected GDP Levels		
	2009	**2050 (Forecast)**
GDP (U.S., Japan, Germany, U.K., France, Italy, Canada)	$29.0 trillion	$69.3 trillion
GDP (China, India, Russia, Indonesia, Mexico, Turkey)	$20.9 trillion	$138.2 trillion
Source: "Five Megatrends and Possible Implications," PricewaterhouseCoopers, April 2014.		

And this is not just about China. According to the U.S. Department of Agriculture's macroeconomic projections, by the year 2030 India will become the world's third-largest economy, while Brazil's economy will rank sixth. To varying degrees, the Association of Southeast Asian Nations (ASEAN) countries, Latin America, and Africa are helping to drive this economic shift as well, and the shift in consumer power is likely to be even greater.

Although incomes have stagnated for years in many advanced countries, incomes and the size of the middle class are growing rapidly in emerging-country markets. Over the next two decades, it is estimated that the middle class will expand by another 3

---

[222] "Hitting the Sweet Spot: The Growth of the Middle Class in Emerging Markets," Ernst & Young, 2013.

billion people, coming almost exclusively from the emerging world. Ernst & Young projects that, by the year 2030, two-thirds of the global middle class will be residents of the Asia Pacific region, up from just under one-third in the year 2009. China and India will become the powerhouses of middle-class consumerism. Regardless of exactly how the forecasts play out, it is clear that there will be radical shifts in the distribution of wealth and the economic balance.[223]

Homes of the World's Largest Companies: The Fortune Global 500

Year	1980	2000	2013	2025 (Forecast)
Emerging-Country Markets	23	24	130	229
Developed Country Markets	477	476	370	271

Source: *No Ordinary Disruption: The Four Global Forces Breaking All the Trends*, by Richard Dobbs, James Manyika, and Jonathan Woetzel, PublicAffairs, 2015.

Emerging-country markets are not homogeneous, and even though all seemed to be rising in unison several years ago, their performance is increasingly diverging. Growth in China is slowing as the leadership seeks to shift the economy away from a dependence on capital investment and low-cost exports toward domestic consumption and innovation. India is looking to boost foreign investment and leverage its talent pool. Meanwhile, Brazil is facing stagflation and a crisis in confidence, as corrupt activities tear at the country's fabric. Each market has unique characteristics that boards and management must understand and be prepared to meet.

The economic shift accompanies the rise of powerful new political actors and business practices, standards, and values that are decidedly not Western. Many important economic and trade linkages are decreasingly led by or dependent upon Western participants. In many emerging-country markets, Western firms face local incumbents that enjoy state sponsorship, and the shift in economic and political power is making it easier for these upstarts to compete both at home and abroad.

Additionally, risks in these markets often are downplayed as a result of their high growth rates. Western ideals and regulatory transparency are looming larger and more difficult to drive on a global basis.

While many institutions describe themselves as global, in reality they are multinational. With such organizational complexity come new risks. Boards and management will need to concentrate on markets where they have comparative advantages and where the risks can be properly identified, calibrated, and mitigated. They also will need to redouble efforts to imbue a uniform culture and operating principles even as the number of geographies and cultural orientations of staff and management expand. "Strategies need to become simpler and more focused even as management navigates the nuances of a greater number of markets," noted Ronald L. Merriman, a board member of Pentair Inc., Aircastle Limited, Harmonetics Corporation, and Realty Income Corporation.

---

[223] Ibid.

Demographic Changes

Countries have very different demographic trajectories. Some countries are young and growing, creating ever larger labor forces and consumer markets. Their economies are expanding. Others are aging rapidly and their workforces are constrained as a share of the population. Their economies are shrinking.

Within the next decade, the world's population will be 10% larger, but it will also be different. Even more important from a business perspective will be the reduction in poverty and the rise of emerging-market middle classes. An often less appreciated, but highly disruptive, demographic trend is the aging of the world's population.

Demographic shifts caused by slow—or no—population growth in some countries are causing a massive redistribution of the world's workforce. And since work is what generates wealth, this will have an immense bearing on future consumption patterns as well. In a survey of CEOs conducted by PricewaterhouseCoopers, 60% of the respondents cite demographic shifts as a very important trend transforming business.[224]

Population aging, which translates into not having enough workers, exacerbates the problem. Given current trends, by the year 2050 developed-country markets will have twice as many older people than children.[225]

Total World Population Aged 60 Years or More			
Year	**1950**	**2000**	**2050 (Forecast)**
Proportion of total	8%	10%	21%
Source: "Five Megatrends and Possible Implications," PricewaterhouseCoopers, April 2014.			

Businesses will need to understand the types of products and services these new consumers seek because preferences in these markets vary. Many boards and management are only beginning to grapple with the complexity of developing for the middle classes in these markets products and services that are preferred to those of their local competitors. Capitalizing on these new consumer markets requires management to go beyond the conventional approach of developing products and services at reduced costs and then exporting affordable, scaled-down versions. This will add complexity, which can be difficult to identify and manage.

Reaching these new consumers will require investments in new skills and capabilities. Boards and management must, in order to get the model right, reevaluate their approaches to marketing, R&D, branding, logistics, and other core business functions.

Changes in demographics serve to reinforce the precept that talent is and will continue to be the main engine of business. Management regularly cites lack of talent as their top constraint to growth. Despite the expanding global population, however, the availability of skilled workers is actually shrinking as business and economic opportu-

[224] "Fit for the Future: Capitalizing on Global Trends," Annual Global CEO Survey, PricewaterhouseCoopers, 2014.
[225] "World Population Prospects," United Nations Department of Economic and Social Affairs, Population Division, June 2013.

nities grow. The war for talent is becoming increasingly acute in a number of important geographies and sectors that require high skill levels and advanced education.

The need for knowledge workers will continue. Recruiting, training, and retaining top talent is becoming a critical and daunting challenge, particularly in emerging-country markets where businesses are growing fastest.

In aging economies, the workforce needs to be retooled in order to address the growing mismatch between the skills employers need and the talent that is available. Older workers will need to learn new skills and work longer. More women need to enter the workforce, and the migration of workers needs to be accelerated in some geographies.

A number of strategies are being deployed to address the aging workforce. For example, policies and practices are being considered or put into place to 1) assess the impact of retiring workers; 2) address skill shortages due to attrition; 3) create an environment that attracts talent of all ages; 4) manage a multigenerational workforce; and 5) build a brand that attracts and retains talent. None of these strategies is easy to implement, but for directors and managements all have become essential.

Proliferation of Information

Technology, with its emphasis on digital, continues to drive the acceleration of innovation, interconnectivity, and investment. It is spurring the proliferation of information. Boards and management across all sectors are grappling with how breakthroughs with the Internet, mobile devices, data analytics, and cloud computing are transforming business and how this is impacting consumers in different geographies and cultures.

Nicholas G. Moore, who serves on the boards of Bechtel Group Inc. and Gilead Sciences Inc., has witnessed the proliferation of data in multiple industries. "Satisfying the technology needs of consumers and businesses is leading to a spectacular expansion in the growth in information and analytics, new competition, and the disruption and realignment of industries," he said.

Megatrends: The Digital Future

- The digital transformation is changing business models.
- Declining personal computer usage and increasing adoption of mobile devices is driving a "mobile first" world.
- Digital disruption is changing the market context and competitive landscape in most industries.
- As cyber threats continue to multiply, it is becoming more difficult to safeguard data, intellectual property, and personal information.
- Work styles and the means to engage talent are becoming more agile in the digital world.
- Digital and robotic technologies will increasingly augment or replace workers.

Source: "Megatrends 2015: Making Sense of a World in Motion," Ernst & Young, 2015.

The digital push has put more power in the hands of more people than ever before. The amount of data will continue to explode, forcing management to transform business models to optimize performance. Cloud computing and mobile technologies have become mainstream, while mobile devices are increasingly replacing personal computers. The sophistication of data analytics and the reach of social media are extending into every aspect of business.

Advances in technology spurring the information revolution have lowered the barriers to entry in many industries. Some of the most disruptive new players are coming from completely unexpected quarters. However, in some sectors, such as financial services, the requisite large investments associated with information, technology, and storage can be obstacles to entry, differentiation, and sustainability. Only those institutions that make large and sustained investments in new hardware and software, new data analytics tools and storage, cybersecurity, and skilled talent can realistically aspire to remain competitive and relevant.

In the PricewaterhouseCoopers survey, 81% of the CEOs cite technological advances as the global trend most transforming business. Business analytics attracts the greatest investment.[226]

The ability to gather and analyze data in real time has become a differentiating competitive advantage and of crucial importance. Research reports, records, and sensors embedded in cars, appliances, and even clothing make up an increasing percentage of the business value in many products and services. The proliferation of information has given birth to a new generation of consumers. Technology raises the expectations of consumers, sharpening their demands for personalized information that is tailored to their specific needs. Consumers are swapping information and advice on the virtual airwaves. They now want ever more accessible, portable, flexible, and customized products, services, and experiences.

A survey by New Vantage Partners finds that the number of institutions using big data in the past three years has surged 58 percentage points to a 63% penetration. Meanwhile, 70% of the respondents say that big data is of critical importance to their firms, a jump from 21% noted in the year 2012.[227]

Rise of the Connected Devices

Year	2003	2010	2020 (Forecast)
World population (in billions)	6.3	6.8	7.6
Connected devices per person	0.08	1.84	6.58

Source: Cisco Internet Business Solutions Group, 2014.

While consumers want more powerful devices and applications, businesses seek more powerful and cost-effective solutions to harness the onslaught of data. Technology is driving the transformation of the delivery of goods and services. Although technology and information will not always deliver massive cost reductions, they can allow for much

---

[226] "Fit for the Future: Capitalizing on Global Trends," 2014.
[227] "The Big Data Future Has Arrived," *The Wall Street Journal*, February 23, 2016.

better results at similar costs. In addition, access to information and systems can enable the flattening of organizational structures.

Along with the opportunities, a world filled with an abundance of information and new technologies poses new and significant risks associated with breaches of security and the misuse of information. This is especially the case in the area of cybersecurity, where corporate reputation is increasingly connected to market performance.

Although some directors may feel uncomfortable or inadequate in this domain, it is essential that all board members become sufficiently knowledgeable to ask informed questions. "Information and technology have clearly moved from the back office to the corner office and now to the boardroom. Irrespective of the industry or sector, all institutions have become technology centric," said Bala Iyer, a board member of Skyworks Solutions, IHS Inc., and Power Integrations Inc.

Leveraging the Megatrends

Muhtar Kent, chairman and CEO, The Coca-Cola Company, said that as economic growth shifts rapidly, consumer products and goods companies need to adapt with the right products in the right stores at the right prices and at the right time to meet the needs of new consumers. [228]

Boards and management that can align around an accurate vision of the future by understanding the opportunities and appreciating the risks, and have the agility to act on them, will have a distinctly strategic advantage. The Boston Consulting Group articulates best practices for leveraging megatrends, as follows:

- Treat every megatrend as a new phenomenon, even if it has been around for a while. The question is not whether it is new but whether strategic plans have kept up with its growth and development.
- Develop a network of experts on critical trends who can challenge management and keep them up-to-date on the latest developments, providing an information advantage over competitors.
- Explore emerging megatrends, even if they seem too small to move the dial. They will get bigger.
- Explore the business model implications of important megatrends. Which competitors, products, and services are well positioned? Can the current business model capture the opportunities and risks either as is or with no more than modest changes? Is an entirely new model required?
- Directors need to see for themselves. "Learning journeys" with customers, markets, and trend experts foster a visceral understanding and alignment around the strategic implications of megatrends.
- Look across categories and industries to obtain a holistic view of a megatrend's influence. Know the institution's blind spots and threats.
- Act quickly once a megatrend promises an opportunity or a threat. The exponential growth of these trends shortens the window for response time.[229]

---

[228] "Fit for the Future: Capitalizing on Global Trends," 2014.
[229] "Megatrends: Tailwinds for Growth in a Low-Growth Environment," The Boston Consulting Group, 2010.

Implications for Directors

The global landscape is changing as new customers and markets emerge, creating enormous opportunities and, along with them, new competitors and new risks. The biggest challenge facing directors is not responding to what is known but rather learning how to respond in an environment where the circumstances and competition are changing daily.

The megatrends are inevitably creating a far more complex and diverse operating environment. The future includes powerful technologies, more information, and new actors. It is not a straightforward rollout of Western products, practices, standards, and values. Understanding the sources of volatility and how to mitigate them is essential.

As boards and management look to the future, it has become evident that executing on established assumptions may no longer be sufficient. "Multiple business strategies are prudent and should be developed. Given the uncertainties and likely disruptions ahead, it is unwise to develop strategic plans around a single set of assumptions or only one or two possible scenarios," advised James T. Morris, chairman and CEO of Pacific Life Insurance Company.

Operating any business requires taking risks. Institutions that identify and manage these risks are well positioned to grow and remain successful. Directors are challenged with overseeing a rapidly changing global landscape. The risks include market volatility, geopolitical crisis, economic changes, regulatory reforms, and cyber threats.

"Megatrends, such as the expansion of the emerging-country markets, the aging of the population and use of data, the rise of hyper-connectivity, and geographic mobility, are all having direct impacts. While these trends and developments represent threats, they also present unique opportunities provided the risks are properly and thoughtfully managed," noted Andrew G. McMaster, a board member of both UBS Americas Holding and Black & Veatch Corporation.

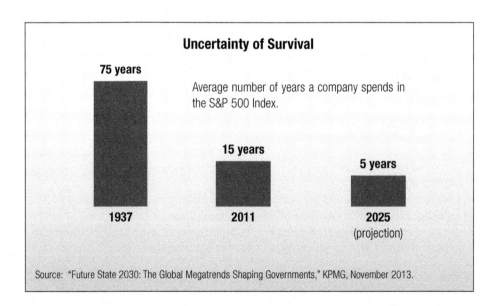

Uncertainty of Survival

75 years

Average number of years a company spends in the S&P 500 Index.

15 years

5 years

1937

2011

2025
(projection)

Source: "Future State 2030: The Global Megatrends Shaping Governments," KPMG, November 2013.

In the new world, it is essential for boards and managements to avoid having their businesses "die in good health." In other words, the business possesses accurate financials with the proper disclosures, but it is executing on an antiquated strategy. The most significant risk may be from "slow failures" or "creeping risks," where the longer-term implications of the megatrends have been vastly underestimated or even ignored.

The responsibility of directors is to engage in critical and relevant discussions, form independent opinions, and work closely with management to ensure goals are well formulated and subsequently met. Directors must gain sufficient insight to ensure they are in a position to provide management with thoughtful, meaningful counsel—and also to exercise skepticism regarding the company's plans, which can be particularly difficult given that global megatrends are often complex, subject to rapid change, and occur in far-off places. Directors need not be experts on emerging-country markets, demographics, and information technology, but it is essential that they have the ability and strength to ask informed, and sometimes difficult, questions.

Boards need to be populated with directors who have insight into worldly developments and trends and who possess both a strategic and international perspective, which is sometimes difficult to find in the boardroom. "Boards today need directors with a global view given the megatrends and the rapid pace of change. Although sometimes this experience and expertise may be lacking, boards that are committed to adding an international perspective find ways to overcome the obstacles," noted Caroline A. Nahas, vice chairman, Korn/Ferry International, and a board member of Dine Equity Inc.

Directors can counsel management to stay the course and attempt to deliver on the current business models, or instead adapt and adjust to the new operating reality. Change is a double-edged sword. It presents an opportunity to take a business to another level. Conversely, it can be a sign of the beginning of the end. Whichever side of the change curve directors and management find themselves, few disagree that the megatrends and disruptive changes cannot be taken lightly. The essential point is to embrace their inevitability.

*Portions of this chapter were taken from an article written by Dean A. Yoost and D.J. Peterson, "Embracing Global Megatrends," for *NACD Directorship*, March/April 2015.

Questions Directors Should Ask About the Global Megatrends

Strategy

- Which opportunities and threats are presented by the global megatrends? Are the existing long- and short-term strategies relevant, given these trends?
- Does management have a clear view of the global landscape, including nontraditional challenges from other markets, sectors, or competitors? Are appropriate strategies in place to respond to competitive actions?
- In what ways are the operating model and costs aligned with changing markets? Are they responsive to consumer demands?

Shift in economic power

- Is management prepared for emerging-country markets becoming core markets? How is the institution positioned in each of these markets?
- Does the institution have the right talent, cultural understanding, age profile, experience, and skills to establish credibility and relationships with critical stakeholders, such as the regulators and key business leaders in emerging-country markets?
- How are the unique risks and higher risk profiles managed in the emerging-country markets?

Demographic changes

- Which threats are presented by the demographic changes?
- How are products and services modified to fit the new consumer markets?
- How well prepared is management to recruit, train, and retain tomorrow's workforce while dealing with today's talent challenges?
- How are the aging workforce, rising education levels, and enhanced requisite skills addressed in global resource planning?

Proliferation of information

- How does management use information and metrics on performance, trends, customers, and competitors? What are the plans for deploying analytics to provide competitive advantage?
- Does management have a digital strategy and the skills to execute?
- How is management leveraging the newer technologies, such as social media and cloud-based services, data analytics, security and privacy, and virtualization solutions?
- How is management addressing the new risks in using big data?

Risks in Emerging-Country Markets

"Do not go where the path may lead, but go instead where there is no path and leave a trail."

RALPH WALDO EMERSON

Once attractive only for their natural resources and as a source of cheap labor and low-cost manufacturing, emerging countries are now seen as promising markets in their own right. Rapid population growth, sustained economic development, and a growing middle class are making boards and management look at emerging-country markets in a whole new way.

The boards of global companies are struggling with evolutionary changes affecting their businesses, as domestic growth prospects wane in the U.S. and opportunities expand in the emerging countries. Ernst & Young predicts that 70% of world growth will come from these emerging markets, with China and India accounting for 40% of that growth.[230] Honeywell International, a multinational conglomerate, has doubled the size of its non-U.S. business in the past 10 years, driven by growth in the emerging-country markets. The company's businesses in China and India have been growing more than 20% annually since the year 2004.[231]

But these are challenging times. China's economy is expanding at the slowest pace in some time, and the annual growth in once-booming emerging markets like Brazil and Russia has slowed. The challenges, however, go beyond volatility. Fundamental, longer-term changes are transforming the competitive landscape. In many emerging-country markets, local businesses with low cost structures and intimate knowledge of the market are more aggressive and improving their capabilities. Competition for increasingly scarce talent is fierce and driving up labor costs.[232]

Emerging-country markets promise access to new customers with rising levels of consumption, access to low-cost labor and materials, outsourcing opportunities, and increasingly sophisticated research and development capabilities and capacity. However, these markets pose unique and significant risks that sometimes are ignored in the rush

---

[230] "Tracking Global Trends: How Six Key Developments Are Shaping the Business World," Ernst & Young, 2011.
[231] "Guide to Emerging Markets: The Business Outlook, Opportunities, and Obstacles," *The Economist*, 2014.
[232] "Time to Reengage with, Not Retreat from, Emerging Markets," Bernd Waltermann, David Michael, and Dinesh Khanna, The Boston Consulting Group, 2014.

to seize an opportunity. Given the allure, boards and management tend to overemphasize potential rewards and underestimate the inherent risks.

Investments and commitments in these markets will continue to evolve from new, exciting opportunities into business imperatives. "Although the growth prospects can be seductive, they cannot be painted with the same brush. Some of these markets are riskier than others, and the levels of risk change over time. Directors need to understand the nature of the risks and provide thoughtful commentary on the challenges and mitigations," noted Gregory M. E. Spierkel, board member of PACCAR Inc., MGM Resorts International, and Schneider Electric.

The traditional approaches to doing business in emerging-country markets are now being challenged by multiple market-based, macroeconomic, and competitive factors, such as the following:

- Local businesses in emerging-country markets are growing stronger and more competitive. They have the advantage of lower overhead costs and lower wages. Stiffer price competition also exists as foreign investors expand middle markets, where a need for lower prices decreases profitability.
- As the economies of emerging-country markets become more advanced, foreign investors find rising labor costs at the same time revenues are declining. Meanwhile, the productivity of skilled workers in emerging-country markets lags behind that of developed-country markets.
- Foreign investors are losing their ability to recruit employees as local companies gain ground. Also, increased confidence in local businesses has led governments to be less accommodating to foreign investors in policies and regulations.[233]

Although success in these markets has become more challenging than in the past, greater opportunities exist and remain much stronger in most emerging-country markets than in those markets that already have been developed.

While the board's risk oversight in emerging-country markets may not be substantially different from that exercised in developed-country markets, it does require consideration of distinctive characteristics and an international view. "The board's oversight of global matters is challenging, complex, and multilayered, so that directors need to be aware and proactive. Boards often are stretched to provide the proper perspective," said Gary Daichendt, a board member of NCR Corp., Juniper Networks, and Polycom Inc.

Among the more formidable risks in these markets are political and policy instability, bribery and corruption, non-transparency of information, culture and customs, influence of government, talent shortages, intellectual property protection, failure to diversify, dominance of family conglomerates, overspending of resources, and local competitive threats.

Political and Policy Instability

"Political risk" refers to uncertainty regarding adverse political decisions. The risk that a government will indiscriminately change the laws, regulations, or contracts—or fail to enforce them—is referred to as "policy risk."

---

[233] "Transformation in Emerging Markets: From Growth to Competitiveness," by Christoph Nettesheim, Lars Faeste, Dinesh Khanna, Bernd Waltermann, and Peter Ullrich, The Boston Consulting Group, February 2016.

Overt seizures of assets by governments in emerging-country markets are remnants of the past and have essentially disappeared. However, other risks to assets and investments, such as potential regulatory actions, have dramatically increased.[234] Potential destabilizers include the possibility of war, tax increases, loss of subsidies, a change in market policies, inability to control inflation, and changes in laws regarding resource extraction.

Developed countries tend to follow a free-market discipline of low government interruption, whereas emerging-country markets are not infrequently privatized upon demand. In many of the emerging-country markets, the basic ingredients necessary to allow productivity to rise are absent. Many of these economies remain highly regulated and are often run for the benefit of their leaders. They can also be socially fractious or may pursue noneconomic priorities such as territorial ambitions. Recognizing the imperfections in these environments, boards and management need to be able to identify those geographies with the best chances of sustained growth and containable risks.[235]

The absence of reliable or consistent governance from recognized government authorities adds to business risks and costs, reducing management's ability to forecast business conditions and predict results.

Political instability frequently is associated with corruption and weak legal frameworks, discouraging investment and the further development of a healthy, reliable business environment. In Russia, for example, evolving conditions often threaten business plans, as bureaucratic practices have long favored well-connected, domestic companies, harming the confidence of international investors. The turmoil in Ukraine is an example of difficulties that boards and management of global companies can face in emerging-country markets. Russia's move into Crimea may have been a surprise, but after a similar move into Georgia in 2008, it should hardly have come as a shock.[236]

Governments tend to play rougher in the emerging-country markets. In their enthusiasm to exploit the opportunities, boards and management sometimes do not take the political and policy risks seriously enough.

Bribery and Corruption

Anticipating and addressing corrupt activities requires a constancy of board awareness, as corrupt politicians, bureaucrats, and business leaders exist and operate overtly in many of the emerging-country markets. Tax collectors in China, for example, regularly ask for bribes to relax inspections and assessments, to refrain from pursuing acts of tax avoidance, or to give advice through separate consulting arrangements on the possibilities of reducing tax obligations. Sometimes, high-level politicians and local business leaders are swept up in the investigations of corrupt activities, as in Brazil when a bid-

---

[234] "The Hidden Risks in Emerging Markets," by Witold J. Henisz and Bennet A. Zelner, *Harvard Business Review*, April 2010.
[235] "Guide to Emerging Country Markets: The Business Outlook, Opportunities, and Obstacles," 2014._
[236] "Submerging Hopes," *The Economist*, March 8, 2014.

rigging-and-bribery scandal probe centered on the state oil company Petrobras, which sent the country spiraling downward into a crisis over graft.[237]

Directors are ultimately responsible, but they are sometimes viewed as out of touch with conditions on the ground. While it is inevitable that directors will have a less detailed understanding of the business and the conditions on the ground than management, board members need to be deep enough into the details of the operations to be able to focus on key areas of potential bad behavior.

The board of any U.S. company seeking to do business in emerging-country markets needs to have a clear understanding of its duties and responsibilities under the Foreign Corrupt Practices Act (FCPA), signed into law in 1977, and other international laws, such as the United Kingdom's Bribery Act of 2010. The reputational and economic ramifications of misinterpreting these duties and responsibilities can have long-lasting impacts on operations and reputations.

The FCPA has a wide reach and applies to U.S. issuers, other domestic concerns (both individuals and businesses), U.S. parent companies of foreign subsidiaries, and foreign companies and individuals, including their agents. While these laws apply to the bribery of foreign government officials, they do not apply to bribery of third parties in business relationships.

Investigations and prosecutions, the number of fines, and the size of the penalties under the FCPA have risen dramatically. As evidenced by the U.K.'s Bribery Act, regulators' heightened focus on corrupt activities is not confined to the United States. Regulators in some of these markets are following the U.S. and U.K. regulators in stepping up their efforts. India introduced legislation to establish an anti-corruption watchdog. Brazil is often cited for its strong legal framework aimed at eliminating corruption and sometimes is used as a model when establishing legal anti-corruption frameworks. However, Brazil's enforcement of the laws is inconsistent and, for the most part, disappointing and blatantly ineffective.

To protect against charges of bribery and corruption, companies need to keep books, records, and accounts that accurately reflect transactions and the disposition of assets. Internal accounting and management controls must be maintained and aimed at preventing and detecting FCPA violations, establishing policies and procedures that explain how business is to be conducted, performing due diligence on and monitoring of third parties, and conducting training for employees and business partners.

There is no doubt the board has a duty with respect to FCPA compliance. The Federal Sentencing Guidelines indicate that a board must be knowledgeable about the company's compliance program and must exercise reasonable oversight.

In 2012, the Department of Justice and the Securities and Exchange Commission jointly released their "Resource Guide to the U.S. Foreign Corrupt Practices Act." The guide demonstrates their shared commitment in fighting corruption through continued vigorous enforcement of the FCPA. Although the guide does not have the force of law, it does represent the evolving views of the DOJ and SEC based on years of enforcement activity and reviews of private and public companies' compliance programs. Perhaps most significantly, the guide underscores the importance of a compliance program to

---

[237] "Brazil Descends into Crisis Over Graft," *The Wall Street Journal*, March 18, 2016.

prevent and detect corrupt activity as a factor in determining the size and force of any enforcement actions.

Ten Elements of Effective Compliance Programs

- *Commitment from management and a clearly articulated policy against corruption.* Management and directors alike are responsible for conveying a strong message that corruption will not be tolerated.
- *Code of conduct and compliance policies and procedures.* A code of conduct provides ethical guidelines for those conducting business on the company's behalf. A company may also have specific anti-corruption policies and procedures that address the most significant risks and outline proper internal controls and monitoring procedures.
- *Oversight, autonomy, and resources.* Responsibility for the compliance program should be assigned to an appropriate senior individual or group to provide the authority and autonomy to oversee the program and report to the company's governing body.
- *Risk assessment.* A company's compliance program should be designed around and commensurate with its unique risk profile, taking into account factors such as its size, structure, industry, geography, interactions with foreign governments, and involvement of business partners. A thorough risk assessment adds efficiency and credibility to anti-corruption compliance efforts.
- *Training and continuing advice.* A company should take steps to ensure that all employees are aware of the company's anti-corruption policies and procedures, which is often accomplished through periodic training. Certain key roles, such as management, sales, business development, and personnel, may receive enhanced training.
- *Incentives and disciplinary actions.* To avoid the appearance of a "paper program," the corporate compliance program must be enforced unequivocally throughout the organization and clear disciplinary procedures for violators applied in a timely and consistent way. Positive incentives, both financial and other merit-based rewards, may reinforce a culture of compliance.
- *Third-party due diligence and payments.* A risk-based due diligence approach identifies and devotes attention to third parties posing the greatest corruption risk.
- *Confidential reporting and internal investigation.* Employees and third parties should be encouraged to share tips or suspected violations in a secure and confidential manner. Significant issues should ultimately be investigated by qualified individuals.
- *Continuous improvement through periodic testing and review.* Companies should perform periodic testing or anti-corruption audits to monitor compliance with the various elements and controls of the program and to uncover potential violations and red flags signaling new corruption risks.
- *Pre-acquisition due diligence and post-acquisition integration.* An acquirer is responsible for conducting thorough due diligence of a potential target company, which extends to evaluating potential corrupt activity by the target.

Source: "Resource Guide to the U.S. Foreign Corrupt Practices Act," Department of Justice and the Securities and Exchange Commission, November 14, 2012.

Many elements in the resource guide are similar to leading practices already accepted by most global companies, but it also provides important direction on how to further develop and implement governance programs. The guide also acknowledges that small and medium-size companies will have compliance programs different from those of large multinationals and, in doing so, implies that cost and size are factors in the measures companies should take to achieve compliance.

The guide suggests that more than 90% of reported FCPA cases involve the use of third-party intermediaries such as agents or consultants. As a result, this is a central focus of many anti-corruption efforts, and the degree of due diligence for each third party should be commensurate with the risks posed by that third party. The guide supports a risk-based approach that includes the following:

- Pre-contract due diligence to assess the third party's qualifications, reputation, and connections to foreign officials.
- An understanding of the business purpose and services being provided by the third party and a guarantee that payment terms are in line with the services provided.
- Monitoring of third parties with controls such as periodic due diligence, training for third parties, and exercising contractual audit rights.

While the implementation of an effective compliance program is an operational imperative, the related legal issues are complex and often open to interpretation. Informed and experienced legal guidance is essential. Moreover, legal considerations do not end at interpretation of the FCPA but may also be related to other laws. For example, it is not uncommon for an internal whistleblower to expose compliance issues. In a 12-month period ending September 2012, the SEC's Office of the Whistleblower received 115 specific FCPA whistleblower claims, with China one of the most prominent sources.[238] Whistleblowers have specific protections and incentives under the 2010 amendment of the Securities Exchange Act of 1934, the Dodd-Frank Act, and the Consumer Protection Act. Effective handling of whistleblower claims is an added level of complexity in managing compliance issues and should be visible to the board.

The internal and external costs of investigating whistleblower allegations in these markets are not insignificant, requiring bicultural and bilingual resources. Many claims are unfounded and the result of misunderstandings or misinterpretations of company policy. However, given the potential criticality of whistleblower allegations, they must be extensively pursued and dealt with as a cost of doing business. These costs can be mitigated by hiring and educating the right employees.

Compliance is an area that requires both locally focused and expert advice. Ultimately, the successful implementation of a robust day-to-day compliance program is the responsibility of management—formed by the company's culture, established by board leadership, and enabled by management and external subject experts.

The establishment of effective compliance management systems, and management's monitoring and auditing of compliance, should be apparent to the board. Proper structuring of the reporting relationships of the compliance function indicates, both internally and externally, the importance of compliance. The board should ensure that the talent committed to compliance management and reporting relationships is commensurate with the level of compliance risk.

---

[238] "Annual Report on the Dodd-Frank Whistleblower Program," Securities and Exchange Commission, 2012.

"It is important to achieve balance between expectations, financial incentives, and compliance risk. Overly optimistic growth expectations combined with high individual rewards can lead to noncompliant behavior. Often, this is a root cause of compliance issues in emerging-country markets. Setting the right balance is a management issue, but validating this balance is a board issue," said Michael Ray, general counsel, Western Digital Corporation.

A compliant culture must include the ability of management to refuse expedient and potentially noncompliant short-term business. Boards and management should make it clear that if an employee's refusal to pay a bribe was the cause of not achieving targets, there would be no financial penalty for that individual. In some instances, policies may be developed in these markets of not pursuing business relationships if complete and reliable information cannot be obtained about how the individual or company obtained its financial strength.

The board must be aware not only of the resulting costs of penalties and litigation associated with corruption and bad behavior, but perhaps more importantly, their potential impact on the culture and the risk to the company's reputation, including the reputations of directors and management. In the end, the difficulties in dealing with corruption and complying with U.S. laws may result in directors and management deciding to forgo the business opportunities in some of these markets.

Non-transparency of Information

Even when bribery and corruption are not present, the board's oversight responsibilities in emerging-country markets can be tested because the quality of information often is opaque—if not inadequate, incorrect, or nonexistent. There can be little, if any, information available on the government's inner workings and relationships, partner profiles, and reputations. Estimating the true potential of market demand can pose challenges. Unique country conditions such as limited availability of data sources and reliable information make it difficult to gather market insights. Often, improvisation is required.

Corporate structures tend to be overly complex. In highly granular, regulated environments like China, local companies create constellations of special-purpose but related entities, including but not limited to sales companies, finance companies, management service companies, and technology and R&D companies. Within these groups, individual entities are controlled by different combinations of owners, risking manipulation of transfer pricing, asset transfers, and incomplete financial reporting.

For example, it has been reported that Chinese insurer Anbang Insurance Group has a very unusual and nontransparent ownership structure represented by a mask of corporate shareholders, involving multiple layers of holding companies registered throughout the country. Asked to comment by *The Wall Street Journal*, a company spokesperson responded nebulously that it is owned by 30 corporate investors that do not participate in the company's daily operations.[239]

Audited financials of local companies, particularly if performed by regional or local attestation firms, can be questionable and need to be reviewed with skepticism. In these

---

[239] "The Starwood's Mysterious Suiter," *The Wall Street Journal*, March 29, 2016.

markets, the extensive underground economy created to avoid paying taxes makes it almost impossible to track financial information. When due diligence is performed, workstreams need to be much more forensic and investigative than in developed markets.

Disclosures of improprieties in financial reporting by companies based in emerging-country markets have suggested conditions that indicate highly elevated fraud risk. The Public Company Accounting Oversight Board published a Staff Audit Practice Alert to increase auditors' awareness of these risks when performing external audits of companies having operations in emerging markets. The alert says that the local business practices and cultural norms can differ widely from those in more developed markets.[240]

The levels of internal controls typically do not meet international standards or investor expectations. Recurring control problems tend to be weaknesses in processes, lack of remediation planning, and control improvements that suffer from inconsistent attention. The result often is a mixed quality of reporting.

The non-transparency of information, which can lead to inaccuracies and poor decisions, requires board vigilance. Opaqueness may indicate under-performance, differing agendas, or poor behavior. Directors accustomed to very stringent reporting guidelines should understand it may be impossible to meet those standards, and they may need to accept exceptions to normal practices.

Five Ways to Manage Risks in Emerging-Country Markets

- Prevent, control, and contain losses related to bribery and corruption.
- Know the local and regional jurisdictional nuances.
- Watch operating model efficiency amid pressure to sustain profits.
- Bring local talent into the business and take leadership to the streets.
- Be a model of absolute business ethics.
- Build a culture that supports the corporate values and principles.

Source: "Navigating the Risks and Opportunities in Emerging Markets," by Harry Broadman, PricewaterhouseCoopers, 2012.

Culture and Customs

When it comes to emerging-country markets, directors need to have heightened sensitivity to obvious and subtle cultural differences, both in thought and action. Closing gaps in culture and customs requires an appreciation of the local value system, not merely a superficial adherence to etiquette rules.

These markets do not have a long history of Western business and legal practices, so a certain number of surprises, misunderstandings, and perceptions of unusual or inappropriate behavior can be expected. In some of these markets, transactions are based far more on relationships than on contracts or policies and procedures. Contracts are subject to change, so negotiations are sometimes restarted immediately after signing.

---

[240] "Audit Risks in Certain Emerging Markets," Staff Audit Practice Alert No. 8, Public Company Accounting Oversight Board, October 3, 2011.

Often, management must contend not only with cultural differences between an emerging country and other parts of the world, but with differences within the country itself.

"Gaps in culture and customs involve much more than language barriers. Directors need to have not only a sense of these differences, but also an understanding of how the business adapts its normal practices to these environments," commented Khanh T. Tran, CEO, Aviation Capital Group.

Influence of Government

Many boards tend to underestimate the influence of government and the breadth and intensity of regulatory risk, especially when the regulator and the partner are one and the same. In emerging-country markets, this risk can be particularly troublesome.

Burdensome administrative rules, as well as excessive and time-consuming approval processes, can delay business activities. Delays in licensing approvals, which have become virtually folklore in India, are usually associated with lack of transparency, suggesting that legal and political systems may not be open and accountable to the public. Government intervention and intrusions are daunting challenges, as laws, regulations, and contracts governing an investment can be changed quickly without notification.

In China, the government's heavy hand has intervened to nationalize strategic resources, inhibiting private investments. And in Brazil, the government has raised its tax on foreign investors twice within one month, at short notice with little warning. In fact, Brazil regularly ranks near the bottom in the World Economic Forum's Annual Global Competitiveness Report, which grades the burden of government regulation and the extent and effect of taxation.

In India, foreign investors have long complained about red tape. Now, some retailers are dropping their plans to open outlets in the country. Regulations have been adopted requiring that at least 30% of the value of retail inventories is to be manufactured in India and the value target must be attained within five years.[241]

Additionally, Indonesia unveiled a rule requiring franchisees to obtain 80% of their goods locally, although the time frame for meeting the requirements remains unclear. Exceptions have been granted by the government after some franchisees successfully argued that the policy thwarts business.[242]

As a result, many companies find that it is critical to build meaningful relationships with the appropriate branches of the local governments. The government often becomes a business partner or serves as the agent in introductions to local companies that become business partners. In many jurisdictions, government connections are perceived as essential for success.

Boards and management need to learn to work within and across multiple and often divergent geographies and regulatory environments. In some of these markets, like India and China, there are many different regulatory regimes across the country's regions and administrative districts.

---

[241] "Ikea's India Bet Hits Thicket of Rules," *The Wall Street Journal*, February 24, 2016.
[242] Ibid.

Talent Shortages

The board needs to understand and appreciate the unique challenges associated with talent in the emerging markets. The recruitment, training, and retention of talent in these markets often represent a primary constraint to growth and the single most significant execution risk.

Not only may local hires have difficulty understanding corporate values, but they also need to learn Western business practices and ethics. The workforces tend to be young and inexperienced, and bilingual pools of resources are often limited. Loyalty is hard to instill. Annual turnover of senior managers in these markets often is excessive, not infrequently exceeding 40%. Even nominal increases in compensation and benefits offered by competitors can result in employee resignations.

Deploying bilingual nationals who have been educated in the U.S. can fill gaps and address critical resource challenges, but can result in significant gaps in compensation and career expectations when these employees integrate into the local operations. Their higher compensation levels can cause discomfort and even resentment.

Success is dependent on more than language proficiency. English skills should not be misinterpreted as functional capabilities. Achieving the right balance between expatriate and local talent is among the most critical factors for sustaining growth and managing risk. Over-reliance on local hires who are proficient in English but who are not locally connected, do not understand the local market and customs, or do not possess specialized or industry expertise can lead to under-performance and disappointment.

Restructuring or downsizing can also be challenging. Local unions in some markets are aggressive in frustrating such plans. In India, companies with more than 100 employees need government approval to lay off workers. This puts them at the mercy of corrupt government officials with an incentive to say no.

The human resources function in these markets generally is underdeveloped, so it is virtually impossible to find HR professionals who are experienced in recruiting, training, and retaining talent without significant guidance and support. As a result, boards and management need to prioritize the importance of HR leadership in their strategic plans.

Intellectual Property Protection

A primary threat in emerging-country markets is the theft of intellectual property. Successful brands and products are frequently counterfeited and sold on unprecedented scales due to the enormous size of the local markets, high price sensitivities, and lack of effort and coordination among the regulatory agencies. Counterfeiting of software, DVDs, and CDs is common practice, particularly in China, Russia, and Indonesia. In India, weak patent protection makes doing business difficult, to say the least. Beyond lost sales, IP theft can expose a company to reputation risk as counterfeit and potentially defective products bearing its brand flood the marketplace.

Although some of these markets are making attempts at enhancing IP protection, there generally is no consistency in the implementation and enforcement of standards by the local authorities. In some instances, the rules may be in place, but they are not being effectively enforced.

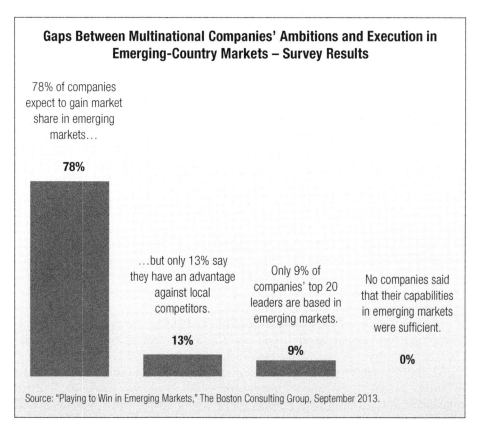

Gaps Between Multinational Companies' Ambitions and Execution in Emerging-Country Markets – Survey Results

78% of companies expect to gain market share in emerging markets...

78%

...but only 13% say they have an advantage against local competitors.

13%

Only 9% of companies' top 20 leaders are based in emerging markets.

9%

No companies said that their capabilities in emerging markets were sufficient.

0%

Source: "Playing to Win in Emerging Markets," The Boston Consulting Group, September 2013.

IP theft is an area requiring a fundamental rethinking of strategies for IP owners and board oversight. There are absolute limits to how long and how well IP can be protected, so the challenge is to render as much value as possible while products, designs, and other advantages remain exclusive and distinct. Businesses need to integrate every aspect of new product development, marketing strategies, channel management, technology, and manufacturing and partnering processes to manage the value of their IP for the best outcomes.

Failure to Diversify

A consequential risk in emerging-country markets is dependency on a single regulator or business partner. Although this may be unavoidable due to local regulations in certain industries, establishing multiple relationships is strategically prudent. Multiple relationships with diverse purposes can be particularly useful within a territory, as they provide leverage with local governments and business partners who know that withdrawal is a legitimate option.

Partner selection requires the board's understanding of the process and the important elements of the decision-making. Local partners who understand the market and customs, and have good relationships with government officials, can help mitigate the risks of these markets. However, in some places, qualified partners are not readily available and the risk profile increases with each partner selection. Disputes with partners can be protracted and costly, as in Brazil, where partner disputes taken to court can extend upwards of 10 years, owing to the complexity and uniqueness of the judicial system. Obstructive bureaucrats in India are known to often become embroiled in partner disputes, resulting in notoriously slow and unseemly resolutions.

The leverage that comes with having alternative relationships in these markets is a requisite to avoid the pitfalls of a singular approach or strategy.

Dominance of Family Conglomerates

Some emerging-country markets are dominated by family owned rather than publicly owned businesses. Depending upon the perspective, this could be viewed as a reality, a threat, or both.

A family conglomerate is a large, privately owned company that is highly diversified. Their businesses can range from manufacturing to banking to construction. These conglomerates control the majority of economic activity and employment in emerging countries like South Korea (where they are called chaebols), in India (business houses), in Latin America (grupos), and in Turkey (holding companies). A typical conglomerate may hold the largest market share in each of several industries in its home country. In South Korea, for example, the top 30 family conglomerates account for almost half of the assets and industry revenues in the entire Korean economy.

The fact that family conglomerates exist and dominate the commercial landscape in emerging-country markets can present formidable challenges. They can be fierce competitors or capable partners, possibly with a disproportionate bargaining power. In many cases, the conglomerates provide substantial local tax revenues and facilitate natural economic development, which explains why governments are eager to support them.

Overspending of Resources

Despite the dynamic growth prospects in emerging-country markets, when chasing opportunities there is a tendency to overspend by investing more than is required. Management's enthusiasm to pursue the growth opportunities in these markets needs to be balanced with sober financial modeling. The board's oversight of the spending of resources can be particularly critical given the volatility in these markets. The challenge is "how to do more with less."

The Economist points out that the growth in emerging-country markets has led to an abundance of disappointment, based on Western firms' belief that they should rush into these markets. As a consequence, *The Economist* suggests careful screening of potential investments for strategic relevance and financial returns, as well as an emphasis on the strengthening of existing operations.[243]

Often, boards and management are persuaded that if they invest heavily upfront, investments will be recouped. This is not always the case. In China, as soon as the local

---

[243] "Submerging Hopes," 2014.

firms figure out how the business model works, it will be copied. Therefore, it is wise to develop plans to accelerate the path toward profitability and avoid overspending.

Local Competitive Threats

The competition from both global and local companies in these markets is intense and increasing. Global peers are trying hard to increase their share in emerging-country markets, and local businesses are rapidly becoming much more serious competitors. Local competitors enjoy advantages such as better cultural understanding, more appropriate business models, better relationships with the government, entrenched protectionism, and possibly fewer restrictions on how they operate.[244]

According to a survey by the Boston Consulting Group, 78% of the respondents said their companies expected to gain share in emerging markets, but only 13% were confident that they could take on local competitors. No respondents stated that their capabilities in emerging-country markets were sufficient for success. The biggest concern is not the ambition but the risks associated with the growing threat from local competitors.[245]

In order to mitigate the execution risks, investing needs to begin, as a "best practice," in one market (or at most two or possibly three) to ensure that gaps in local competitiveness are addressed and a robust methodology is developed for subsequent rollout throughout the company to other emerging-country markets. Once one market demonstrates results and positive momentum, the approach can be transferred to other countries. To take advantage of "lessons learned" in the first country or group of countries, the same templates and tools can be used. Management should develop handbooks and lessons for quick learning and ensure some continuity by transferring people who have experience in those markets.[246]

Final Comments

Pursuing the opportunities in emerging-country markets is an imperative for many boards and management, but extreme care must be exercised and tendencies toward excessive exuberance need to be restrained. Some of these markets may be considerably less attractive once questionable business practices and the risks are considered. Directors need to be cognizant of the unique threats in these markets and help guide management in the quest to exploit the vast and growing opportunities.

*Portions of this chapter were taken from an article written by the author, "Board Oversight of Risks in Emerging-Country Markets," *NACD Directorship*, July-August 2012.

---

[244] "Guide to Emerging Markets: The Business Outlook, Opportunities, and Obstacles," 2014.
[245] "Playing to Win in Emerging Markets," The Boston Consulting Group, September 2013.
[246] "Transformation in Emerging Markets: From Growth to Competitiveness," February 2016.

Questions Directors Should Ask About Risks in Emerging-Country Markets

- How much risk is the board willing to accept in each of the emerging-country markets? What is the risk appetite? What is the balance of opportunities versus risks? Are the risk thresholds applied consistently in each of the emerging-country markets?
- Does the board understand the degree and types of compliance risks that exist in each of its emerging-country markets? Are those evaluating compliance independent of the operations so that they can provide objective viewpoints?
- What technology is used to manage compliance risks? Do directors understand how it works, and do they think the technology is calibrated to the size and complexity of the local operations?
- What are the global compliance safeguards and protections? How will the board and management hold local management accountable for enforcing these measures?
- How does the board evaluate the political environment? What are the risks of instability?
- Are global business ethics and practices embedded in the local operations?
- What is the board's comfort level with the quantity and quality of the information provided in these markets?
- Which indicators suggest that directors and managers understand and appreciate the local cultures and customs?
- What are the relationships with local government officials? Are safeguards in place against corruption?
- What distinct strategies are in place to recruit, train, and retain talent?
- How often does the board review potential IP violations in these markets? How extensive are the reviews?
- What is the breadth and depth of other relationships in these markets so that there is a diversification of risks?
- Does the board understand the amount of investment? What are acceptable levels of investment?
- How do directors obtain information on how different macroeconomic scenarios might impact each emerging-country market? What processes are in place to anticipate and identify likely and seemingly unlikely game-changing events?
- How is the board responding both globally and within each emerging-country market to the prospect of new rules and higher expectations of board governance?
- What are the experience and expertise on the board in emerging-country markets? How can this experience be leveraged?

A Chinese Joint Venture Means Big Work for the Board

"Dreaming different dreams while in the same bed."
—CHINESE PROVERB

Virtually every U.S. company investing in China confronts a myriad of challenges and risks with joint ventures. Historically, joint ventures have been the optimum or, in many cases, the mandatory investment vehicle. More recently, however, direct investment is gaining popularity as valuable on-the-ground experience in China has been achieved, restrictions on foreign investments are easing, and the difficulties of negotiating, establishing, and managing joint ventures have become evident.

State-owned enterprises have consolidated, creating national champions in many industries. These enterprises are increasingly pursuing their own investments in R&D and innovation, as well as directly investing overseas. The desire for foreign investment and the perceived need for domestic joint ventures have receded in some industries. Nevertheless, in many cases, joint ventures remain attractive, particularly as the costs of greenfield investments rise and valuations remain elevated for acquisitions of Chinese targets.

In dozens of sectors ranging from health care to financial services, government restrictions make joint ventures the only feasible option. But when foreign investors in unrestricted industries consider venturing with Chinese partners, they often stop cold when confronted with the potential challenges. The list of issues is long, including misaligned agendas between the global and local partners, poor governance or organizational control among the partners, contract noncompliance, technology infringement, and the risk that the partner may become an eventual competitor in the same market.[247]

The fact remains that joint ventures in China, when properly planned and managed, can be the quickest path to success for foreign investors. Given the likely importance of China to the company's future, the board has an important role in ensuring a joint venture's success.

PricewaterhouseCoopers commissioned a report, written by the Economist Intelligence Unit, that surveyed and explored the motives and the challenges of Chinese-and-foreign partnerships. Here are some key findings:

---

[247] "Deals for Getting Big in China Fast," by Phil Leung, Weiwen Han and Raymond Tsang, Bain & Company, January 28, 2013.

- *There are no signs of a slowdown when it comes to using joint ventures.* Despite China's slowing economy, recent scrutiny of foreign companies, and rising labor costs, forming business partnerships through joint ventures remains an attractive way to do business in China. As of 2015, over three-quarters of foreign investors plan to enter into a business partnership in China.
- *Divergent objectives can exist from the very beginning.* A main strategic objective of foreign investors is access to the domestic market, while for Chinese partners it is international expansion.
- *For foreign investors, the primary driver for choosing a joint-venture business model versus other entry modes is regulatory requirements.* Joint ventures also offer foreign investors the benefit of sharing resources and skills while limiting risks.
- *Both foreign and Chinese partners are worried most about the costs and complexities of setting up a joint venture.* As with most businesses, costs remain a key factor for all parties and an important area of consideration prior to establishing operations.
- *Foreign investors are focusing more on business compatibility with potential partners than in the past.* When considering their Chinese partners, foreign investors are looking beyond local business, political, and social networks and focusing more on strategic features of Chinese partners, such as their market responsiveness and open-mindedness.
- *Strategic misalignment and cultural differences are among the main reasons why partnerships are not formed.* Both foreign and Chinese parties agree that the likelihood of being successful is virtually nonexistent without a shared strategy and the ability to deal with cultural differences.
- *Financial performance is a top concern.* No matter how complementary the relationship between partners, the joint venture must ultimately deliver on its financial objectives. Poor financial performance is the top factor cited for terminating joint ventures.[248]

Directors need to understand the nature of the risks and provide thoughtful commentary to management on the challenges and mitigations. Among the crucial areas for boards and management to consider when pursuing a joint venture in China are selecting a partner and diversifying, addressing compliance, acquiring ownership, protecting intellectual property, nurturing government relations, addressing talent shortages, assuming leadership, exhibiting agility, planning for the inevitable, and avoiding pitfalls.

Selecting a Partner and Diversifying

Boards and management have more choices of how to invest in China than in the past, when joint ventures were required to enter into most industries. Options ranging from commercial relationships and alliances to cooperative ventures to wholly owned enterprises are possible and now common. Non-joint venture forms of investment are inherently easier to form, allow partner relationships to develop before committing, and

---

[248] "Courting China Inc: Expectations, Pitfalls, and Success Factors of Sino-Foreign Business Partnerships in China," PricewaterhouseCoopers, 2015.

provide more flexibility to address the fast-moving business environment, regardless of the degree of success of the initial relationship. The tangible and intangible costs of joint ventures can be significant and should not be underestimated. Board oversight is necessary to ensure that management has explored all the options. Moreover, the board needs to have confidence in the unique benefits to come from the joint venture and to confirm that a joint venture is indeed the best route to market before committing to complex and demanding structures.

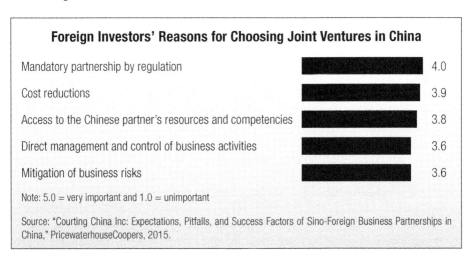

Foreign Investors' Reasons for Choosing Joint Ventures in China

Mandatory partnership by regulation	4.0
Cost reductions	3.9
Access to the Chinese partner's resources and competencies	3.8
Direct management and control of business activities	3.6
Mitigation of business risks	3.6

Note: 5.0 = very important and 1.0 = unimportant

Source: "Courting China Inc: Expectations, Pitfalls, and Success Factors of Sino-Foreign Business Partnerships in China," PricewaterhouseCoopers, 2015.

Historically, joint ventures were greenfield relationships, creating a new legal entity with some form and amount of technology, capital, and local operations and facilities contributed by both parties. Increasingly, joint ventures are now formed through the acquisition of a portion of an existing Chinese legal entity. While the acquisition of an entire target often appears more expedient, it is also much more complicated and inherently more risky. The foreign investor will also be buying into all the problems and issues of the target—in many cases, with direct successor liability.

The foreign investor most certainly will have higher governance requirements and business standards than the Chinese partner, including adherence to social contracts.

A foreign investor will also be held to a higher standard of compliance to laws and regulations. This will most likely mean the venture's existing cost structure and, at times, commercial business model will need to change. The board and management must be explicitly aware of the impact of these changes on the basic economics of the joint venture and not make the false choice of investing in an existing operation that is no longer economically viable, given the foreign partner's higher governance, compliance, and operating requirements.

Partner selection requires the board's understanding of the process, the critical elements of the decision-making, and why management recommends a joint venture approach. There are many good reasons to have a joint venture. Local partners that understand the market and customs, and have good relationships with government officials and other intermediaries, can be attractive partners and help mitigate the risks of entering the Chinese market. Many industries have dominant and increasingly international competitors raising the barriers to entry, which may also be a good reason to form a joint venture. However, it is imperative that foreign investing companies select partners that explicitly share their strategic and commercial goals. This does not necessarily eliminate as potential partners large, well-established Chinese companies. But it does open the door to faster-growing, privately owned, and smaller local companies that bring a strong commercial mind-set and tangible business assets to joint ventures.[249]

Some foreign investors emphasize profitability, even when growth is slow, while their Chinese partners emphasize growth, even without profitability. Foreign investors often will have a longer-term view of a joint venture's financial returns, willing to reinvest profits and increase registered capital, while the Chinese partner will be more focused on the short term and dividends. The result can be different priorities for investments and a lack of cooperation, both between the joint venture partners and within the mixed management team.[250]

It is important to avoid being in the same bed dreaming different dreams. Before committing, foreign investing companies frequently fail to spend sufficient time with potential partners to build a shared understanding of the future business, the markets to compete in, and how the business will evolve over time. Inadequate time and attention is given to developing business plans and preparing for probable changes in the market dynamics. Differences of opinion rooted in competing expectations of future performance can seriously affect the joint venture's focus and strategy and potentially lead to failure.

In any relationship, the inevitable question of how to handle partner disagreements must be addressed. Most arise from differences of opinion about how to finance growth, often involving disagreements about reinvesting retained earnings and additional capital requirements. Since venture financing is often critical, and subject by law to unanimous agreement of the partners, a way to handle disagreements and the process to get to an agreement need to be explicitly addressed prior to consummating the joint venture.

Also essential is the ongoing oversight and cultivation of partner relationships, as joint ventures will invariably go through difficult strategic and business issues, particularly in the initial years. Problems between joint venture partners often will be solved based on a mutual understanding of respective aspirations for the joint venture. Board oversight is necessary to ensure that management makes the proper investment in partner relationships.

Additionally, as Chinese partners become increasingly successful and confident, many of the smaller ones themselves hope to become regional, national, or even global players. These aspirations can make it difficult to agree on the scope of the joint venture—that is, whether it is to be limited to China or to specific products and services. A suggested approach is to outline the extent of cooperation both domestically and internationally. This normally entails determining whether the joint venture will have access to overseas

---

[249] "Past Lessons for China's New Joint Ventures," by Stephan Bosshart, Thomas Luedi, and Emma Wang, McKinsey & Company, December 2010.
[250] Ibid.

channels, noncompete clauses for specific markets, and agreement in principle on potential expansion into additional product or service lines.[251]

An unforeseen risk can be building a business whose success is dependent on a single regulator or business partner. Although there may be unavoidable situations due to local regulations in certain industries, establishing multiple relationships through diversification generally is strategically prudent. Care must be taken, however, not to spread relationship capital too thin, because building scope and scale with the joint venture partner and the local government and regulatory authorities can be the basis for growing the business and receiving political support and investment incentives.

Addressing Compliance

Deng Xiaoping, China's paramount leader until his retirement in 1992, said that if leadership did not punish corruption, the Chinese government will run the risk of failure to achieve its objectives. In China, eradicating corrupt behavior is a voyage filled with rogue waves.

In a survey conducted by Deloitte, 55% of respondents noted that their company was extremely concerned about the potential impact corruption in China would have on their business. Further, the survey suggests that these concerns are growing.[252]

Many directors are not doing enough to properly understand the way management conducts business in diverse and complex environments like China. This is important because the board needs a detailed understanding of the business if it is to be an effective safeguard against fraud and corrupt practices. The mishandling of compliance issues can have significant impact on the business and the reputation of the company, management, and the directors themselves.

The board of any U.S. company entering into a joint venture in China needs to have a clear understanding of its duties and responsibilities under the Foreign Corrupt Practices Act (FCPA) and other international laws, such as the United Kingdom's Bribery Act of 2010. China also has its own version of anti-bribery laws, which, in many instances, are more strict and severe than international laws.

The FCPA applies to the bribery of foreign government officials. It does not include nongovernmental entities, an area where commercial bribery is often far more pervasive and corrosive. In China, compliance risks are aggravated by the ubiquitous involvement of the government in business, exposing many transactions to government influence that would be purely commercial in other jurisdictions and adjudicated through legal recourse. The government's extensive ownership of assets and businesses in China also complicates the landscape. The Department of Justice is clear that employees of state-owned enterprises are government employees and subject to the FCPA. Thus, the FCPA has a wide and deep impact on the daily management of businesses in China, and it must be a key consideration in how boards and management address on-the-ground governance issues.

---

[251] Ibid.
[252] "Anti-Corruption Practices Survey 2011: Cloudy with a Chance of Prosecution?" Deloitte, 2011.

The reality remains that business practices in China are widely noncompliant. Practices that are commonly regarded as corrupt by global standards, or at least serious if not blatant conflicts of interest, tend to be the norm. Anticipating and addressing corrupt activities requires board awareness. The board is responsible for ensuring that the company is compliant, so directors need to establish a clear commitment to a culture that values compliance and ensure the existence of a robust management system to monitor and ensure compliance.

The board needs to be comfortable that the joint venture promotes business ethics among its managers and develops a written, unambiguous program, including a code of conduct, to build a culture of compliance. Regulators may not expect perfect execution, especially in the early period of the joint venture, but a well-developed program can be an essential protection in the event of misbehavior.

Incentives may change after a joint venture is consummated and governments can become predatory, even if technically within the law. It is essential for directors to understand what the interests of government are and how these may change over time.

Getting Out Front of Corruption in China

- *Foster open communication.* This is both a top-down and a bottom-up dynamic. Directors and management set the tone by communicating a robust framework of rules and employee standards. An engaged compliance function and an effective whistleblower program feed information to the board and management about how well those standards are being adopted.
- *Encourage local solutions.* Making compliance relevant to local teams means engaging them to design specific procedures. It is not the board's role to devise tactics. Rather, directors set consistent guiding principles that apply globally, which management can then achieve in a rational, locally efficient manner.
- *Bolster technology.* Businesses operating in China have moved well beyond the point where compliance functions are able to monitor effectively using manual methods. Companies with large Chinese operations are increasingly using technology to detect potential problems much earlier in key functions such as third-party due diligence, vendor transactions, and employee expenses. Directors are uniquely positioned to make the case that such proactive measures are more cost-effective than an investigation of corrupt activities.
- *Conduct regular assessments.* Reviews should be vigorous and frequent to determine whether existing internal controls are effective in detecting and thwarting bribery and corruption. Management should share those findings with the directors and, if necessary, design remedial actions. Engage local independent third parties to undertake assessments so that local regulations are followed.
- *Make everyone accountable.* Ethical practices are just as essential to the business as branding and cost management. All employees should be involved. The board should see that specific responsibilities in executing the compliance program are clearly communicated by management throughout the organization and that they are a part of employee performance measures.

Source: "Getting Out Front: Proactive Approaches to Address Bribery and Corruption Risks in China," *Board Matters Quarterly*, Ernst & Young, June 2014.

The board should be prepared for a large number of anonymous reports of misconduct and noncompliant behavior originating in China. Many of these reports may be of questionable veracity. Management should strike a realistic balance between adopting an appropriately rigorous method of investigation and fulfilling FCPA standards. Getting this balance wrong will only serve to undercut the effectiveness of the joint venture. The board should be aware of this issue when overseeing management's decisions.

If fraud, corruption, or other malfeasance is suspected, it is often difficult to investigate and obtain sufficient information to identify the violators and validate the violations. Local employees are often culturally impaired when it comes to providing information to investigators that would implicate coworkers. In addition, many joint ventures led by local management teams are adept at appearing compliant while hiding unacceptable business practices. Often, decisions and actions on compliance violations are a matter of judgment based on information gleaned from multiple sources.

The auditing of books and records—and often multiple sets of accounting records—without a detailed and operational understanding of the underlying business is insufficient to identify real compliance risks. The board should be aware that a well-crafted compliance program must be complemented with extensive employee training and regular auditing of actual practices, not just a review of the documentation.

Educating local employees in China on why a U.S. law applies to their behavior outside of the U.S. is a constant challenge when implementing an FCPA-driven compliance framework. Local employee reactions sometimes can have a patriotic component. Interestingly, social media comments regarding actions and penalties imposed by the U.S. Department of Justice have raised questions among local employees as to why the Chinese government is not earning the penalties from those enforcement actions.

Compliance is an area that requires both locally focused and expert advice. The establishment of effective compliance management systems, monitoring, employee education, and regular auditing should be visible to the board and regularly reinforced.

Acquiring Ownership

The Boston Consulting Group notes that prospective foreign investors are frequently deterred by the view that value-generating acquisitions and joint ventures in China are nearly impossible. Foreign investors see the regulatory process as painstaking to navigate in the absence of deep personal connections. The Boston Consulting Group indicates that foreign investors believe that asking prices remain excessively high for equity stakes and can be justified only by realizing a degree of synergies that is somewhere between difficult and impossible to achieve. BCG also notes that foreign investors doubt their ability to bridge differences in culture and management processes and systems.[253]

In any event, many joint ventures are formed through the acquisition of a local Chinese business that invariably will have some level of compliance-related issues. How to bring these businesses into compliance is often a major and defining risk in the formation of the joint venture. The main reasons why acquisitions and joint ventures fail often

---

[253] "M&A in China: Getting Deals Done, Making Them Work," The Boston Consulting Group, January 2015.

Financial Services at a Glance

For directors, the critical point to understanding the financial services sector in China is that the banks, including the central bank and all major commercial banks, are the government's most cherished assets and their main agents for influencing the economy. Accordingly, from the earliest attempts by First Chicago to the most recent attempts by Silicon Valley Bank, nondomestic financial institutions have encountered a regulatory thicket when trying to navigate China. That is not changing in a major and immediate way. Dr. Kenneth J. DeWoskin, advisor to both Deloitte & Touche and the Conference Board, observes the following:

- For a foreign bank to do domestic business in China, a joint venture is required. Business scope remains strictly constrained.
- By necessity, in the wake of the global financial crisis, regulators tolerated an explosive diversification of financial services, providing trust services, securitizations, and a range of commercial services, grouped under social funding and/or shadow banking.
- To reduce the risks inherent in the current imbalances, capital flight, and a badly bloated domestic money supply, China is in need of new channels to attract foreign investment into the economy, especially in the financial sector.
- China's desire to assert its potential influence as the world's second-largest economy has led to its stronger participation in Key International Economic Organizations, including some of its own making, such as the Asia Infrastructure Investment Bank and the BRICs Bank.
- At the enterprise and family levels, outbound investment continues to grow, in both real estate assets and operating companies, moving a growing number of Chinese business leaders up the learning curve in terms of international business norms.
- From health care needs to large property and casualty risks, China will need to diversify and rationalize the insurance sector. Foreign insurers already play a major role in certain categories of insurance.
- The Shanghai Pilot Free Trade Zone, as well as recently approved ones in Tianjin, Zhuhai, and Shenzhen, will provide some room for local development officials to push regulatory limits and pilot what could be attractive openings related to currency and other financial activities ahead of the national regulators.
- HSBC, Citibank, UBS, and Deutsche Bank, as well as Aetna, AIG, and Cigna, have all built substantial businesses in China by ensuring that they have a deep understanding of the economy, regulations, and government goals. None of these institutions operate freely, but all have managed to create some regulatory space for themselves, and many are driving liberalization activities in the Free Trade Zone.

include 1) the inability to understand actual business practices; 2) the impact of these practices on the core business; and 3) ineffectiveness in dealing with transition plans.

Conducting due diligence is always difficult in China since, by definition, the infrastructures are nascent and the information sources are less developed. Because of unofficial payments and other hidden costs of doing business in China, published financial statements are not as transparent as they are in the developed-country markets. Evading corporate income tax is pervasive in China, and manipulation of value-added taxes is not uncommon. Boards and management must pay particular attention to VAT issues because these violations may be criminal in nature and have successor implications for both the company and the managers of the joint venture.

Targeted due diligence into key aspects of a joint venture deal, while likely more time-consuming and expensive, is essential to mitigate risks. It is imperative for boards and management to understand the reality that stands behind the numbers. Combined with strategic and commercial due diligence, financial due diligence will often provide an understanding of the financial accounts and lay the foundation for a meaningful assessment of the opportunities. It also can provide insight into how potential partners operate their businesses, treat employees, and handle fiscal and legal responsibilities.[254]

Due diligence specifically focused on FCPA compliance also should be conducted. When issues surface as a result of an acquisition, the regulators will evaluate whether the acquiring company conducted sufficient pre-acquisition FCPA due diligence and whether the acquiring company promptly integrated the acquired company into its compliance program, including implementing policies, requiring training, and performing audits.

Numerous recent fraud allegations in China have hinged on the legitimacy of supposedly official documentation—for example, documentation in regard to property ownership or the use of natural resources, and even fraudulent verification of bank balances. Such documents vary widely across China, ranging from deeds that are centrally catalogued and hard to forge to pro forma templates that can be easily reproduced. This can create significant difficulties for due diligence teams trying to authenticate documentation.[255]

Boards and management cannot avoid successor liability simply by reorganizing or buying only parts of the business. Actions have been taken against successor companies, in limited circumstances, that involve egregious and sustained violations, or in instances where the successor company directly participated in the violations or failed to stop the misconduct from continuing after the acquisitions.

Additionally, valuations of contributions made by joint venture partners also can be uniquely challenging to confirm, because even claims of asset ownership like land use rights are difficult to verify. Significant unrecorded liabilities can go unnoticed, dramatically altering the economics of the relationship.

Protecting Intellectual Property

Foreign investors continue to struggle in attempts to protect their intellectual property in China, where joint ventures are particularly vulnerable. The concept of intellectual property protection is still relatively new, and recourse to the legal system can be lengthy and unsatisfactory. Although China is making attempts to enhance IP protection, there tends to be no consistency in the implementation and enforcement of standards by the local authorities.

---

[254] "Navigating the Risks and Opportunities in Emerging Markets," by Harry Broadman, PricewaterhouseCoopers, 2012.
[255] "Growing Beyond: A Place for Integrity," Ernst & Young, 2012.

Foreign investors are increasingly investing in R&D in China for domestic purposes and also for the rest of the world. The board should understand the dynamics of this important shift and what it means for the protection of IP. Aligning the joint venture partner's interests with the protection of the joint venture's development of IP is a step in the right direction.

McKinsey & Company suggests the following practices to protect IP:

Bring only older technology to China. This approach works for products that may have been available in developed markets for some time but are still competitive in the Chinese market. It also works in industries where innovation cycles are short. The attractiveness of older technology, however, will diminish as China's industries continue to mature.

Leave the blueprints at home. Foreign investors can protect their intellectual property by delivering equipment or technology ready to be installed, without including detailed design specifications. Negotiating these agreements can signal a lack of trust in the local partners, however, and can increase costs if spare parts and maintenance must be furnished from overseas.

Keep critical intellectual property out of a joint venture. Some foreign investors have established joint ventures that are restricted to those steps in the value chain that involve limited intellectual property, such as assembling, packaging, or tailoring. This approach may be feasible when local innovation lags behind global standards and when critical IP components can easily be separated into a step in the value chain.

Charge for intellectual property upfront. Some foreign investors have chosen to sell their intellectual property to joint ventures, either through upfront cash payments or licensing fees. However, this approach can be challenging to execute. While it may resonate with local partners, they generally are willing to pay for technology upfront only at a significant discount.[256]

Nurturing Government Relations

It is imperative to build business-partner relationships with the appropriate sections or branches of the local and national governments. Understanding the roles and relationships within the government is necessary when working with officials to achieve the joint venture's goals while satisfying the government's needs.

Foreign investors need to learn to work within and across multiple and often divergent regulatory geographies and environments. The interpretation of the laws and the rigor with which they are implemented and enforced can vary between cities like Beijing or Shanghai and the second- or third-tier cities.

Nevertheless, government intrusions can be daunting challenges. Laws and regulations governing a joint venture can be changed quickly without notification, impeding progress and significantly reducing financial viability. Once the joint venture is formed, government oversight can be expected to increase and may be followed by attempts to enhance bureaucratic revenues through increased taxation or other regulation-driven methods. Handling these issues and avoiding unnecessary or arbitrary taxes and penal-

---

[256] "Past Lessons for China's New Joint Ventures," December 2010.

ties can be a major drain on local management's time. Accordingly, proper management of government relationships can be foundational to the success of the joint venture.

Additionally, the company's managers involved in government relations, and the regulators and bureaucrats themselves, are subject to change. Ensuring that the relationship map with government officials is resilient and that relationships are corporatized are important objectives requiring board oversight and an emphasis on their importance.

Addressing Talent Shortages

The board and management need to understand and appreciate the unique challenges associated with talent. Talent shortages invariably are among the most important risks to the success of virtually every joint venture.

Before the joint venture is launched, the partners need to agree on selections for the leadership roles and whether those individuals have the skill sets and temperaments required to establish and lead the operations. Because fostering trust among the stakeholders demands a tremendous amount of work and personal interaction, the leaders should be skilled at building constructive relationships. They need to be thoroughly familiar with the objectives and operational needs of the joint venture. And they need to understand the fiduciary duties of leadership and how the governance structure is intended to function.[257]

Many foreign investors lack the ability to mobilize and relocate the right talent to China who can cope with and thrive within joint ventures. Deploying secondees or expatriates can be cost-prohibitive, so there is a strong preference toward employing local talent. Given the high demand for local employees, salaries have risen dramatically, which makes hiring the right talent, regardless of the source, particularly challenging. Achieving the right balance between expatriate and local talent is among the most important factors for sustaining growth and managing risk.

In the past, many foreign investors simply dispatched available executives, often not the top performers but average executives searching for new challenges. Most of these executives had limited credibility with overseas management and were ill-prepared to manage demanding joint-venture partners. Today, leading companies recognize that a successful joint venture requires credible, high-performing executives supported by strong local teams.

Foreign investors must continue their commitment even after candidates are hired. This means sending some of a company's best people to the joint venture to create a strong team, compensating employees at or above relevant market rates, fast-tracking the advancement of high performers, and even breaking away from more tenure-based advancement systems. Additionally, given the likely importance of China to the company's future, boards and management should consider how to integrate the China experience into the development of its next generation of corporate executives.

The best local candidates prefer employers that have a strong image and offer good prospects for career progression. Therefore, joint ventures must not only invest in their

---

[257] "Human Capital Challenges of Joint Ventures," Towers Watson, February 2012.

corporate brands but also partner with top universities to sponsor undergraduate and graduate students and to establish a training platform for current employees.

Assuming Leadership

Agreement on management positions and executive authority is an essential element of the joint-venture agreement to avoid misunderstandings and false expectations. Often, ownership percentages will dictate many components of this agreement. Foreign investing companies sometimes have agreed to invest in joint ventures as minority or even equal stakeholders, often failing to secure authority and management positions that were sufficiently meaningful. These investors often found themselves relegated to providing know-how and capital, with little influence other than board voting rights.

Moreover, the ability to influence the course of a joint venture depends largely on the partners' ability to build trust-based relationships at the working level, the joint-venture board level, and even outside the joint venture, and with the government or other industry players. Successful foreign investors map out critical stakeholders in and around the joint venture, from local management to central regulatory bodies and industry leaders, and assign relationship responsibilities at multiple levels. This approach requires developing interaction protocols, such as the composition of delegations, the number of visits, the specific topics to be discussed, and so on, depending on the relative importance of the stakeholders and their specific agendas.[258]

Exhibiting Agility

Decision-making processes for Chinese parent companies might include more people, but once decisions are made, managers tend to execute them quickly. In contrast, foreign investors may be slower to react, often encumbered by layers of country and regional management. It is not uncommon for the foreign managers of a joint venture to report back to the multinational's China head, who reports to the head of the international unit, who then eventually reports back to the global CEO.

Once a joint venture is up and running, foreign investors should aspire to manage it as if it were their own, putting in place short lines of reporting from the joint venture back to the parent company. An agile reporting structure is important to give management and the board the information they need, and in a timely manner, to assess performance and make informed decisions. This is especially true in China, where the fast pace in many sectors requires both partners to react quickly to changes in the marketplace and the regulatory environment.

Some foreign investing companies provide for direct reporting lines to their CEOs. Others have assigned responsibility for China to a member of their senior executive team, sometimes with a dual reporting line into the regional organization. This can result in improved cooperation with regulators and faster approvals, more frequent interactions and deeper relationships between the senior managements of the parent companies, and closer alignment within the joint venture's mixed management teams.[259]

---

[258] "Past Lessons for China's New Joint Ventures," December 2010.
[259] Ibid.

Planning for the Inevitable

Even in developed-country markets, joint ventures are inevitably restructured and, more than infrequently, dissolved. In a market as dynamic as China, terms negotiated today might be ineffective in only a few months or years, and even strong partners may struggle to survive. This dynamism and uncertainty means that the joint venture agreement must include provisions for restructuring its contractual terms if the competitive or regulatory landscape change.

Some foreign investing companies have had to enter into difficult negotiations with their Chinese partners to reach agreement on exit conditions. Others have languished in joint ventures that continued as formal partnerships while one party (or both) pursued other avenues for growth. These situations need to be avoided, and they can be with proper anticipation and planning at the outset.

Key issues like decision-rights and changes in the financial structure should be addressed before the formation of the joint venture. While these discussions may be difficult before the venture is formed, they are even more problematic, if not impossible,

---

Questions Directors Should Ask About Chinese Joint Ventures

- Why is the formation of a joint venture the preferred investment strategy? What are the alternatives?
- How confident are directors that the potential partner shares the same strategic and commercial goals?
- How is market information of the joint venture obtained, corroborated, and tested?
- What are the plans to conduct targeted due diligence into key aspects of the joint venture agreement?
- What threats of bribery and corruption in China are the most significant facing management?
- Are the joint venture's business ethics and code of conduct sufficiently developed? How are they communicated?
- Are directors confident that management is taking the necessary steps to prevent bribery and corruption, rather than waiting to react to an incident?
- Is the board aware of increased efforts by Chinese leadership to crack down on corruption and how that may impact compliance risks?
- What is the internal control environment? What improvements are necessary?
- How will the joint venture protect intellectual property? What technology will be or has been transferred?
- How will management be sensitized to gaps in the joint venture's culture and customs?
- How are control and management of the joint ventures shared?
- What are the plans to initiate and cultivate relations with important local government officials?
- What are the local and expatriate talent strategies? How will top local universities be engaged?
- What are the plans to prevent the joint venture partner from competing?
- Are directors in agreement with the spending commitments required of the joint venture?
- What are the exit strategies to the joint venture?

later on. Early clarity is necessary and may indicate basic differences in how each partner views the joint venture and whether it is indeed viable.

As the business grows, the joint venture will need to make funding decisions on additional debt or equity contributions. Often the Chinese partner will desire higher leverage than the foreign investor and, conversely, lower equity. The risk of the partners not agreeing on how to fund growth is significant, and it should be explicitly addressed prior to formation of the venture.[260]

Avoiding Pitfalls

Directors and management should develop sources of information independent from local management in order to assess the market and investment risks. Periodic briefings, corporate participation in relevant organizations, and just walking the halls of the joint venture can be important. Directors increasingly are holding periodic board meetings in China to get a firsthand and in-depth view.

Joint ventures in China, as elsewhere, are notoriously difficult to manage and oversee. With control shared between what are often commercially competitive shareholders/owners, the risks of conflict are rife. To avoid some of the pitfalls, Pinsent Masons recommends the following:

Explore alternatives. Because there are multiple inherent risks, joint ventures should only be entered into if absolutely necessary. Foreign investors should actively explore all reasonable alternatives.

Focus on long-term competition. Joint venture partners are often potential competitors. Perhaps the greatest long-term risk of the joint venture is inadvertently establishing or enabling a future competitor.

Know your partner's motives. Chinese partners' rationale for entering into joint ventures rarely begin or end with a profit motive. The local partner frequently seeks technology, know-how, and, ultimately, new products, services, and processes.

Commit to the process. Joint ventures are complex and their negotiation is a time- and resource-intensive process. This process cannot be completed without a serious commitment by the joint venture partners.

Negotiate rigorously but flexibly. It is advisable to begin negotiations based on dual-language standard contract precedents. This will ensure the comprehensive treatment of all standard structural and operational issues and also provide a solid framework for any necessary variations.[261]

Final Comments

Despite China's slowing economy, recent scrutiny by financial investors, and rising labor costs, the pursuit of joint ventures remains an attractive way to do business in China. However, directors and management need to approach China with their eyes wide open. It is essential to develop plans to address the risks as soon as it appears negotiations may lead to the formation of a joint venture. Establishing, managing, and overseeing a

---

[260] Ibid.
[261] "Successful Joint Ventures in China," Pinsent Masons, February 2013.

joint venture in China requires trust, commitment, and communication. Courageous and thoughtful leadership is a requisite. The ability to anticipate, prevent, and resolve the issues associated with joint ventures requires the full attention and support of the directors, as well as the dedication, cultural awareness, and steady hands of management.

*Portions of this chapter were taken from two articles written by Dean A. Yoost and Eric V. Zwisler: "A Chinese JV Means Big Work for the Board," *Directors & Boards*, First Quarter 2013, and "Corruption in China and Elsewhere Demands Board Oversight," *NACD Directorship*, July/August 2013.

Risks of Passage
Through India

"We cannot change the direction of the wind, but we can adjust the sails."

— INDIAN PROVERB

I ndia is a land of contradictions. While business opportunities abound and the market is fundamentally sound, the challenges and risks that businesses face are immense and varied.

India is prominent on board agendas as the emerging-country market to watch. Boards and management often view India with admiration and skepticism, admiring the country for its democratic values, cultural heritage, young and highly skilled workforce, lower cost structures, and English-speaking population. However, they have concerns about the difficulties in doing business in India, its pervasive and systemic corruption, and its troubling failures in protecting intellectual property rights.

A decade ago, India was positioned by global companies as an ideal location for the outsourcing of routine activities and back-office operations, which presented an important opportunity to reduce costs. Some multinationals have expanded and enhanced these investments into higher-value assembly operations and engineering by transferring portions of intellectual property and hiring skilled workers. Today, India continues to embody these initiatives, as well as the growth opportunities presented by its expanding consumer market.

By the year 2020, it is projected that India will surpass China and become the world's most populous country.[262] It is a youthful country, with nearly 65% of its 1.3 billion people younger than 35. As other growing markets confront a rapidly aging population, India's youthful population is fulfilling the intense global demand for skilled, lower-paid workers.[263]

Since 1991, India's gross national product per capita has increased nearly fivefold, and annual foreign direct investment inflows have surged by a factor of 200.[264] Prospects are

---

[262] "World's Population Projected to Reach 9.7 billion by 2050," United Nations Department of Economic and Social Affairs, July 2015.
[263] "Future of India: The Winning Leap," PricewaterhouseCoopers, 2015.
[264] "How the Indian Economy Changed in 1991-2011," *Economic Times* (Mumbai), July 24, 2011.

bright. Estimates are that India will become the world's third-largest economy by the year 2030.[265]

The population boom is generating significant business opportunities. General Motors Company announced in July 2015 that it will be investing $1 billion in India as part of a move to strengthen its business in global markets, aiming to double its market share in India within the next five years. Deloitte Consulting has more than 10,000 employees in India to support its global information technology consulting practice. India now is the world's third-largest market for smartphones. And, in the past year, Twitter, Facebook, Yahoo, and other Silicon Valley firms have made significant investments in Indian e-commerce and social networking ventures. The country accounts for Facebook's second-largest user base after the U.S.

Comparatives: India, Brazil, and China (2015)

	India	Brazil	China
Population	1.31 billion	207 million	1.37 billion
Gross national income per capita (US$)	$1,590	$9,850	$7,820

Source: World Bank Group, 2016.

According to a recent study conducted by the United Nations Conference on Trade and Development, India ranks among the top three countries as the most attractive destination for investment because of its emerging middle class, competitiveness, and huge pool of talent.

An Ernst & Young survey rates India as the foremost market for investment. However, although the respondents conclude that India's macroeconomics, political stability, and bureaucratic processes are improving, almost half of the respondents believe India needs to continue improving on the difficulties in doing business and to enhance transparency.[266]

Many of the risks in India are being addressed by far-reaching government initiatives, particularly the "Make in India" program. This initiative is the most comprehensive economic and business reform India has experienced since gaining its independence almost 70 years ago. Prime Minister Narendra Modi, who was elected in May 2014, knows he cannot sell the incredible India story and accelerate growth unless the difficulty of conducting business is improved, the corruption epidemic is eradicated, and intellectual property is properly protected.

---

[265] "India to Become Third Largest Economy by 2030: PricewaterhouseCoopers," *The Hindu* (Chennai), July 5, 2014.
[266] "India: Ready, Set, Grow," EY's Attractiveness Survey, Ernst & Young, 2015.

'Make in India' Program

Make in India is the Indian government's flagship program, focusing on the following: • Promote the manufacturing of low-cost, eco-friendly and zero-defect products. • Foster innovation. • Enhance skill development. • Protect intellectual property. • Build best-in-class manufacturing infrastructure.	In support of the Make in India initiative, the government has embarked on a series of actions: 1. A new trade policy. 2. New labor laws. 3. Simplification of regulatory compliance. 4. Improvement of its resource management programs. 5. Focus on skills development.

Source: "Make in India" Web site, June 2015.

Difficulty in Doing Business

A pronounced problem in doing business in India is its polychromic culture. Things there are done differently. Indian business culture and etiquette are the product of thousands of years of Hindu influence with an overlay of Islam, the British Raj, and the more recent Western business systems. Having an understanding of the hierarchical mind-set, the complex communication patterns, and the myriad of other cultural subtleties is essential for directors and management when navigating the opportunities and calibrating the risks.[267]

India has an almost forlorn reputation for being a very difficult market in which to operate. Red tape is excessive, so companies both large and small inherently take on greater execution risks. Investment plans are frequently abandoned, not because the business proposition lacks merit, but because the environment and the bureaucracy present excessive barriers. Regulations, tax compliance and audits, along with labor laws and constantly changing government policies, create unnecessary complexity. Rather than being helpful advocates of economic progress, many bureaucrats become pettifoggers in the approval process of requests and applications.

There are many Indias within the country, owing to cultural, linguistic, geographical, and economic diversity. India, as a collection of states, is a complex place to do business because it tends to operate under local laws with little national uniformity. "Policymaking is highly decentralized, and the country is characterized by large regional differences in governance, culture, and business practices," noted Shashank Tripathi, partner, PricewaterhouseCoopers in Mumbai.

In a survey conducted by KPMG and the Confederation of Indian Industry (CII), the respondents indicate that 1) taxation is challenging and not conducive to fostering growth; 2) the costs incurred in starting a business are significantly high; 3) the lack of effective land acquisition processes makes land acquisition overly complex and time consuming; and 4) contract enforcement is complicated and time consuming.[268]

---

[267] "Doing Business in India," World Business Culture, 2013.
[268] "Ease of Doing Business in India," KPMG, May 2014.

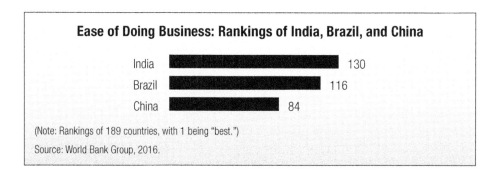

As an example, the long-term leasing of land for commercial purposes can face a precarious journey through laborious and notoriously tricky processes. Buying private land in India is even more complicated because of the fragmentation of land ownership. It is possible, and not improbable, that a piece of land may be jointly owned by numerous family members. At times, land is bought from one family member and, after a number of years, other family members claim ownership and litigate, which can take decades to adjudicate.[269]

The business environment puts India at a clear disadvantage relative to other emerging-country markets. In many sectors, management is forced to deal with multiple layers of stakeholders, regulators, and even members of civil society, introducing unforeseen costs and delays. Not infrequently, it is difficult for management to focus on building local businesses because excessive time is expended in addressing bureaucratic layers and barriers. Multinationals go elsewhere, and even some Indian companies locate their primary activities overseas.

India's poor performance is reflected in the World Bank's 2016 "Ease of Doing Business" rankings. India ranks 130 out of 189 countries, below Brazil and China, and even below Uganda (ranked 122) and Cambodia (ranked 127). The primary reasons for its poor performance are cited by the World Bank as unnecessary costs, the difficulty complying with a complex web of regulations, and frequent and long delays in regulatory decisions. The challenges of doing business in India extend across multiple components of the World Bank's rankings, and in certain areas India ranks near the very bottom. Starting a business (ranked 155), paying taxes (ranked 157), enforcing contracts (ranked 178), and dealing with construction permits (ranked 183) are examples.

The World Bank's criteria for its rankings regarding enforcing contracts focus on the efficiency of the commercial court system, the extent of procedures, the time and costs to resolve a commercial dispute, and aspects of the quality of the judicial processes. The World Bank suggests that it takes nearly four years on average to enforce a contract in India, compared with 1.25 years in China. The cost of contract enforcement in India, as a percentage of the claim, is 2.5 times that in China. Moreover, the magnitude of the contract risk cascades because businesses can have difficulty in quantifying the risk of their business relationships. Managements must go to extraordinary lengths to prove that

---

[269] "Doing Business in India: Some Key Issues for U.S. Companies," Osborne Clark, April 8, 2013.

they, and third-party relationships, are reliable partners. Complex business activities that require multiple, interlinked commercial agreements become substantially riskier.

Reinforcing these World Bank rankings, a majority of the respondents to the KPMG/CII survey indicate that enforcement of contract judgments is not as smooth as the existing procedures assure, and the costs for engaging and retaining lawyers, for miscellaneous costs, and for contract enforcement pose significant challenges. KPMG/CII notes that it often takes multiple years for commercial litigation to be resolved. This occurs not because of bias or lack of jurisprudence in the courts, but rather because Indian courts are grossly overburdened. Therefore, they tend to readily allow procedural delays, impeding the hearing process. "If a lawsuit aims at seeking damages, it literally can stretch a lifetime, in some cases, to reach a satisfactory resolution," said Rabindra Jhunjhunwala, attorney at Khaitan & Co. in Mumbai.

Contract Enforcement: Rankings of India, Brazil, and China

	Rank	Time (days)	Cost (% of Claim)
India	178	1,420	39.6%
Brazil	45	731	20.7%
China	7	453	16.2%

(Note: Rankings of 189 countries, with 1 being "best.")

Source: Doing Business Project, World Bank Group, 2016.

Muhtar Kent wrote that the market in India can never be entirely understood. If you come to India with some grand, predetermined strategy or master plan, prepare to be distracted, deterred, and even demoralized.[270]

Given the hurdles, some global companies find it virtually impossible to go it alone in India given the difficulties in doing business. Accordingly, local collaboration in the form of joint ventures, acquisitions, and alliances becomes almost an imperative. However, more than a handful of the multinationals that opted for joint ventures have exited the Indian market, while others have bought out their partners or established themselves as the majority shareholder.[271] "In our experience, local Indian businesses that have commercial interests outside of India tend to be the best partners because their reputation abroad is at risk if they fail to deliver at home," noted James V. Mazzo, global president of ophthalmology, Carl Zeiss Meditec, Inc. He previously served in executive positions with both Allergan Inc. and Abbott Medical Optics.

Insidious Corruption

Corruption, a significant concern in many emerging-country markets, is among the most challenging issues and significant risks in India.

---

[270] "Thinking Outside the Bottle," *McKinsey Quarterly*, December 2013.
[271] "How Multinationals Can Win in India," *McKinsey Quarterly*, 2012, Number 2.

Businesses routinely get into trouble in India when they make payments to win a business contract, to gain regulatory approval of a product, to reduce their taxes, or to avoid custom duties. Often, relatively small payments are used to facilitate routine transactions and services. In some cases, politicians and bureaucrats may seek to extract money by making threats. Some believe the biggest corruption risk, however, is not the bribe or the facilitation payment, but rather the risk that the company's own employees may be on the take.[272]

Although India is making strides to counter corruption, bad behavior continues to metastasize. Corruption, red tape, and bribery are especially prevalent in the judiciary, police, public services, and public procurement sectors. Owing to varying levels of both corruption and the quality of government operations, business conditions vary between and within states. The computerization of some public offices and records has, to some extent, helped reduce facilitation payments in physical encounters with public officials. Nevertheless, because of low levels of enforcement and monitoring, integrity in all state bodies is lacking and facilitation payments and bribes continue to plague businesses.

In July 2013, the Federation of Indian Chambers of Commerce and Industry and Ernst & Young released a bribery and corruption report based on the findings of a survey of local and foreign-owned companies with operations in India. The report revealed the following:

- A large number of the respondents are aware of unethical business conduct, including irregular accounting to hide corrupt activities, gifts paid to seek favors, and the use of third parties to pay bribes.
- More than half of the respondents believe that it is the reluctance to obtain approvals and licenses "the right way" that leads to corrupt activities.
- Complicated licensing and taxing systems are key contributors to corruption.
- More than 80% of the respondents believe that bribery and corruption negatively impact investment.
- The sectors most vulnerable to corruption include infrastructure and real estate, metals and mining, aerospace and defense, and power and utilities.
- Almost 90% of the respondents believe there needs to be greater enforcement of existing laws to curb the proliferation of corrupt activities.[273]

Transparency International's Corruption Perceptions Index 2015, which measures the perceived levels of public-sector corruption in 167 countries and territories, ranks India at 76, above China, tied with Brazil, and below El Salvador and Mongolia (both ranked 72).

The Economist reports that, in a recent poll, 96% of Indians say corruption holds their country back, and 92% believe it has worsened in the past five years. *The Economist* notes that graft in India does not function, as some claim it does elsewhere, as an unseemly but expedient market solution to inert bureaucracy. In fact, the survey suggests that it stalls progress.[274]

---

[272] "Confronting Corruption," by Venkatesan Ravi, *McKinsey Quarterly*, January 2015.
[273] "Bribery and Corruption: Ground Reality in India," Ernst & Young, 2013.
[274] "Fighting Corruption in India: A Bad Boom," *The Economist*, March 15, 2014.

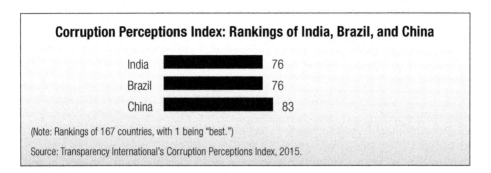

Corruption Perceptions Index: Rankings of India, Brazil, and China

India   76
Brazil   76
China   83

(Note: Rankings of 167 countries, with 1 being "best.")

Source: Transparency International's Corruption Perceptions Index, 2015.

There are many causes of corrupt activities in India, including a bottom-heavy bureaucracy, widespread red tape, a higher tolerance for corruption, and lax and inconsistent anti-bribery enforcement. Other factors contributing to India's corruption are excessive regulations, complicated tax and licensing systems, a multitude of government departments each with opaque powers, monopolies by government-controlled institutions on certain services and goods, and the lack of transparent laws and processes. Additionally, according to the World Bank, only 35% of adults in India have had access to a formal bank account. Therefore, a significant percentage of the population is vulnerable to exploitation from people involved in informal channels that fall outside regulatory control, such as money lenders or operators of fraudulent savings schemes. This situation exacerbates the threat of bad behavior.

The corruption risks associated with third parties in India is particularly troublesome. Frequent contact with all levels of the government, either directly or through third-party relationships, is customary. Third-party intermediaries such as agents, consultants, lawyers, dealers, accountants, distributors, and custom agents, who are often hired to deal with government agencies and officials, can make the detection of corrupt activities even more problematic.

As part of due diligence on third parties, it is not uncommon to include the search and review of public information databases, media reports in local languages, and/or discreet inquiries made by experienced former law enforcement agents. In India, however, only very limited information may be available on third parties, severely restricting the effectiveness of what would be considered normal due diligence.[275]

Several laws in India address corrupt activities. The principal law governing the corruption of public officials is the Prevention of Corruption Act. Unlike the U.S. Foreign Corrupt Practices Act, which is focused on the bribe giver, the primary focus of the Prevention of Corruption Act is on the bribe taker (the recipient), which prohibits the receipt of any gratification by public officials, as well as other related acts. Private-sector corruption is addressed by the Companies Act. The Indian Penal Code, the Right to Information Act, and the Prevention of Money Laundering Act also address corruption. In addition, the Modi Administration has committed to taking strong anti-corruption measures, although new initiatives remain pending.

---

[275]"Managing Corruption Risks in India," by Anthony Campanelli, Deloitte, 2014.

Common Corrupt Practices in India

Paying bribes

- Paying high salaries to selected employees, with an understanding that the excess amount will be used to make improper payments.
- Routing improper payments through payment facilitators, such as vendors or material suppliers, who pass on the cash to liaising agents, keeping themselves out of the loop.
- Paying a periodic performance bonus to vendors assisting in the procurement of licenses.
- Presenting gift cards, such as prepaid cash cards issued by banks, to government officials with whom there is frequent interaction.

Hiding bribes

- Capitalizing bribes paid to set up a factory, offices, or shops.
- Bribes paid in cash and recorded fictitiously under "repairs and maintenance."
- Bribes paid through dealers and distributors and recorded as "performance bonus payments."
- Expenditures for gifts recorded under reimbursement for "meals, entertainment, or travel."
- Funds spent on liaising with government officials, recorded as "retainer fees."

Source: "Bribery and Corruption: Ground Reality in India," Ernst & Young, 2013.

Corruption is an area that requires both locally focused and expert advice. The board and management of any U.S. company doing business in India need to have a clear understanding of their duties and responsibilities under the FCPA.

Given the environment in India, anti-corruption compliance programs need to be customized and calibrated and not simply part of a "one size fits all" program. A customized program should include a critical assessment of the corruption exposures and an analysis of the services and products that require frequent contact with government agencies and officials and therefore present unique risks. Making compliance relevant to local teams means engaging them to design specific procedures. It is not the board's role to devise tactics. Rather, the board should establish guiding principles, which management can then follow in a rational, locally efficient manner.

The board and management need to be aware, however, that putting compliance policies and procedures into place may be insufficient if the program is not effectively monitored and regularly reviewed. Board oversight should be persistent in determining whether internal controls are effectively detecting and thwarting corrupt activities. Management should share its findings with the board and explain how it is remediating the gaps.

"The difficulties in dealing with bad behavior and complying with U.S. and Indian anti-corruption laws are big concerns for directors, requiring both their understanding of the environment and persistence," noted Rahul Merchant, a board member of Jupiter Networks Inc.

Outlier on IP Protection

Another consequential risk in India is the theft of intellectual property. Some of the important factors to consider include the considerable time it takes to register IP, frequent instances of reported IP theft and infringement, and India's legal bureaucracy associated with the enforcement of IP rights.

Financial Services at a Glance

The percentage ownership of local banks by foreign investors is restricted to 74% in private banks and 20% in public banks, subject to the approval of the Foreign Investment Promotion Board. Foreign banks have less than 17% of the total branch network in India, about 7% of the total banking sector assets, and 11% of bank profits. Citibank, JP Morgan, and Bank of America are invested primarily to serve their multinational clients, while their relationships with Indian corporate clients are pivoted around their ability to provide access to global capital and debt markets.

According to Shashank Tripathi, "As competitiveness in the banking sector grows, there is likely to be a liberalization of the regulatory restrictions. Inorganic opportunities via acquisitions will become more important as foreign banks continue to find the branch licensing requirements difficult to navigate."

He also noted that, "Foreign investment in the insurance sector, including insurance companies, insurance brokers, third-party administrators, surveyors, and loss assessors, is permitted up to 49%, subject to obtaining a license from the Insurance Regulatory and Development Authority. However, the breadth and complexity of the license application process can take significant time to prepare for, which has often discouraged interested parties."

According to KPMG/CII, the IP laws in India are not yet able to keep pace with global trends and standards, as the rights and liabilities of licensees of IP in proprietary technology are unclear and often inadequate. Many believe that this has restricted investment. Most companies will invest in emerging-country markets only if they believe that the IP will be protected by laws and there will be timely intervention by the judiciary to enforce such laws.

The Global Intellectual Property Center, the principal institution of the U.S. Chamber of Commerce handling issues relating to intellectual property, ranks the IP environment in India 37th out of 38 economies, based on an evaluation of 30 indicators that reflect a robust IP system. Only Venezuela ranks below India. Brazil ranks 28th and China 21st. Among the 30 indicators are patents, trademarks, copyrights, enforcement, and international treaty participation.[276]

Continued weak IP laws and enforcement that is, at best, well below average, limits investment in R&D and discourages foreign investors from bringing their technology into the country. "Although India is making genuine attempts to enhance IP protection, there remain serious challenges with respect to implementation. Even where protective rules are in place, enforcement through the Indian court system can be time consuming and unpredictable as to outcomes," commented Pretap Amin, a partner in Freshfields Bruckhaus Deringer.

Given a number of measures initiated by the government, greater emphasis has been placed on the enforcement of India's copyright and patent laws. For example, various mechanisms such as the digitization of trademark and patent registers along with e-filing platforms are significantly improving the IP filing processes. The Modi Administration released a draft national policy on intellectual property, which recognizes the fundamental links between IP, innovation, and the successful development of innovative

---

[276] "The U.S. Chamber International IP Index: Infinite Possibilities," U.S. Chamber of Commerce, February 10, 2016.

products. It is hoped and expected that the formation of a high-level IP working group as part of the Trade Policy Forum will elicit further measurable and sustainable changes to India's IP system.

As local Indian companies continue to innovate and invest in their own R&D pipelines, they will also need IP protection. As in other emerging-country markets, this may very well stimulate constructive change and the greater enforcement of IP laws. The relatively early stage of India's pipeline, however, suggests that policies and enforcement changes will not occur rapidly.

Final Comments

India represents an exciting and important opportunity for businesses, particularly as the government's "Make in India" program gains momentum. Although growth prospects are exceptionally appealing, directors and managements need to understand the nature, breadth, and depth of the risks, which can be debilitating.

Directors and managements who expect to succeed simply by transplanting their normal ways of doing business into India using global templates likely will be disappointed in the results. The risks associated with bureaucratic delays and regulatory barriers, corrupt activities, and inadequate protection of intellectual property are imposing threats and immense obstacles for multinationals. It is imperative for directors and management to understand the Indian mind-set, adapt their practices to local conditions, and remain alert to changes in the environment.

Questions Directors Should Ask About the Risks in India

- How are market entry and penetration achieved most effectively and efficiently? What are the benefits and detriments of entering into local partnerships, joint ventures, alliances, or other relationships?
- What initiatives are being explored or are already in place to simplify and safeguard the payment of taxes?
- What are the challenges with contract enforcement? How are contracts validated and enforced?
- What is the nature and magnitude of compliance risk? Does management periodically identify and prioritize the key corruption risks? What are the local practices and customs that could increase corruption risks?
- Have all relations with government agencies and officials been identified, prioritized, and assessed? Which products sold and services delivered require frequent contact with government agencies and officials that present opportunities for bad behavior? What is the potential for conflicts of interest?
- What anti-corruption programs are in place and how effective is the monitoring of these programs?
- What intellectual property has been or will be transferred and what are the risk mitigations against infringements? Are limits on IP transfers workable?
- Are the experiences of board members sufficient to understand, identify, and help address the risks of doing business in India? If not, how will the board address these gaps?

Responding to
an Aging World

"And, in the end, it is not the years in your life that count. It is the life in your years."

—Abraham Lincoln

Many directors are vaguely aware that titanic demographic shifts are transforming societies and their businesses, yet they downplay the threats of an aging world. Boards and management cannot turn back or slow down the clock. But they need to respond to demographic risks that are resulting from retirements and changes in productivity as employees age, as well as seize the opportunities inherent with an aging population.

Demography seeks to understand population changes by investigating age, gender, ethnicity, home ownership, mobility, disabilities, language knowledge, employment, and location. These elements, and how they change, constitute vital information about the population of a given location, which influences all human activity, including the economic, social, political, and cultural aspects.

Ben S. Bernanke, former chairman of the Federal Reserve, predicted over 10 years ago that, in the coming decades, many forces will shape our economy and our society, but in all likelihood no single factor will have as pervasive an effect as the aging of the population. He notes that adequate preparation for the coming demographic transition may well involve significant adjustments in patterns of work effort, consumption, and savings.[277]

The basic forces behind today's demographic shifts are simply that people are living longer and having fewer children. The specific reasons vary among countries and societies, but they include better health care, marrying later in life, the availability of family planning, economic uncertainties, and more women in the workplace.

In the developed world, the average life expectancy increased from about 66 years in 1950 to roughly 78 years by 2010. Over the same period, fertility rates fell from 2.8 to 1.7, measured as number of children per female. Given that a fertility rate of 2.1 indicates a stable population, and excluding the effects of immigration, populations in developed countries are in decline.

---

[277] "The Coming Demographic Transition: Will We Treat Future Generations Fairly?" Remarks by Ben S. Bernanke, Washington Economic Club, Washington, D.C., October 4, 2006.

Comparative Demographics

		U.S.	Germany	China	India
Fertility rate	2011	2.1	1.4	1.5	2.6
Year in which labor force began decline		—	1999	2015	—
65+ age group as % of 15-to-64 population	2010	19%	31%	12%	8%
	2050 (Est.)	33%	53%	45%	22%

Source: "Headwinds, Tailwinds and the Riddles of Demographics," by Jorrit Volkers and Ardie van Berkel, Deloitte, 2012.

Today, about 60% of the world's population lives in countries with fertility rates below the replacement rate. While aging has been evident in the developed world for some time, Japan and Russia have seen their populations actually decline. The demographic deficit is now spreading to China and will soon reach Latin America. For the first time, the population could plateau in most of the world.

The European Commission expects that, by 2060, Germany's population will shrink by 19%, and the number of its people of working age will fall from 54 million in 2010 to 36 million. Although China's workforce-age population has grown by more than 100% since the year 1970, it is expected to contract 11% by 2050 even as the country's economy continues to expand.[278]

As life spans grow and birthrates fall, an aging working population will be supporting ever higher numbers of retirees. Among the developed countries, only the U.S. has a demographic profile favorable to long-term economic growth, although the U.S. adds about 1.6 million retirees annually. For the rest of these developed economies, expected productivity improvements will not bridge the gap. Without the continued participation of older workers, the introduction of more female workers, and the acceptance of more immigrant workers, the workforces and economic growth of many regions and countries, and the prosperity of their private sectors, are expected to be seriously limited.[279]

Demographic factors play a significant role in determining how the future will take shape. The aging population has far-reaching impacts, ranging from growing pressure on critical resources to sweeping changes in goals and aspirations at the personal and social level. Beyond sheer demographics, technology advances are adding to the aging trends by helping people live healthier and longer. The combined effects of both demographics and technology advances on business strategies, which represent both an opportunity and a threat, are significant.

---

[278] *No Ordinary Disruption: The Four Global Forces Breaking All the Trends*, by Richard Dobbs, James Manyiks, and Jonathan Woetzel, PublicAffairs, 2015.
[279] "Shifting Tides: Global Economic Scenarios for 2015-25," by Luis Enriquez, Sven Smit, and Jonathan Ablett, McKinsey & Company, September 2015.

Countries with Forecasts for Workforce Declines
(Years 2010 to 2050)

	Total Decline (-)
Japan	−32%
Russia	−27%
Germany	−27%
Italy	−20%
China	−15%

Note: Assumes no significant changes in migration or policy.

Source: *No Ordinary Disruption: The Four Global Forces Breaking All the Trends*, by Richard Dobbs, James Manyiks, and Jonathan Woetzel, PublicAffairs, 2015.

Business Impacts

Global aging is not just about the retirement of baby boomers in the U.S. and Europe, nor does it represent a temporary bubble. Global aging represents an unprecedented shift in the demographic equilibrium that will not only have social, political, and economic ramifications, but also impact global businesses in the areas of workforce planning and consumer opportunities.

Workforce Planning

The growth rate of the workforce-age segment in the U.S. population has slowed significantly, and in other countries, like Japan and Germany, the size of the workforce is shrinking. Death rates are as significant as birth rates. Longer life expectancies increase the population, but not necessarily the workforce.

As employees age, businesses can face significant losses of critical knowledge and skills, as well as decreased productivity. Workforce aging can be exacerbated by the relentless focus on cost reductions, particularly in the post-financial-crisis era where growth rates have stagnated in many industries and geographies. In their zeal to become lean, boards and management initiate and lead round after round of layoffs, without appreciating that in a few years these businesses may confront skills or labor shortages or, if mostly younger workers are shed, be left with an excessively aged workforce. In other cases, when employees retire in droves, there may be no one left who knows how to solicit and manage important customer relationships, develop new products and render services, address the concerns of regulators, or manage risk processes.[280]

As the workforce ages, two categories of demographic risk become apparent: 1) the risks associated with increasing numbers of retiring employees, and 2) the risks having to do with the productivity or performance of older employees.

---

[280] "Managing Demographic Risk," by Rainer Strack, Jens Baier, and Andres Fahlander, *Harvard Business Review*, February 2008.

When an employee retires, the business loses intellectual capital and accumulated knowledge and expertise. If more than a few employees retire and are not replaced, there will be "capacity risks," or the diminished ability to carry on the production of goods and services.

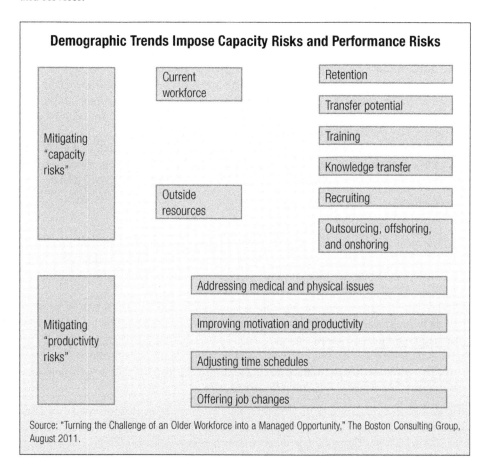

Demographic Trends Impose Capacity Risks and Performance Risks

Source: "Turning the Challenge of an Older Workforce into a Managed Opportunity," The Boston Consulting Group, August 2011.

In addition, even before aging employees begin retiring in large numbers, they can pose other troubling and distinctive challenges. Although age brings experience and wisdom that make employees valuable in a variety of ways, productivity can suffer. Older employees may lack skills owing to technology advances. They may become less motivated because of fewer career opportunities ahead. They also tend to demonstrate greater resistance against organizational change and are more likely to be susceptible to the risks of absenteeism and declining health. As a consequence, even though age and experience can make workers wiser and more effective, an aging workforce can also create "productivity risks."[281]

---

[281] Ibid.

This combination of a generally older workforce and disproportionate levels of retirements and productivity issues requires a rethinking and potentially a reconfiguration of human resource paradigms.

The Boston Consulting Group highlights several workforce capacity risks and possible strategic responses:

- Today, there is an adequate supply of qualified employees for most job categories. In the future, qualified employees for many positions will become scarcer, intensifying the competition for top talent and increasing labor costs.
- Today, older workers are offered early retirement incentives so that cheaper labor can be hired. In the future, businesses will do their best to retain older workers through a variety of incentives, including offering jobs with more time flexibility and creating new advisory positions.
- Today, resource requirements generally cannot be accurately foreshadowed more than two to three years out. In the future, requirements will have to be planned five to 10 years in advance and include targeted job specifications and required skills.

In terms of workforce productivity risks, Boston Consulting Group has made the following suggestions:

- Today, older workers' productivity is generally assumed to decline. In the future, retaining older workers and investing to maintain their productivity, through new education, workplace adaptation, and internal transfers, will become a source of competitive advantage.
- Today, job mobility is typically moving upward. In the future, careers will be more likely to progress horizontally, such as to an advisory position, or downward to a less demanding post with a lower salary.
- Today, salaries generally increase with age and seniority, potentially making older workers less attractive for employers. In the future, performance-based compensation regardless of age will become the norm.

The Boston Consulting Group emphasizes that businesses that approach capacity and productivity issues as an opportunity to get the most out of older workers' experience will be best positioned as talent becomes progressively scarcer.[282]

In addition to capacity and productivity risks, a complicating factor in transitioning to the next generation of workers is that those entering the workforce today are far less committed to one employer than, for instance, the baby boomers were. "The new generation of workers puts much greater value on their employer's commitment to community, personal wellness, and better work/life integration. From a career perspective, they want to be the architect of their careers and as a result will change employers much more quickly," said Annemieke van der Werff, chief human resources officer, MUFG Union Bank. This will require adjustments in planning the workforce of the future by replacing historical assumptions about career aspirations and employment mobility with new assumptions.

---

[282] "Global Aging: How Companies Can Adapt to the New Reality," The Boston Consulting Group, 2011.

Consumer Opportunities

Over the next 20 years, the 65-and-over segment of the population is expected to account for a significant share of the growth in consumer spending. They will make up a large portion of the market and will be active consumers for a longer duration. Boards need to understand the dynamics of this age group and ask management to develop strategies, market and delivery approaches, and products and services to meet this segment's evolving needs.

The notion of what it means to be "old" is becoming no longer static but dynamic. Boards and management should realize that the older consumers of tomorrow will be different from this segment today. In the coming years, many people in their 60s and 70s may be perceived as still in their prime years, continuing to pursue their education, working in new and different careers, and maintaining an overall activity level not previously associated with those age groups. Businesses need to consider this when targeting older consumers.

At the same time, strategies need to take into account the fact that aging typically brings increased physical limitations and adjust their product and service offerings to handle the challenges related to housing, health care, everyday purchases and activities, and other domains.

Older consumers generally look for products and services that are functional, simple, accessible, and convenient. They also have a lower propensity to change brands. And although they do not want to be patronized in any way because of their age, they want their special needs to be acknowledged. Businesses will need to respond to this in a way that emphasizes the positive rather than the negative aspects of aging.

In response, boards and management need to direct a careful review of product and service offerings. Some may be ill suited to this segment, so a simple repackaging will not be enough to attract older consumers. A new product development process that is efficient and age appropriate can help bring innovative products and services to the market designed specifically for older buyers. For example, age-friendly customization of products and services in retail banking is increasingly common. Telephone, online, ATM, and physical touch points are getting a makeover to cater to customers' differing visual, hearing, and accessibility needs. TD Canada Trust has developed a toolbar, designed with a television remote in mind, to specifically help aging customers navigate the Web, adjust font size and volume, and instantly access help.[283]

In addition, marketing targeted specifically to an aging demographic will be essential. If more older people are likely to be working longer, they will have greater disposable incomes. As these customers' preferences and needs change over time, the market strategies and the channel strategies will require recalibration.[284]

A Hyper-aging Japan

Barring the unimaginable, just 30 years from now, Japan will be a far less populated and a vastly more aged country than today. Aging and population decline will profoundly alter the realm of the possible for Japan and will have major reverberations on its social and eco-

---

[283] *No Ordinary Disruption: The Four Global Forces Breaking All the Trends*, 2015.
[284] "Global Aging: How Companies Can Adapt to the New Reality," 2011.

nomic positions[285] and the well-being of its businesses. Japan's ability to craft a successful aging strategy has global implications since other countries will soon follow its path.

The hyper-aging society in Japan presents an acute challenge for boards and managements with operations based there. It also provides some useful lessons for businesses in other geographies.

Japan is the world's oldest country, with 25% of its people aged 65 or over, compared with 15% in the U.S. By 2040, that ratio is estimated to rise to the historically high level of 36%. The population of Japan nearly tripled in the 20th century, despite the attrition caused during the war years, peaking at 128 million in 2010. But with a falling birth rate, one of the world's longest life expectancies, and close to zero net immigration, Japan is headed for not only a uniquely high ratio of seniors, but also a sharp downturn in its total population. This is putting tremendous strains on Japan's ability to manage its rising debt and social security obligations, while also creating growing scarcities of labor.[286]

The official census figures released in February 2016 indicate that Japan's population shrank by 947,000, or 0.7%, compared with the last census in 2010, an unprecedented drop for a society not ravaged by war or some other deadly crisis. Because Japan's low birthrate means each generation is smaller than the last, the bulging cohort of older Japanese is expected to be supported by a narrowing base of younger working people.[287]

"The growing shortages of talent in Japan require emphasis on increasing the overall working-age population by encouraging more females into the workforce, relaxing immigration policies, and raising the workforce participation by seniors," commented Hiroyuki Suzuki, who recently retired from his post as chairman, PricewaterhouseCoopers in Tokyo.

Japan is making headway on greater female participation in the workforce—much faster progress than South Korea, but far slower progress than China, Taiwan, and the Philippines. Japan is also addressing the need to render the labor market a friendlier place for females by enacting changes in policy. As part of the Japanese growth strategy championed by Prime Minister Shinzo Abe, the government has pledged to create more flexible working environments for women and promote them to leadership roles. A third of employers in Japan plan to hire more women and foreign workers as the labor market responds to Abenomics, according to a survey conducted by Korn Ferry Hay Group.[288]

Given Japan's history as one of the world's most homogeneous cultures, revising the country's rigid immigration laws is proving to be problematic. Alone among the developed countries, Japan has reported net out-migration over the past four decades. It remains to be seen if the rigid work barriers imposed on foreign workers will be relaxed by policy makers.

Moreover, programs that make the senior population more productive, while helping to staff jobs that otherwise would be impossible to fill as the population shrinks, continue to confront obstacles because of general resistance from employers and the lack of a large market to outplace seniors. As a benchmark, France took a century to double the

---

[285] "Demography and Japan's Future," by Nicholas Eberstadt, McKinsey & Company, 2011.

[286] "Japan: Lessons from a Hyper-aging Society," by Misato Adachi, Ryo Ishida, and Genki Oka, McKinsey & Company, March 2015.

[287] "Japan Lost Nearly a Million People in 5 Years, Census Says," *New York Times*, February 26, 2016.

[288] "Abenomics' Impact on Hiring Activity," *Japan Today*, September 19, 2013.

share of its over-60 workers. Japan needs to accomplish close to the same goal in a much shorter time frame.

Hiroyuki Murata, author of some of Japan's best-selling books, including *The Business of Aging: 10 Successful Strategies for a Diverse Market*, commented that Japan needs to change its view from anti-aging to smart aging.[289]

Another important aspect of addressing the shortage of talent is Japan's emphasis on technology to increase productivity. Technology has traditionally been thought of as an effective way to substitute for labor and reduce labor costs. However, Japan is emphasizing the use of technology to make the most of skills that workers have and to improve their productivity, both blue and white collar. In this regard, Japanese companies are leading the way in exploring innovative applications in specialty areas such as robotics.[290]

Some illustrations highlight the importance of leveraging aging workers and supplementing the work force, and the initiatives being pursued by Japanese companies.

Toyota Motor Corporation, which used to maintain strict age-based retirement programs, is implementing re-employment programs that enable retiring workers to apply for positions at the company and its affiliates. Toyota is retiring about half of its aging employees through the program, allowing the company to retain their skills and experience as it maintains flexibility. In return, the retiring employees gain income, social interaction, and the opportunity to continue working on a part-time basis.[291]

The NEC Corporation has established the Lifetime Career Support program, which provides employees opportunities to gather information and plan their future careers while still working at the company. When employees turn 50, they become eligible for training that includes personal financial planning; classes on work, family, and community themes; and coaching toward life goals. They are also given help with developing specific career plans. When they reach age 55, they can participate in Life Design seminars in which they can study topics such as pension and severance benefits systems and possible extended employment.[292]

Bank of Tokyo Mitsubishi UFJ, Japan's largest financial institution, employs a small robot speaking 19 languages to greet customers. Komatsu Ltd. is developing self-driving vehicles for construction sites, while industrial robot maker Fanuc Corporation, which specializes in automation solutions, is designing machines that repair each other.[293]

How Japan responds to this unprecedented demographic shift can help guide responses in other aging geographies. Boards and management may be able to learn from Japan's experience and apply these practices in other markets impacted by aging demographics.

U.S. Demographics

For the first time in its history, the U.S. is facing a situation where the percentage of the working-age population is shrinking.

---

[289] "Graying Japan Looks for a Silver Lining," *The Wall Street Journal*, November 30, 2015.

[290] "Turning the Challenge of an Older Workforce into a Managed Opportunity," The Boston Consulting Group, August 2011.

[291] *No Ordinary Disruption: Four Global Forces Breaking All the Trends*, 2015.

[292] "Turning the Challenge of an Older Workforce into a Managed Opportunity," August 2011.

[293] "Graying Japan Looks for a Silver Lining," November 30, 2015.

According to Paul Taylor, former executive vice president of Pew Research Center, two major demographic trends are happening in the U.S. First, the country's population is aging. Older generations have always needed the younger generations to drive the economy. However, Taylor noted that millennials, the youngest generation in today's workforce, are collectively experiencing great difficulty in launching their careers and remain largely dependent on their families. Second, Taylor points out that, by the year 2050, immigrants will constitute the largest ever share of the American population, which will alter the dynamics of the country's consumer base.[294]

In March 2011, the Congressional Research Service issued "The Changing Demographic Profile of the United States," a report for members and committees of Congress that describes three trends shaping demographics:

1. The U.S. is getting bigger. The growth is due to the trends in the interplay of increased births, decreased deaths, and increased net immigration. The employment rates of women will continue to rise.
2. The U.S. is getting older. The rapid aging of the population, as reflected by an increasing proportion of persons 65 and older, and an increasing median age of the population are profound demographic changes. The number of Americans who are 65 or over is expected to be one in five by the year 2050.
3. The U.S. is becoming more racially and ethnically diverse. Immigration is a major influence on both the size and the age of the population. If current demographic trends continue, the Hispanic population as a percentage of the total population through the year 2050 will increase from 12.6% in the year 2000 to 30.2%.

U.S. Population by Age Group

Percent in Age Group	1975	2000	2025 (Est.)	2050 (Est.)
0 – 19	35.0	28.6	26.4	25.7
20 – 64	54.5	59.0	55.8	54.1
65+	10.5	12.4	17.9	20.2

Source: "The Changing Demographic Profile of the United States," by Laura B. Shrestha and Elayne J. Heisler, Congressional Research Center, March 31, 2011

The report notes that the declining labor force participation of older men is one of the most dramatic trends of past decades. The report highlights that the decision to remain in the workforce or retire is based on a complex interaction of factors, such as eligibility for social security benefits, availability of employer benefits such as pensions, work incentives to stay in the labor force, the status of one's health, availability of government programs, and leisure versus employment trade-offs.

Accenture foreshadows dramatic changes in the quantity and quality of talent in the U.S. workforce. As baby boomers retire, the working-age population (15 to 64 years) is shrinking as a share of the total population. In fact, Accenture predicts that the working-age population will decline to an historic low of 61% by 2030. Additionally, as the workforce declines, the largest drop will be among young people. In combination, these

[294] "Expert Advice on Leveraging Disruption," *NACD Directorship*, May/June 2015.

factors suggest that the base of talent in the U.S. is in a steady decline. Moreover, Accenture noted that the growth rate in productivity of the workforce has been unreliable, falling below 1% for five of the last 10 years.[295]

The Wall Street Journal asked experts how they thought demographic shifts in the U.S. will influence business in the next decade. The responses provide some unique perspectives.

Rosabeth Moss Kanter, a professor at the Harvard Business School, noted that the two largest demographic changes are the entry of women into the U.S. workforce and vastly increased longevity, which means 20 to 30 productive years beyond conventional retirement age. She notes that businesses need to increase their work flexibility, permit virtual work, reduce schedules, and adopt a variety of other human resource policies that take these changes into account. To thrive going forward, she suggests emphasizing the importance of being multicultural—that is, providing a better education and opportunities for everyone regardless of race or geography.

Jay Hooley, president and CEO, State Street Corporation, commented that in the next 10 years, as the U.S. becomes even more diverse, so will the workforce and the products and services that institutions offer. More women will rise through the ranks of leadership, and new cultural perspectives will permeate every level of the most successful institutions, from the boardroom to the mailroom.

Bruce Nolop, former CFO of both Pitney Bowes Inc. and E*Trade Financial Corp., said that the aging population has profound implications for business, particularly on human resource strategies as businesses seek to retain sufficiently productive and skilled employees to meet their talent needs. He suggests that the demographic transition will not occur naturally and instead will require creative destruction of traditional practices. Given that many older people will continue working, he recommends a reevaluation of employee-value propositions for a dramatically altered workforce, including the following:

- Shifting more employees to part-time positions that may better suit the lifestyle expectations of older workers.
- Offering more flexible benefits packages that tailor medical and savings programs to different age groups.
- Accelerating the integration of medical benefits with government health care programs.
- Providing additional training to long-time employees to keep them current on new technologies and redesigned processes.
- Revising management development programs to reflect longer career trajectories that anticipate greater intergenerational competition for coveted positions.

Robert A. Howell, a visiting professor at the Tuck School of Business at Dartmouth, said that three major demographic shifts in the U.S. will significantly influence businesses in the next decade. First, the aging population known as the "baby boomers" will move into super-senior status. Second, the proportion of nonwhites will increase. And third, the advanced technological competencies of the millennials and their successors will have significant impacts. Howell notes that businesses need to recognize

---

[295] "U.S. States: For Richer, For Poorer? Winning the Battle for Talent and Securing our Standard of Living," Accenture, 2014.

and address these major shifts and that the inability to do so will ultimately result in business failures.

Noreena Hertz of the Center for the Study of Decision-Making at University College in London highlighted that the risk of depending on aging workers is not having the skills needed for advances in technology. She notes that productivity may suffer as older workers find it difficult to cope with physically demanding jobs and their health problems result in increased absenteeism or reduced roles. She believes there is a real danger of knowledge shortages within the workplace as large swaths of the workforce start to leave businesses all at once.

And Wayne Mekjian, executive vice president and head of information services, Wells Fargo & Company, commented that the next generation has such a strong connection to mobile devices that they have completely different outlooks and expectations. Mobility has changed everything. He emphasizes that mobile banking at Wells Fargo is its fastest-growing channel, growing 38% annually. He adds that products and services are being developed based, in large part, on how customers want to interact with the providers of these products and services.[296]

Creative responses to the aging workforce in the U.S. require special attention and sensitivities from directors and management. "In considering the retention of older workers using downward progression, lower compensation, and addressing physical limitations, directors and management need to carefully consider employment laws and regulations which can, in some instances, work against these approaches," cautioned Sharon A. Cheever, senior vice president and general counsel, Pacific Life Insurance Company. The use of contingent workers, temporary or part-time, who work under contract for a fixed period or a specific project, in some cases, may be an attractive alternative.

Implications for Directors

Falling fertility rates, slowing population growth, and aging populations will all have profound effects on tomorrow's workforce. New workers will enter at a slower pace, older workers will work longer than today, and the definition of the workforce itself will change.

Boards and management cannot afford to stand still and watch as employees and customers age. Fundamental changes are required in the way employees, stakeholders, and customers are managed over their life spans. Strategic assumptions that drive decisions on crucial talent issues will need to be updated and revised. "The aging of the population requires a different perspective on the elderly as employees, stakeholders, consumers, and customers. Shifts in longevity will affect business models and talent goals and ambitions," said Henry R. Keizer, board member of both Hertz Corporation and WABCO Holdings Inc.

Directors need to recognize that the workforce likely will need to be retooled. In the aging economies, older workers will need to learn new skills and remain longer, and their work may have to be supplemented by migrant populations. In some geographies, more emphasis will need to be placed on the recruitment, development, and retention of females. In emerging-country markets, the gaps between supply and demand for educated workers will have to be filled.[297]

---

[296] "How Will Changing Demographics in the U.S. Influence Business in the Coming Decade?" *The Wall Street Journal*, November 29, 2013.

[297] "Five Megatrends and Possible Implications," PricewaterhouseCoopers, April 2014

According to PricewaterhouseCoopers' annual global CEO survey, 62% of respondents are planning to increase headcount, and most recognize the need to change or are already changing their strategies for attracting and retaining talent. Almost two-thirds are concerned that the lack of key skills could threaten growth prospects.[298]

A KPMG survey suggests that 30% of the U.S. respondents believe that talent management and development is their biggest challenge and a fundamental risk.[299]

Questions Directors Should Ask About Aging Demographics

- What is the impact on the global workforce of the different strategic scenarios and initiatives? What are the critical talent assumptions underlying the strategy?
- How will the workforce develop over the next 10 years, judging by attrition rates, retirements, and other factors? What is the impact of aging on the availability, capability requirements, and the overall quality of talent?
- How is management preparing for the expected changes and threats posed by the aging workforce?
- How is technology used to make the most of employees' skills and improve productivity? How is technology impacting workflow and functions in general?
- Which initiatives and programs are deployed to promote greater female participation in the workforce and render the workplace more inclusive?
- Which qualifications, tools, and metrics are used to monitor and manage strategic workforce planning?
- How are directors able to provide support and guidance to management regarding demographic shifts? How has the board challenged itself and management about the opportunities and threats posed by the demographic changes?
- What is management's approach to employing immigrants? What are the barriers or inhibitors?
- Which elements of the strategic plan are targeted at marketing to aging consumers? Which products and services are customized specifically for seniors?
- In what ways are data and third-party advisors used to shape strategic plans resulting from the aging workforce?
- What are management's succession plans and do they describe competencies needed in the changing environment? Should mandatory retirement ages for management and employees be reconsidered?
- Should changes to the board's mandatory retirement age be considered given demographic trends? How should the board approach this decision? What are the important factors?

Directors should direct management, as a matter of some urgency, to focus on global workforce planning. The Boston Consulting Group observes that fewer than 10% of businesses deploy sophisticated workforce supply-and-demand models and plan their workforce needs more than a few years in advance. Many businesses continue to operate on old assumptions and prejudices. Not many can confidently say where their older workers are concentrated or how likely it is that a wave of retirements will happen. According to

---

[298] "Good to Grow: Annual Global CEO Survey," PricewaterhouseCoopers, 2014.
[299] "Global Audit Committee Survey," Audit Committee Institute, KPMG, 2015.

BCG, in many workplaces there is no clarity about where older employees' attributes are most beneficial and where they may be less suitable.[300]

In a graying world, rather than viewing older employees as legacy costs, they must be seen by directors and management as assets and resources. Aging employees often possess critical skills, education, talent, and experience. In order to engage workers who are older, and for whom the attraction of a full-time position may be decreasing over time, directors and management need to become comfortable dealing with more flexible employment packages. Such arrangements can help retain older employees, but on terms possibly more appealing to them. Another important element may be to offer specific training to help retain older workers, redefine their roles, and keep their skills updated. Smart innovation with this labor pool can be a differentiator.

Directors are often challenged to understand, appreciate, and evaluate the pervasive effect that the aging of the population is having and will have on strategy, execution, and risk management. In addition to providing new consumer opportunities, the aging of the population will radically reshape global workforces, requiring management to undertake multi-year talent programs to maximize the opportunities and mitigate the threats. As a result, demographic risk management needs to be an integral part of strategy and be viewed not as a one-time analysis or initiative, but rather as an ongoing and important component of strategy and risk discussions.

"Setting aside time at board meetings to discuss the changing external environment and significant trends can help directors and management ensure the continuous viability of their institution versus allowing it to become irrelevant," commented Michael R. Gallagher, a board member of Allergan Inc.

Honda Lifts Retirement Age as Japan Inc. Copes with Aging

Honda Motor Company plans to shake up employment terms and lift its retirement age by five years to 65, making the carmaker one of Japan Inc.'s largest companies to take action in coping with the country's aging demographics.

Other proposed changes applying to about 40,000 employees at Honda and five of its group companies include a shift to child care and nursing allowances, rather than family allowances. Honda also plans to introduce a work-from-home and a partial-workday system, and adopt a salary and bonus structure that widens the pay gap between higher and lower performers.

These moves position Honda as one of the most aggressive companies seeking programs and policies to help deal with a population in Japan that is aging at the fastest pace in the developed world. More flexible work arrangements also contribute to the government's initiatives to boost the proportion of women in the workplace.

Retirement-age systems are almost universal in Japan. For about 91% of companies with at least 1,000 workers, the retirement age is 60. Programs directed at working from home and support for employees with children are an exception in Japan.

Source: *Bloomberg Business*, November 30, 2015.

---

[300] "Turning the Challenge of an Older Workforce into a Managed Opportunity," The Boston Consulting Company, August 2011.

Risks in Using Big Data and Advanced Analytics

"Information is not knowledge."
—ALBERT EINSTEIN

Big data. Just because you can, does not mean you should. As a board member, do you really know what your data scientists are up to? Which specific data elements are they collecting and analyzing? What are the data sources? More importantly, how are they using the analyses? Have the algorithms outpaced the institution's ability to manage them wisely?

The bigness of data is growing faster than boards and management realize. Today, more data is generated in 10 minutes than all of humanity created through the year 2003.[301] The Computer Services Corp. predicts that, by 2020, the annual generation of data will increase by 4,300%. Drivers include the switch from analog to digital technologies and the rapid increase in data generation by individuals and corporations alike.[302]

Individuals are using global digital platforms to learn, find work, showcase their talent, and build personal networks. Some 600 million people have international connections on social media, and 360 million take part in cross-border e-commerce.[303] Digital platforms for both traditional employment and freelance assignments are beginning to create a more global labor market.

The promise of big data is that it can combine multiple, disparate data sets to yield answers that could never come from studying separate piles of data alone. The ability to collect, manage, and analyze data effectively can lead to better business decisions and competitive advantage. Indeed, Ernst & Young's research shows that companies that successfully use data are outperforming their peers by as much as 20%.[304] Although this movement makes it possible for businesses to reach markets with business models that are less capital-intensive, it poses important new risks and policy challenges as well.

---

[301] "Big Data: Changing the Way Businesses Compete and Operate," Ernst & Young, April 2014.
[302] "The Rapid Growth of Global Data," Computer Services Corp., 2012.
[303] "Digital Globalization: The New Era of Global Flows," by James Manyika, Susan Lund, Jacques Bughin, Jonathan Woetzel, Kalin Stamenov, and Dhruv Dhingra, McKinsey Global Institute, February 2016.
[304] "Ready for Takeoff? Overcoming the Practical and Legal Difficulties in Identifying and Realizing the Value of Data," Ernst & Young, 2014.

What Is Big Data?

Big data refers to the dynamic, large, and disparate volumes of data being created by people, tools, and machines. It requires new, innovative, and scalable technology to collect, host, and analytically process the vast amount of data gathered in order to derive real-time business insights that relate to consumers, risk, profit, performance, productivity management, and enhanced shareholder value. Big data includes information garnered from social media, data from Internet-enabled devices (including smartphones and tablets), machine data, video and voice recordings, and the continued preservation and logging of structured and unstructured data. It is typically characterized by the four "V's":

Volume   The amount of big data being created is vast compared to traditional data sources.

Variety   Data comes from different sources and is being created by machines as well as people.

Velocity   Data generation is extremely fast, a process that never stops even while we sleep.

Veracity   Big data is sourced from many different places, requiring tests of its veracity and quality.

Source: "Big Data: Changing the Way Businesses Compete and Operate," Ernst & Young, April 2014.

Big data is being generated by everything around us at all times. Every digital process and social media exchange produces it. Systems, sensors, and mobile devices transmit it. Big data is deriving from multiple sources at an alarming volume, variety, velocity, and veracity.

In this increasingly digital era of globalization, businesses can manage their international operations in leaner, more efficient ways. Using digital platforms and tools, businesses can sell in fast-growing markets while keeping virtual teams connected in real time. This may be the moment for boards and managements to rethink their organizational structures, products and services, assets, competitors, and the associated risks.[305]

Businesses are gaining unprecedented opportunities to understand consumer needs, preferences, and behaviors. The amount and types of customer data available from sources, including social media, online shopping behavior, and geolocation information, are expanding at exponential rates. Making sense of the volume and variety of this data, however, is a significant challenge. By some estimates, more than 80% of the data within institutions is unstructured and unfit for traditional processing.[306]

Businesses that can extract value from this information using data analytics will benefit greatly. They will gain a more precise understanding of customer segments. Products and services can be tailored to the level of the individual. Altogether, they can derive a much richer customer experience. This is important because consumers' expectations are growing. They are demanding greater choice and control, more transparency, and anytime, anywhere access to information. They also want their voices heard, and digital technologies are making it easier to gather and understand consumer feedback.

---

[305] Ibid.
[306] "Big Data: Changing the Way Businesses Compete and Operate," April 2014.

Recent developments in machine learning have enabled incredible insights of customers, employees, suppliers, business processes, and the compilation of risks. On a human dimension, big data allows for very detailed composite profiles of who people are, their demographics and travels, how they behave, what they look at, and which actions they take. These composite profiles have far greater value than raw or individual data elements. However, these profiles are subject to potentially greater abuse, possible conflict with regulations, and greater security threats than the raw data itself.

In some institutions, sales and marketing organizations may be buying analytic capabilities from the cloud and using these as they see fit. But is the institution in control? What privacy and data security is being applied to protect the most valuable assets? Who, at a management level, is accountable for decisions about big data and the use of advanced analytics and the associated risks?

The open frontier of institutions collecting as much data as they want, and reusing it, is about to be fenced in. This is especially true if the data security is breached and consumers are exposed to financial or personal losses. While there is some legislation at the state level, the U.S. Congress has not yet passed comprehensive legislation regarding privacy and data security. However, the Federal Trade Commission has won a court judgment seeking to take action against unfair and deceptive business practices with data. And the Consumer Financial Protection Bureau has won judgments against the use of selected data in setting consumer loan rates and consumer insurance.

Protecting Personal Data

- *Increasing significance of personal data.* The protection of personal data is a central concern for customers and consumers.
- *The need to define and manage personal data carefully.* Big data and cloud computing increase the risks in how data is defined and managed.
- *The volume of data.* Those businesses that do not keep track of what they hold, or fail to keep checks on the accuracy of this information, cannot guarantee compliance with the law.
- *The changing legislative environment.* Legislators and regulators are scrambling to keep pace with efforts to exploit the value of data.
- *The need to protect the institution's own data.* As threats of cyber attacks grow, the data of institutions may be vulnerable, leaving them open to legal and reputational risks.
- *The possibility of a big data backlash.* Consumers are becoming more selective and careful about the parties with whom they share their data.

Source: "Ready for Takeoff? Overcoming the Practical and Legal Difficulties in Identifying and Realizing the Value of Data," Ernst & Young, 2014.

Some countries severely regulate what can be tracked. Brazil requires individuals to have notarized statements indicating they want to "opt in." Otherwise, tracking is prohibited. In the European Union, there are regulations requiring the trackers to selectively "forget" some data. The U.S. may eventually impose restrictions on which big data analytics are allowed.

Simply asking at the next board meeting "What are we doing with big data?" is proving to be insufficient. It severely underestimates the importance and complexity of the opportunity and the full downside of the risks. Directors need to understand which big data is being collected, how it is being processed, how it is used for business purposes, how it impacts strategy, how risks escalate when this information is used, and what types of controls are in place.

In a survey of directors conducted by PricewaterhouseCoopers, directors of companies in all sectors and industries recognize that big data and cloud technologies could use more attention. Over a quarter say they are not sufficiently engaged in these areas. And only 53% of directors indicate that IT strategy and risk mitigation approaches even "moderately" take sufficient advantage of big data.[307] However, as the use of big data and advanced analytics proliferates, the risks also will expand.

Big Data and Advanced Analytics

"Big data" describes the accumulation and processing of very large data sets, usually a composite of information from every possible source—such as traditional operations and process information from within the business, data from outside the business (such as from suppliers and third parties), and structured and unstructured data (such as images, voice records, memos, call center records, click stream patterns, social media sources, etc.). Big data becomes useful when unique insights are derived from analytics and predictive analytics are applied to the totality of these different data sources, because patterns can emerge that are not visible from the individual data elements alone.

Approaches to Analyzing Big Data			
Descriptive Analytics	**Diagnostic Analytics**	**Predictive Analytics**	**Prescriptive Analytics**
What happened?	Why did it happen?	What will happen?	How can we make it happen?

Source: "Mining Big Data," by Steve Weber, *NACD Directorship*, September/October 2013.

Applications of "advanced analytics" range from pattern recognition in historical data to real-time decision support. Predictive analytics software provides forecasts of likely outcomes based on the calculated patterns. Prescriptive analytics determine which decisions or actions will produce the most effective result against a specific set of objectives and constraints. The most advanced systems today are based on "deep learning," a form of artificial intelligence that masters tasks by analyzing enormous quantities of information across a vast network of machines.

Deep-learning systems roughly mimic the web of neurons in the human brain. Sometimes, these systems blend human and machine capabilities by helping institutions with call center activities, identifying images such as face imagery, recognizing speech, target-

---

[307] "Trends Shaping Governance and the Board of the Future," Annual Corporate Directors Survey, PricewaterhouseCoopers, 2014.

ing ads, or resolving problems. The analytic engines used on the data have developed capabilities exponentially.

Without the need to pre-program intelligence into software, new deep-learning capabilities develop optimized results on their own. In one recent gaming example, data scientists have turned machine deep-learning capabilities loose, without predisposing the software, and the systems have learned, on their own, how to play games better than any human.

What Directors Should Do Today About Big Data

- *Provide leeway.* Scrutiny should be tempered by an openness to pursue new discoveries that point in unexpected directions.
- *Ask who is responsible and why.* Boards should ask who is in charge, inquire about credentials, and determine how expertise in this important field is being factored into succession planning.
- *Determine whether the budget is realistic.* While big data needs to be given leeway, boards must be confident that appropriate resources are being committed to its implementation.
- *Integrate into the culture.* The board should look for a growing familiarity with big data that is meaningfully reflected in areas expected to benefit, such as marketing or finance.
- *Be skeptical.* While being supportive, it is important to question whether big-data results are based on mathematically valid methods, are internally consistent, can be independently reproduced, and are ultimately actionable.
- *Renew the focus on enterprise risk management.* The concentration and widespread availability of information in big data should prompt directors to make informatics security an even greater concern.
- *Task the audit committee.* The board should have the same confidence in the accuracy of any big-data conclusions as it does in the company's financials. Internal or external audits by firms with a requisite level of scrutiny can also be engaged to ensure that a company's big-data shop is relying on an appropriate mix of curiosity and scientific discipline.
- *Ensure privacy and sanctions.* Boards should ask their management teams about policies that ensure customer, employee, and stakeholder privacy, including what sanctions exist if those policies are violated.
- *Reduce incentives.* Boards should ask if any compensation incentives are unwittingly promoting unethical or fraudulent behavior by persons who are reporting big-data-related outcomes. In addition, the "tone at the top" should not only embrace the culture of big data, but also ensure that its use is both ethical and lawful.
- *Find an expert.* A significant commitment to big data may warrant having an individual on the board who has the requisite level of competence in analytics.

Source: "Beyond Skepticism: How Boards Should Oversee Big Data," by Jaan Sidorou, *NACD Directorship*, July 18, 2014.

Why Directors Should Worry

There are several reasons why directors should carefully examine and assess management's pursuit of the use of big data.

Technology gap: Under ideal circumstances, executives are chosen based on leadership, management skills, expertise, and character. While these traits are vital, leveraging big data, and mitigating the risks, calls for a comfortable working knowledge of computer technology, informatics, and statistics. Such experience may not have been cultivated during the careers of many directors and management.

Data security and privacy: The collection, storage, and analysis of data are a significant temptation for criminals and hackers. The recent travails of Target Corporation over a breach in its customer database prove that privacy and security should be top concerns. Not only can an institution's competitive advantage be sold to the highest bidder, any unintentional release of customer data can lead to an instantaneous loss of reputation, regulatory scrutiny, and time-consuming lawsuits.

Garbage in, garbage out: Since incomplete data and faulty analytics can lead to spurious associations, it is important to understand and weigh the underlying assumptions, inputs, analytics, exclusion criteria, and strengths of any observations.

Fraud: As interest and investment in big data grow, the temptation for employees to deliberately generate false results, massage the numbers to support a predetermined conclusion, or "spin" the information for undue personal gain is likely to increase.[308]

Gartner suggests that boards and management focus on the risk and compliance implications of using big data in the following four areas:

1. People and machines should be able to find and use information when needed, but unauthorized use must not occur.
2. There is an abundance of regulations at local, state, and national levels.
3. Big data analytics is increasingly about letting people interactively explore data that presents information governance challenges beyond traditional business intelligence.
4. Many innovative big-data solutions come from start-ups that might cease to exist in the near future. Some of these start-ups have only a vague idea about enterprise-grade requirements for security, availability, and other customer IT expectations.[309]

Big Data in Banking

The same capabilities that power game winning can be used to identify risks and understand and create improved business operations patterns. Big data and advanced analytics are useful in virtually all businesses, but in banking and other financial institutions their use is exploding. Every bank and financial institution has the need for more and better-quality information; thus, directors have a duty to bring into the boardroom fresh ideas and early warnings of coming trends and risks.

"Larger and regional banks are becoming more diverse and complex, and technological change has radically increased the speed of operations and the rate at which data is amassed, stored, processed, and analyzed," said John C. Erickson, president of Consumer Banking and president, California, CIT Bank.

---

[308] "Beyond Skepticism: How Boards Should Oversee Big Data," by Jaan Sidorou, *NACD Directorship*, July 18, 2014.
[309] "Information Governance in the Age of Big Data," Gartner, May 30, 2013.

By applying new analytical tools and service delivery methods, banks are converting data into knowledge in their pursuit of market and service-differentiating capabilities. These efforts require both the support of the board and management and a cultural shift toward evidence-based decisions.

Big Data: Implications for Businesses

- Test the current analytics against the state of the art. The field is moving so quickly that even well-versed businesses can fall behind.
- Consolidate databases across the institution. Big data yields advantages from scope as well as scale, so siloed, business-unit-specific databases are quickly becoming antiquated.
- Form partnerships to gain scale. The power of aggregation lies in the million non-intuitive relationships between seemingly unconnected things.
- Manage data as a trustee. Personal data collected by businesses cannot be treated as mere property. Data storing will succeed only if the businesses involved earn the informed trust of their clients and customers.

Source: "Navigating a World of Digital Disruption," by Philip Evans and Patrick Forth, The Boston Consulting Group, February 2016.

The use of big data and advanced analytics in banking extends to monitoring money-laundering activities, recognizing unusual trading activity, improving risk aggregation, and enhancing regulatory reporting. In addition, predictive analytics are now being used to help bank credit officers assess which customers are most likely to default. "Although still in the early stages, banks are applying big data and advanced analytics across customer-facing channels such as mobile, the Web, e-mail, and physical locations, up and down the supply chain, and in risk and compliance functions," commented J. Michael Shepherd, chairman, BancWest and Bank of the West and a board member of Pacific Life Insurance Company.

Some financial institutions have redesigned their business models on the basis of insights gleaned from data, such as structuring divisions around customer segments rather than types of product. Other businesses are entering the financial services area by using big data and analytics to make significant advances in the payments space.[310]

Three primary factors are driving the importance of advanced analytics in the banking industry:

1. Regulatory reform: The regulators are asking institutions to demonstrate a better understanding of data, to turn that data into information that supports decisions, and to manage risk more effectively.
2. Customer profitability: Personalized offerings are expected to play a big role in attracting and retaining the most preferred customers.
3. Operational efficiency: While institutions have been reducing costs, there remains opportunity for improvement, including reducing duplicative systems, manual reconciliations, and IT costs.[311]

---

[310] "Ready for Takeoff? Overcoming the Practical and Legal Difficulties in Identifying and Realizing the Value of Data," 2014.

[311] "How Analytics Can Transform the U.S. Retail Banking Sector," Cognizant Reports, August 2011.

Economic headwinds, historic loss rates, and high capital requirements are driving the dramatic increase in institutions' use of data capabilities. The regulators are asking institutions to demonstrate a better understanding of data, to turn that data into information that supports decisions, and to manage risk more effectively using the data. In addition, the regulators are also requesting more transparency and better documentation of how the data is being used.

The "Principles for Effective Risk Data Aggregation and Risk Reporting," published in January 2013 by the Basel Committee on Banking Supervision, is now being referred to routinely by regulators such as the Federal Reserve and the Office of the Comptroller of the Currency and is increasingly informing their expectations of data management capabilities.

The regulators expect an institution to have in place a robust data governance framework and fully supportive data architecture and IT infrastructure. And any data, including big data and advanced analytics, needs to be well defined, clearly owned, and quality-managed. While there is no specific mention of big data or advanced analytics in Basel's guidance, the regulatory expectations are clear.

The objective of a data governance framework is to build a solid foundation of people, practices, processes, and standards that are used to create a consistent enterprise view of data. The regulators tend to avoid providing specific guidance on issues such as the board approval of data policies, except for data-related policies governing information technology and safeguarding customer information. The OCC's minimum standards focus on data and infrastructure, suggesting the need for policies, procedures, and processes to support accurate and useful data aggregation and reporting.

A Change of Mind – Survey Results

Has big data changed decision making at your organization?

64%	Yes
25%	No, but we plan to do so
11%	No, nor do we plan to do so (or do not know)

Top changes to decision making

➡ Making greater use of specialized analytic tools and technologies

➡ Employing a dedicated data insights team to inform strategic decisions

➡ Relying on enhanced data analytics

Source: Economist Intelligence Unit, May 2014.

But key issues remain. Acquisitions activity within the financial services industry has left many institutions with disparate IT systems that are difficult to integrate and transform across the institution, often requiring significant change. Reputational risk is another important issue. Banks, so battered by the financial crisis, are cautious in areas such as data privacy and accessibility, where they fear the risk of further deterioration in customer relationships, even when they comply with the letter of the law.[312]

---

[312] "Ready for Takeoff? Overcoming the Practical and Legal Difficulties in Identifying and Realizing the Value of Data," 2014.

Many institutions continue to struggle with the challenges of aggregating, analyzing, and managing vast amounts of data. "Generally, a root cause for slow progress may stem from a cultural issue of confusion over who owns and has responsibility for data in an institution. In addition, challenges may occur when institutions have been built through acquisitions, causing the institution to miss opportunities to leverage their data to gain the value of deriving better insights into their business operations and processes," said James Sparks, partner, KPMG.

New Types of Risks

The need to secure sensitive data to protect private information, and also to manage data quality, exists whether data sets are big or small. However, the specific attributes of big data create new types of risks.

Ernst & Young summarizes these new risks in seven categories:

1. *Governance*
   - Data can be of great value, but institutions need to consider ownership and privacy issues before using big-data results. Ownership of the data is sometimes unclear, but using the data without the appropriate legal foundation or consent can cause problems.
   - Big data may bring about intellectual property issues, even copyright and database rights infringements. It is a challenge to make sure employees are not sharing inappropriate information.

2. *Management*
   - Simplified access to diverse sources of data may increase the amount of "noise" in the data and lower its overall quality.
   - Many new players in the technology market do not have mature, enterprise-ready capabilities around implementation, support, and training.
   - New big-data methods, architecture, and volume impose additional risks, such as lack of control and governance over data. Given the complex data landscape, it is especially important to establish and maintain data lineage.
   - Institutions may struggle to find the right skills and build internal capabilities for handling big data, as most of the technologies and methods are relatively new and market resources are in short supply.

3. *Architecture*
   - More data can lead to an increased number of data-quality issues, confusion, and lack of consistency in business decision-making, especially when conflicting information is present.
   - Integrated data architecture increases the challenges of data linkages and matching algorithms to distinguish items of relevance from piles of information.
   - A more complex architectural landscape and the growing amount of data bring new challenges around data governance and privacy.
   - Lack of capabilities, internally and externally, make it hard to keep up with rapidly evolving hardware and software technology and methods of implementation.

4. *Usage*
   - Qualified data scientists are in short supply. By trying to handle too much information, institutions can become overloaded and overwhelmed.
   - The challenge of getting the right information to the right person at the right time is made more difficult by the sheer size of big data.
   - The costs associated with managing and monitoring the quality, credibility, and integrity of big data can be prohibitive.
   - There is a need to temper the expectation that big data will solve everything.

5. *Quality*
   - Institutions may not have the knowledge or competencies to deal with big data.
   - The need to interpret and assess unstructured data can be a challenge, and the quality of the unstructured data is often unproven.
   - Structured and unstructured data may not be integrated cohesively.
   - Existing information governance models will not be aligned to manage the quality of newly acquired data.

6. *Security*
   - Diverse sources of data often result in distributed storage and management, compounding security vulnerabilities.
   - Cloud computing puts more data in motion and can create additional security complexities.
   - Lost data results in more direct impacts to the end consumer. When coupled with the behavioral data collected, this can lead to more sophisticated attacks.
   - Increasingly, regulations raise the stakes around security as the cost of dealing with data breaches continues to grow.

7. *Privacy*
   - New technology makes it possible to gather and analyze data from multiple locations, bringing the challenge of meeting different privacy regulations.
   - Sensor and geolocation data may be used to identify an individual, even if no name is attached to the data—thereby increasing the need to define "personal information" that needs to be protected.
   - The ability to collect new sources of information increases the need to evaluate opt-in/opt-out procedures by consumers.[313]

Why You Need to Manage Your Data Diet

- Storage is not cheap
- System performance
- Data privacy
- Litigation risks and costs
- Data security

Source: "Information Governance: It May Be a Duty and It Is Definitely Smart Business," Gibson, Dunn & Crutcher, May 19, 2014.

---

[313] "Big Data: Changing the Way Businesses Compete and Operate," April 2014.

Implications for Directors

The oversight and management of big data is inherently difficult because it is so new and dynamic. These technologies are in the infant stages of application, which means there are few best practices to use as a guide. Directors and managements must balance opportunities while staying alert to the equally fast-moving risks.

"Although digital disruptions are not a new phenomenon, the opportunities and risks they present shift over time. The disruptions caused by the proliferation and use of big data are immense, requiring the close attention of both directors and management," suggested G. Michael Murphy, partner, Deloitte & Touche.

Board members should request clarity of vision and collaboration across all disciplines to maximize the return on any data analytics investment. They also should regularly ask management about the resources being deployed and whether the institution has the best talent in place to execute a high-quality analytics program.[314]

Given the size of potential new risks, directors need to focus on the areas of data management policies, technology policies, and governance.

1. *Data management policies*

   Policies on proprietary and personally identifiable information: The types, amount, and specificity of the data being gathered create even greater concerns about the data's confidentiality and integrity because its value is far greater. In addition to the institution's own privacy policies, what existing and pending regulations may apply? An understanding of ownership rights to data produced by various connected devices is required. Who has what rights to the data when multiple organizations and third parties are part of its creation or processing?

   Policies regarding information security: What access privileges to the data and analytics software are allowed? Especially when it uses third-party systems, such as storage and analytics cloud providers, the institution has a greater risk of compromised systems and data.

   Policies ensuring data accuracy and integrity: Data that has value should be maintained in a way that ensures its quality and protects against alteration. A discipline must be established to keep track of the different data versions and distinguish analytics from source data. Diversified and complex systems and business structures can lead to multiple copies of data and confusion as to the source.

   In addition, an institution is required to retain different categories of information for various periods, depending on the regulators and the jurisdictions where the institution does business, as well as the nature of its products and services. Although unnecessarily kept data dramatically increases the potential costs and consequences of data breaches, data that may be responsive to requests in litigation or investigation must be identified and preserved.

2. *Technology policies*

   Ever-changing landscape of technologies: Big data needs very large storage arrays and massive computing power. Large storage arrays are needed because the

---

[314] "Big Risks, Big Data—and Big Decisions for the Board," Ernst & Young, March 2016.

data is constantly updated and the data sets become additive. The massive computing power is needed to vet, clean, and analyze the data, sometimes in real time for online services. The analytics software is complex and expensive. Both the storage and computing services are now available from several cloud service providers. Social media and Internet-of-things devices allow for the collection and access of data and images by unlimited numbers of people. Choosing the right technologies and technology partners is a key to success. Are policies in place to guide the institution into making the right choices?

Sourcing from the cloud: In order to take advantage of economies of scale and resulting cost savings, many institutions are moving their data into the cloud or procuring services from cloud providers. Data and services may be commingled with those of other institutions, if not under immediate possession or subject to the institution's own rigorous control and policies.

3. *Governance*

Strategy: A major risk is the unbridled enthusiasm of sales, marketing, and research analysts who may go too far with their analyses. Even with privacy disclosures in customer agreements, or lack thereof, there will be huge backlash against probing too deeply into customer behaviors. Many customers do not want to be tracked and analyzed in the detail that is possible, yet the motivation of some analysts is to probe so deeply that they can anticipate every move. Does the institution have a formal strategic and risk mitigation plan for big data? What is the institution investing in specifically? How does the plan support the institution's strategy and create new businesses?

Leadership: Who will lead the institution's big-data initiatives? Should big data be centralized to uniformly manage the investments and risks, or is it best decentralized to allow for optimization to the unique requirements of individual business units? Most institutions will likely find there are already many grassroots efforts under way. Is that too risky to continue? Without disrupting those that may be demonstrating value (or be about to), a formal institutional approach may be needed.

Staffing the big-data competency: Big data requires specialists who understand data and know how to mine it, what to look for and pursue, which models need to be developed, and what information sources are required to answer new sets of questions. However, given the scarcity of trained and experienced data scientists, they are in big demand. While there may be talent within the institution who would welcome the training, the risk is that it will take time and high turnover may result. The institution needs to find a way to combine permanent staff and outside contractors, then incent and motivate them in ways that may be different from the normal HR protocols.

There are technical, ethical, and compliance implications of analyzing new data sources or new combinations of data sources. Privacy is especially impacted when different compliance entities, linked together, lead to noncompliance. Gartner describes one institution that stopped its big-data initiative altogether because of concerns over possible compliance and ethical violations in combining multiple databases. Each of the data sources was compliant, but their combination was not.

Providing thoughtful and careful oversight of the risks associated with big data and advanced analytics is an imperative for directors. The aforementioned categories of risk are a useful start.

Another important consideration is determining who on the board should focus on big data. Is this a topic for the entire board, or should it be delegated to one committee with the specific competence in the technology and the time to focus on it?

Directors are well aware that having board members with financial expertise is, in many cases, a regulatory requirement and best practice. Likewise, a significant commitment to big data and advanced analytics may warrant adding a board member with the requisite skills and expertise. Experience or training in fields such as information technology and data science may be a requirement for this individual.

Alternatively, the board or one of its committees could engage third-party expertise as an advisor. Outside counsel, with specific expertise in big data, security, and privacy, can provide unique and valuable guidance.

"The strategies one institution may choose to follow, and the acceptance or mitigation of particular information-related risks, will differ from the next, depending on each institution's business objectives, specific legal obligations, and its risk appetite," noted Gareth Evans, partner, Gibson, Dunn & Crutcher.

For some directors and management, the best big-data strategy right now may be to proceed cautiously, as the value proposition for using big data and advanced analytics becomes more apparent and the magnitude of the risks are better understood. Of course, this strategy may have unacceptable "lost opportunity" costs, because it is likely the competition—whether a traditional competitor or a start-up—is evaluating this capability. As a result, perhaps the only unacceptable strategy today is to have none at all.

Questions Directors Should Ask About the Risks in Using Big Data and Advanced Analytics

- What policies are in place to guide the acquisition, processing, use, quality control, and disclosure of data?
- How does the use of big data align with the institution's overall strategic plans and risk appetite? What are the consequences of letting users explore big data?
- How is data privacy protected and security ensured? How are the analytics protected?
- What risk mitigations are operative to control data not created by the institution?
- What are the laws and regulations impacting the big data strategy? What are the gaps in compliance? Are the responses to regulatory inquiries and reporting requirements coordinated and sufficiently flexible?
- What are the third-party risk management issues in relying on specialized vendors of big data? How are these risks mitigated?
- How is the model risk management program affected by the use of big data and advanced analytics?
- What would be the response to worst-case scenarios if the data is compromised?

APPENDIX 1

Independence of Directors

Director independence is a key component of effective governance, for these reasons:

- Directors who are independent from management are more likely to act in the corporation's best interests. An independent board is simply more likely to question management's practices and react when those practices run counter to shareholder interests.
- When a crisis occurs, independent board members who are not personally invested in the problem are in the best position to direct the corporation, its future, and what needs to be done to preserve it. Management's own involvement in the crisis, or with the corporation generally, may color its reaction, causing executives to delay in responding, offer half-truths, or engage in finger-pointing.

Independence does not solve problems. Rather, it makes it easier to detect them and find their solutions. Independent directors are more likely to admit to ignorance or uncertainty and to seek advice from fellow directors (recruiting new board members as necessary) or from qualified advisors.

Source: "Risk Oversight: Board Lessons for Turbulent Times," Report of the NACD Blue Ribbon Commission, National Association of Corporate Directors, 2006.

APPENDIX 2

Director's Checklist

- Attend meetings and come prepared.
- Ask thoughtful questions.
- Be a good listener.
- Do not vote on any board or committee actions unless you are informed.
- Insist that the institution create a written job description covering the duties and responsibilities of a director.
- Read the institution's corporate governance guidelines; if there are none, insist that the board develop them.
- Constantly monitor and review the institution's activities.
- Have the institution create and maintain performance review programs for the CEO, the board, and each director.
- Make certain that you are indemnified by the institution and that you understand the extent of the indemnification.
- Make certain that you are covered by adequate directors' and officers' insurance and that you understand the extent of the coverage, the exceptions to the coverage, and the manner in which claims are to be filed.
- Have a basic understanding of the laws impacting your performance and your duties and responsibilities as a director.
- Ask for assistance and information when you need it.
- Be aware of the importance of confidentiality and the rules for observing it.
- Be a team player.
- Always be aware of your responsibility to the institution and its shareholders.
- Keep current with your knowledge of the institution and its continuing relationship with stakeholders, employees, customers, suppliers, the community, the government, and the regulators.
- Insist that the institution create and maintain director educational programs and attendance requirements.
- Keep yourself educated as to what is required of a director and the latest nuances in good corporate governance. *Education, education, education!*
- Be aware of your ethical responsibilities, as well as those of your fellow directors and management.

Source: "A Practical Guide: Fundamentals for Corporate Directors," National Association of Corporate Directors, 2012.

APPENDIX 3

Creating an Effective Information Governance Framework

- Ask the CEO to include with each board meeting package a one-page "meeting introduction" letter summarizing the two or three most important things he or she wants to accomplish at the upcoming meeting.
- Require that board agendas be categorized into three or four sections (for example, board matters, operations, financial and business operations, strategy).
- For the more in-depth operating and financial reports, ask management to include an introductory paragraph or executive summary.
- If the board will be asked to approve a specific resolution, ensure that a draft form of the action and an executive summary, if appropriate, are included with the board materials.
- Allow board agendas to include a reference section for matters that are important but are not required discussion for the meeting. An updated copy of the board's annualized agenda should be standard in the reference section for each meeting.
- Ensure that agencies or reference sections include some non-management-based data (such as an investor perception study, customer satisfaction survey, competitive benchmarks, and industry and market news).
- Remind directors that board materials sent in advance must be read in advance. Remind management not to read previously distributed reports at the meeting.
- Require board materials to be sent one week prior to the meeting. Occasionally, there is a legitimate need for late postings, but this should not be the norm.
- At the end of each meeting, the lead director should ask, "Did we accomplish what was needed to be accomplished today? Did we have the information we needed?" He or she should ensure that every director is heard from on these important questions.
- Require draft minutes to be distributed to the board within one week of the meeting, and ask directors to submit comments promptly. Send final-draft minutes with the board materials so directors can refresh their memories of the discussions at the last meeting before approving for execution.
- Ask the CEO to send the board a brief report at the halfway point between meetings. This helps keep directors focused on the important issues. Some boards may ask that this report be in the form of a conference call.

Source: "Overwhelmed by Board Books? You're Not Alone," by Denise Kuprionis, *NACD Directorship*, May/June 2014.

APPENDIX 4

14 Questions for Every Director

1. Is our board composition right for the challenge?
2. Are we addressing the risks that could send our company over the cliff?
3. Are we prepared to do our job well when a crisis erupts?
4. Are we well prepared to name our next CEO?
5. Does our board really own the company's strategy?
6. How can we get the information we need to govern well?
7. How can our board get CEO compensation right?
8. Why do we need a lead director anyway?
9. Is our governance committee "best in breed"?
10. How do we get the most value out of our limited time?
11. How can executive sessions help the board own up?
12. How can our board self-assessment improve our functioning and output?
13. How do we stop from micromanaging?
14. How prepared are we to work with activist shareholders and their proxies?

Source: *Owning Up: The 14 Questions Every Board Member Needs to Ask*, by Ram Charan, Jossey-Bass, 2009.

APPENDIX 5

Five Steps in Risk Management

Risks are tracked in parallel while new exposures are identified and analyzed.

Identify: Search for and locate risks before they become problems.

Analyze: Transform risk data into decision-making information. Evaluate impact, probability, and timeframe; classify risks; and prioritize risks.

Plan: Translate risk information into decisions and mitigating actions (both present and future) and implement those actions.

Track: Monitor risk indicators and mitigation actions.

Control: Correct for deviations from the risk mitigation plans.

At all times:

Communicate: Provide information and feedback, internal and external, on the risk activities, current risks, and emerging risks. (Communication happens throughout all the functions of risk management.)

Source: The Software Engineering Institute, a federally funded research and development center sponsored by the U.S. Department of Defense and operated by Carnegie Mellon University.

APPENDIX 6

The Director's Role in Compliance and Ethics

A clear mandate has emerged for corporate boards to oversee compliance and ethics programs. To do so effectively, directors must understand the risks posed by the current regulatory environment, including the following:

- The growing volume and complexity of laws and regulations, including criminal laws punishable by jail time. The U.S. government has defined some 3,000 crimes and set forth 300,000 federal regulations enforceable through criminal punishment at the discretion of a federal agency (rather than a court of law).

- The extent to which corporations themselves, in addition to individuals, can be charged with legal violations. Since the year 2000, more than 2,000 corporations have been convicted or have entered guilty pleas, and both the number of convictions and the size of the fines have grown.

- The extent to which regulators are successfully obtaining convictions and levying fines. For example, in the antitrust field, over the past 10 years the U.S. Department of Justice has been initiating fewer cases but winning more of them. Overall, since the year 2000, there have been 379 federal organizational prosecution agreements, of which one-third involve named individuals. Of those, two in five have gone to jail.

- The availability and allure of whistleblowing bounties. Mandated under the Dodd-Frank Act, such bounties have thus far resulted in more than $54 million in payments to 22 whistleblowers "who provided the SEC with unique and useful information that contributed to successful enforcement actions."

- The organizational costs of ensuring compliance. Large companies spend more than $40 million a year to respond to potential regulatory requests.

Source: "Director Essentials: Strengthening Compliance and Ethics Oversight," National Association of Corporate Directors, 2015.

APPENDIX 7

Board's Oversight of Risks

Question: How do you assess your board's performance in selected risk oversight areas?

(% of respondents who indicated "excellent" or "good")

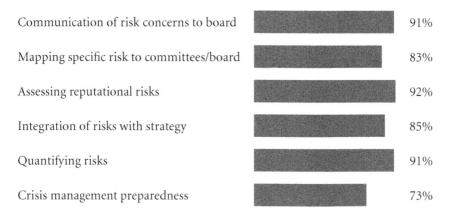

Communication of risk concerns to board	91%
Mapping specific risk to committees/board	83%
Assessing reputational risks	92%
Integration of risks with strategy	85%
Quantifying risks	91%
Crisis management preparedness	73%

Source: "Governing for the Long-term: Looking Down the Road with an Eye on the Rear-view Mirror," Annual Corporate Directors Survey, PricewaterhouseCoopers, 2015.

APPENDIX 8

Identifying Emerging Risks

Institutions are using a wide range of practices to identify emerging risks more systematically:

- Conducting more frequent and more formal risk discussions.
- Instituting committees to identify emerging risks.
- Strengthening stress testing, using more forward-looking scenarios.
- Adopting rigorous screening and on-boarding procedures for new clients and customers.
- Using advanced information technology to conduct real-time monitoring of risks at subsidiaries and branches.
- Upgrading portfolio risk-grading systems.
- Issuing early warning indicator reports.
- Reinforcing product-approval policies and procedures.

Source: "Recover, Adapt, Advance: A Survey of the World's Largest Banks," Ernst & Young, 2011.

APPENDIX 9

How to 'Think Risk' in Fulfilling Director Duties: Questions to Ask

- As we face this crisis, are we adhering to our mission and code of ethics?
- When we select and evaluate members of management, do we consider their personal character?
- In selection and evaluation, do we also consider the CEO's ability to handle a crisis?
- Is our succession plan up-to-date and crisis-ready?
- Are we capable of detecting red flags in financial statements?
- Have we engaged the services of advisors who can and will detect fraud?
- In reviewing the strategy and specific plans, have we considered the risk exposures in the short and long term, internally and externally?
- Have we, as a board, developed a definition of materiality, in compliance with regulatory guidelines, that is suitable for the institution?
- Are we reviewing all transactions that could be considered material?
- Are we confident that compensation awarded to management and directors does not motivate improper behavior or result in excessive remuneration?
- Have we assured ourselves that systems are in place to ensure ethical behavior and compliance with laws and regulations, auditing and accounting principles, and the institution's own governing documents?
- Do we have the traits associated with board effectiveness?
    - Are we independent (avoiding conflicts of interest that can blind us to potential crises)?
    - Are we qualified (possessing characteristics most helpful in preventing or resolving a crisis)?
    - Are we following corporate governance guidelines that meet or exceed current governance standards?
    - Do these guidelines include provisions relating to risk oversight and the prevention and resolution of crises?
- Have we evaluated our effectiveness?

Source: "Risk Oversight: Board Lessons for Turbulent Times," Report of the NACD Blue Ribbon Commission, National Association of Corporate Directors, January 2006.

APPENDIX 10

Characteristics of Country Groups

Characteristic	Advanced markets	Frontier markets	Emerging-country markets
Median age of citizens	38 years	24 years	32 years
Major sector focus	Services, branded products	Agriculture, commodities	Manufacturing, some services
Education level	High	Low	Medium
Economic and political freedom	Free or mostly free	Mostly repressed	Moderately free or mostly not free
Economic/political system	Capitalist	Authoritarian, socialist, or communist	Rapidly transitioning to capitalism
Regulatory environment	Minimal regulations	Highly regulated, burdensome	Achieved much liberalization
Country risk	Low	Moderate to high	Variable
Intellectual property protection	Strong	Weak	Moderate; improving
Infrastructure	Well developed	Inadequate	Moderate; improving

Sources: World Bank, International Monetary Fund, and CIA World Facebook.

APPENDIX 11

Differences Among Country Groups

Dimension	Advanced markets	Frontier markets	Emerging-country markets
Representative countries	Japan, United Kingdom, Angola United States, Canada, France	Nigeria, Bolivia,	China, Brazil, India, Russia
Approximate number of countries	30	150	27
Population (% of world)	14	24	62
Approx. average per capita income (U.S.$, PPP basis)	33,750	6,450	13,250
Approximate share of world GDP (PPP basis)	48	9	43
Population (millions)	892	1,877	3,775

Sources: World Bank and International Monetary Fund.

Conditions Within Country Groups

Trade condition	Advanced markets	Frontier markets	Emerging-country markets
Industry	Highly developed	Poor	Rapidly improving
Competition	Substantial	Limited	Moderate but increasing
Trade barriers	Minimal	Moderate to high	Rapidly liberalizing
Trade volume	High	Low	High
Inward FDI	High	Low	Moderate to high

Sources: World Bank, International Monetary Fund, and CIA World Facebook.

About the Author

D ean A. Yoost is a board member of a large global bank and a large global life insurance company. He is also one of three members of the advisory committee of a captive finance company. He previously served as a board member of two companies listed on the New York Stock Exchange.

Dean is a founder and serves as the chairman of the Corporate Directors Roundtable of Orange County (California). He also is a board member of the National Association of Corporate Directors in Southern California and a trustee and member of the Executive Committee of the University of California Irvine's Foundation.

Dean retired as a partner after 33 years with PricewaterhouseCoopers, where he held numerous client service and firm leadership positions. During this period, he lived and worked in Tokyo and Beijing for 16 years, serving the needs of global clients and establishing and building the firm's businesses. He was elected as a director to the 18-partner Global Oversight Board of PwC International Limited, the top governing body of the global network of firms. At his retirement, Dean was the firm's managing partner in Orange County and the regional leader of its Advisory Services practice.

He has authored and coauthored over 75 articles and editorials published in *The RMA Journal, Asian Wall Street Journal, NACD Directorship, Directors & Boards, Journal of International Taxation, European Business Forum*, and other business publications.

Dean is married to Mei Yoost and they reside in Irvine, California. He can be reached at deanyoost@cox.net.

Acronyms

The following acronyms appear throughout this book:

AFCEA	Armed Forces Communications and Electronics Association
AI	Artificial intelligence
AMA	Advanced measurement approaches
ASEAN	Association of Southeast Asian Nations
ASR	Advanced systems review
ATM	Automated teller machine
BCBS	Basel Committee on Banking Supervision
BCP	Business continuity planning
BHC	Bank holding company
BIS	Bank for International Settlements
BSA	Bank Secrecy Act
CCAR	Comprehensive Capital Analysis and Review
CEO	Chief executive officer
CFPB	Consumer Financial Protection Bureau
CIO	Chief Information Officer
COBIT	Control Objectives for Information and Related Technology
COO	Chief operating officer
COSO	Committee of Sponsoring Organizations
CRO	Chief risk officer
DFAST	Dodd-Frank Act Stress Test
DOJ	Department of Justice
FBI	Federal Bureau of Investigation
FCPA	Foreign Corrupt Practices Act
FDI	Foreign direct investment
FDIC	Federal Deposit Insurance Corporation
FFIEC	Federal Financial Institutions Examination Council
FHLB	Federal Home Loan Bank
FRB	Federal Reserve Bank
FRS	Board of Governors of the Federal Reserve System
FSB	Financial Stability Board
GDP	Gross domestic product
HR	Human resources
ICAAP	Internal capital adequacy assessment process

IP	Intellectual property
IRB	Internal ratings-based
ISACA	Information Systems Audit and Control Association
ISO	International Organization for Standardization
IT	Information technology
JV	Joint venture
MIS	Management information systems
NACD	National Association of Corporate Directors
NCUA	National Credit Union Administration
NIST	National Institute of Standards and Technology
NSA	National Security Agency
OCC	Office of the Comptroller of the Currency
OECD	Organization for Economic Co-operation and Development
OTS	Office of Thrift Supervision
PCAOB	Public Company Accounting Oversight Board
PPP	Purchasing power parity
R&D	Research and development
RAF	Risk appetite framework
RAS	Risk appetite statement
RAROC	Risk-adjusted return on capital
RMA	**The Risk Management Association**
RWA	Risk-weighted assets
SA	Standardized approach
SEC	Securities and Exchange Commission
SOE	State-owned enterprise
SIFI	Systemically important financial institution
S&P	Standard & Poor's
THC	The Clearing House
VAT	Value-added tax